BRITAIN'S THEATRICAL PERIODICALS

1720–1967

A BIBLIOGRAPHY

Britain's Theatrical Periodicals

1720-1967

A Bibliography

By CARL J. STRATMAN, c. s. v.

New York

The New York Public Library

1 9 7 2

PRINTED AT THE NEW YORK PUBLIC LIBRARY
form p755 [vi-1-72 1m]

Table of Contents

PREFACE   vii

INTRODUCTION   ix

LIBRARY SYMBOLS   xix

BRITAIN'S THEATRICAL PERIODICALS
    CHRONOLOGICAL LIST   1

APPENDICES
  I NUMBER OF PERIODICALS PUBLISHED OUTSIDE OF
      LONDON   123
  II NUMBER OF NEW PERIODICALS PUBLISHED EACH
      YEAR   124
  III GENERAL STATISTICS   125
  IV FREQUENCY OF PUBLICATION   125

REFERENCES   127

INDEX   131

Preface

SOME TEN YEARS have passed since the publication of *A Bibliography of British Dramatic Periodicals, 1720–1960*. Most of the work on that edition was prepared here in the United States, by visiting major libraries in this country, and by correspondence with British libraries. During the winter and spring of 1967, while working at the British Museum, I became convinced that a new edition would be necessary, especially in view of the number of periodicals which I was able to discover at the British Museum itself — magazines which are not in the first edition. Further, I felt that the term "dramatic" should be broadened to include such categories as the dance and ballet, vaudeville and magic. Finally, I felt that the coverage should be extended from 1960 to 1967.

Because this new edition has added some 550 titles to the original 674 entries, I also felt that it was imperative to revise the Introduction to the first edition, to bring the comparative figures into line with the increased number of entries and to explain a few points relative to the actual gathering of the material, as well as to changes in a number of the former entries.

I do hope that this new edition — with all its limitations, qualifications and exclusions — may be of some benefit to those who consult its pages.

Introduction

PERHAPS ONE of the richest sources for material on the history of the stage in Great Britain, its theatres, plays, actors, managers, and influence, lies in the theatrical periodicals which have appeared in the last two-and-a-half centuries. In general, these English periodicals cover every phase of theatre life: in them are bills, criticisms of plays and productions, biographies of playwrights and actors, comments on managers and salaries, laws affecting the stage and theatre, anecdotes, portraits, gossip, and, occasionally, an original play. While some of the journals are small daily publications listing playbills and offering but brief criticisms on the evening's performances, others are weeklies or monthlies which devote themselves to every phase of theatrical activity. Each, regardless of size or frequency, has things to offer students of the drama of a particular era, or of individual plays.

To attempt more than a bibliographical analysis of the 1235 periodicals in the present list would be a task far beyond the compiler's intention. An introductory consideration of some of the early journals, however, may serve to indicate the general plan and scope of the theatrical magazines.

The first English periodical which referred specifically to the theatre on its title page was *The Theatre*, begun by Sir Richard Steele, January 2 1720, with the avowed intention of making this semiweekly magazine a vehicle for preserving and improving the English stage in particular, and uplifting manners and morals in general. In single essays Steele attempted to free the actors of the day from the tyranny of capricious audiences, to set the proper tone for the stage, and to state his position on things dramatic. That same year, on February 15, another semiweekly magazine, *The Anti-Theatre*, began to appear, seemingly with the intention of contradicting the position taken by Steele. After twenty-eight issues publication of this periodical came to an end, one day before the demise of *The Theatre*.

No other theatrical journals were published until 1734, when *Cote's Weekly Journal; or, The English Stage Player* and *The Prompter* both appeared on the scene. *Cote's Weekly* had only nine issues, but *The Prompter* ran from November 12 1734 to July 2 1736, for a total of 173 numbers. The latter journal was a semiweekly publication, issued by Aaron Hill and William Popple, with the assistance of Eustace Budgell. In its pages *The Prompter* spoke of actors and acting — with some severe strictures on various actors — of contemporary managers and theatres, and of various current productions. Criticisms were devoted to the works of Shakespeare, Congreve, Wycherley, Dryden, Voltaire, Hill, and Miller. In addition, it contained letters, poetry, dialogues, "characters," and excerpts of dramas. Although the journal was well written, and seems to have had a fair popularity, the only complete set in existence today seems to be at the Bodleian Library.

With the appearance of *The Prompter* the popularity of the theatrical periodical began to grow. By 1763 the pattern was set for all future journals which devoted their pages to dramatic activities; in the introduction to *The Theatrical Review; or, Annals of the Drama*, which began publication that year, the editor promised to present in each issue of his monthly accounts of the lives of the dramatic poets and their writings, together with some biographical notes on the most celebrated actors. Further, he stated that he would assess the talents of the actors in London, Dublin, Edinburgh, Bath, York, and Norwich. All new dramatic pieces, he promised, would be treated and evaluated fairly and objectively. Whimsical incidents, little stories, and interesting anecdotes on matters theatrical completed the features offered during the six months' life of the journal. And, with some variations, this continued to be the format of most of the theatrical journals.

Another of the eighteenth-century periodicals, *The Thespian Magazine and Literary Repository*, which ran from June 1792 until August 1794, was a popular monthly, reviewing plays staged during the preceding month at the various theatres in London, the Provinces, Dublin, and Edinburgh. In a section entitled "Ancient Authors," brief discussions were devoted to early dramatists. A "General Review" of published plays appeared in each issue, as did brief descriptions of the lives of various playwrights, actors, and actresses. Modern authors as well as Shakespeare and his works were covered. Anecdotes, poems, discussions of music, memoirs, letters, and miscellanies, together with the printing of new plays, were among the other features of the journal. Of particular value were the analyses of the plays. An index completed each volume.

One of the early and valuable journals of the nineteenth century was *The Theatrical Repertory*, which followed the pattern set by earlier theatrical periodicals and concerned itself with performances at Drury Lane and Covent Garden Theatres from September 19 1801 until June 28 1802. Thus, playbills appeared for the performances of the past week; essays touching on Shakespeare, his art, and the production of his plays were frequent; criticisms were given of the popular stage. An interesting facet of this journal was the amount of criticism it devoted to revivals of earlier plays. Here the views of an early nineteenth-century critic can be found on the works of such men as Nathaniel Lee, Nicholas Rowe, George Lillo, Edward Young, Edward Moore, and John Home. Gentle fun is poked at the scene-painting in such plays as *The Mountaineers* (Nov 7 1801) at Drury Lane, *The Pirates* (Feb 22 1802) also at Drury Lane, and, on the same day, *The Cabinet* at Covent Garden. And the editor remarks that, although it is standard procedure for the Advertisement of each play to insist that new scenery is being used, one must have a very keen eye to discover more than two scenes out of twenty that "have not slept in the scene room" for at least several years. After twenty-eight weekly numbers, publication of this periodical ended.

Many of the periodicals began with high editorial principles, with attempts to cover all aspects of dramatic activity, and with a vitality suggesting the expectation of many years of fruitful work ahead, yet they shortly had to bow to a lack either of material or of readers. One such, *The Stage; or, Theatrical Touchstone*, which lasted for only four issues, stated in its "Prospectus" that "the strictest impartiality shall guide" the pen of the editor "and pervade his pages." Quite grandiloquently the editor then proceeded to inform the readers that he would discuss the plays in London, and the " 'Drama Provincialis' with a *correctitude* of features hitherto unattempted." Finally, he solemnly swore "that no prejudice or party affiliation shall bias his judgment." It is interesting to note that he attempted to make good his promises by filling the journal with a real miscellany of material, treating of American theatricals, provincial theatres and productions, the German theatre, the Royal Circus, reviews of plays, original poetry, "Green Room Chit-chattery," money made at benefit performances in Boston, and the life of the actor Richard Suett. All was in vain, however, as the fourth issue was the last.

An annual, *The Dramatic Censor; or, Critical and Biographical Illustration of the British Stage: For the Year 1811*, gave what it called "a correct register of every night's performances at our metropolitan theatres." All this material was published, according to the editor, "with a view to sustain the morality and dignity of the drama." There can be no doubt that the magazine became an invaluable dramatic record, for not only did it give the names of plays and the places and dates of staging, but it also criticised each play, discussed the works of Shakespeare, and noted all theatrical happenings of any significance, such the the rebuilding of the Drury Lane, and the issuance of Theatrical Permits. In brief, the journal is replete with incidents which centered in the theatrical world.

Much the same general format as that of London periodicals is to be noticed in journals from the Provinces. Thus, *The Liverpool Investigator, and Review of Amusements*, issued daily except Sundays and Mondays, from May 29 1821 until November 23 1822, included in its four daily pages playbills, a discussion of Shakespeare's plays, a review of the daily stage fare, letters to the editor, and notes on the lives of various actors, together with personal anecdotes about them. One play, John Banim's tragedy of *Damon and Pythias*, so intrigued the editor that he devoted three issues to a discussion of the work.

The year 1821 witnessed the birth of another dramatic periodical in Liverpool, *The Thespian*. This was also a daily, except for Sundays, and ran for ninety-one issues. It too was a four-page paper, giving playbills, reviews of plays staged in Liverpool, poems, analyses of Shakespeare's plays, and short essays on various dramatic topics. It is interesting to note the reactions of both of these Liverpool editors to the same plays.

The Bath Theatrical Review, a weekly of twenty-seven numbers, published from October 1822 to April 1823, contained playbills, reviews of plays performed, criticism and analyses of Shakespeare's plays, together with letters to the editors and essays on actors and their acting. Once again, as in the other periodicals, the editors did not fear to state their preferences in no uncertain terms.

As a final example of a Provincial theatrical magazine, *The Birmingham Spectator*, a weekly which succeeded *The Theatrical Looker-On*, ran from May 29 to November 1824. In the sixteen pages of each issue it reviewed the plays for each evening of the preceding week, discussed the works of Shakespeare, included essays on various theatrical matters, and even printed extracts from various works. Except when reviewing individual plays this paper differed from other periodicals in that it strove for a more humorous tone and tended to emphasize trifles.

As in London and the Provinces, so in Scotland and Ireland, theatrical periodicals touched on every phase of dramatic activity. Some lasted for one or two numbers while others continued several years. Each is valuable in its own way, and each adds something to the total picture of the dramatic activity of its time.

Earlier it was mentioned that many of the periodicals began with high editorial principles but, for one reason or another, were short-lived. A relatively large percentage of the dramatic magazines had, at best, a precarious existence. In the first half of the nineteenth century, when some 272 periodicals began publication, sixty-three of them were issued no more than four times before they became defunct. Of these, twenty-nine appeared but once. Yet so hardy was the spirit of would-be editors that in the second half of the century the race to print theatrical journals continued. In this period some 274 journals appeared for the first time. Of these, sixty-eight appeared for no more than four issues, while forty were printed only once. Even in the twentieth century, in spite of two world wars — only sixteen journals appeared between 1914 and 1917, and only sixteen in the years 1940 through 1944 — by 1967 626 periodicals were born. Of these, 125 appeared no more than four times, and fifty-five others were published but once.

English theatrical periodicals were published not only in London but in the Provinces, in Scotland, and in Ireland. Although London was, and remains, the home of English theatrical periodicals, it is interesting to note that 439 of the 1235 periodicals listed in this bibliography were published outside of London. By 1850 some fifty-four theatrical periodicals made their appearance in the Provinces; after 1850 263 more appeared, for a total of 317. Scotland had fifty-three dramatic periodicals by 1850, and forty-five subsequent to that date. Finally, in Ireland, twenty appeared by 1850, and only twelve after that time.

For those who are interested in the various cities where dramatic activity was sufficiently vigorous to encourage the publication of periodicals devoted to the theatre or theatrical activities, an appendix appears at the end of the bibliography providing this information. The cities which had such publications are listed in alphabetical order, and the total number of periodicals in each city is indicated.

Scotland's theatrical periodicals are to be found primarily in: Aberdeen (1), Dundee (2), Edinburgh (43), and Glasgow (44). In Ireland, aside from three periodicals published in Belfast, dramatic publication was limited to Dublin, where twenty-eight appeared.

With this brief survey of theatrical publication in Great Britain, the scope and format of the present bibliography can now be examined. First, the list is limited to periodicals printed in England, Scotland, and Ireland, in the English language — with only several exceptions. Second, the word "theatrical" is used somewhat loosely, to include periodicals primarily devoted to: 1) acting; 2) actors and actresses; 3) amateur theatre; 4) amusements which are more or less theatrical; 5) ballet; 6) box office; 7) community theatre; 8) dance; 9) drama; 10) magic; 11) managers of theatres; 12) masque; 13) music halls; 14) musical comedy; 15) open air theatre; 16) opera;

17) operetta; 18) pantomime; 19) puppet; 20) scenery; 21) theatre; 22) variety; and 23) vaudeville. No attempt is made to list the hundreds of literary periodicals which, at one time or another, carried a dramatic column (e.g. the *Public Advertiser*), or devoted some issues to theatrical material. Further, I have deliberately excluded from this bibliography periodicals devoted to the movies, radio dramas, television, and the circus. This task will have to fall to the lot of some future scholar.

Perhaps a word should be said about the term "periodical" as used in this bibliography. I use it to include not only all magazines and all annuals but also a number of works listed as newspapers by the British Museum Newspaper Library.

Each entry, as far as possible, includes the following essential information: 1) complete title; 2) title changes; 3) editor, or editors, when indicated; 4) place of publication; 5) number of volumes when issued as volumes; 6) number of issues; 7) dates of first and last issues; 8) date of first issue when the periodical is still in the process of publication; 9) frequency of issue; 10) libraries where the periodical may be located. Because the British Museum has, by far, the greatest collection of theatrical periodicals, I also indicate the periodicals which were once to be found in the British Museum but were destroyed during the Second World War.

The arrangement of entries is chronological, according to the initial date of publication. For a number of periodicals I have not been able to locate the early issues. When such is the case I simply enter the periodical in chronological sequence, beginning with the date of the first issue which I have located. Within each year the periodicals, when more than one appear, are arranged in alphabetical order.

An alphabetical index has been provided which includes the titles (and variant titles) of magazines, and the names of editors, as well as the various cities where the periodicals were published. References are to the entry numbers. Cross references are made in the index.

Library locations are given, for the most part, for libraries which have complete files of a given periodical. When no single library has a complete file, an attempt is made to locate various libraries whose total holdings will represent the complete file of the work. Sometimes, of course, this is impossible, and only one library will have any issues of a particular magazine. Unless otherwise indicated the use of a specific library symbol following a journal indicates that the library has the complete issue of the periodical. Gaps in library holdings are indicated by the use of brackets: round brackets signify which *complete* volumes are in the library, and square brackets signify *incomplete* volumes. For example, MnU (1, 3–[6, 10–12]) means that the University of Minnesota has vol 1 complete; no vol 2; vols 3–5 complete; vol 6 incomplete; no vols 7–9; and vols 10–12 incomplete. For cases in which only incomplete files are listed, The New York Public Library would be most grateful to have information regarding the whereabouts of complete files.

Finally, perhaps some explanation is in order as to the method of compiling this bibliography. The first step in preparing the first edition was to exhaust available printed sources, the most basic and helpful of which are listed under "References." With the list gathered from these, the next step was to visit as many outstanding libraries in the United States as possible, in order to check their holdings. For this purpose I visited the following institutions: Boston Public Library, Chicago Public Library, Columbia University, Folger Shakespeare Library, Harvard University, Library of Congress, Newberry Library, The New York Public Library, Northwestern University, Princeton University, and the University Libraries of Chicago, Colorado, Illinois, Iowa, Kansas, Michigan, Minnesota, Missouri, Pennsylvania, Wisconsin, and Yale.

Another step in the investigation was to check the accuracy of the information in the printed sources, especially for journals, not available in the United States. The problem here was to establish complete titles, dates of first and last issues, as well as frequency of issue. Further, it was necessary to determine which periodicals with such seemingly dramatic titles as *Harlequin*, *Play*, and *Comedy* were actually devoted to the theatre. To accomplish this task numerous libraries in England, Scotland, and Ireland were contacted. As a result of visiting libraries in the United States, and sending queries abroad, the compiler has been able to clear up a number of errors of date and issue, as well as to exclude from the bibliography those periodicals which are in no sense theatrical.

Since the publication of the first edition in 1962, I was able to obtain a sabbatical leave from Loyola University during the winter and spring of 1967. Those months I spent in London, doing research primarily at the British Museum, where I was able to work in the stacks. As a result of my research at the Museum, and at the Newspaper Library at Colindale, I have been able to add a substantial number of periodicals which did not appear in the first edition. Further, after consulting the periodicals personally I have had to make some changes in various entries of the first edition. These changes can be divided as follows: 1) Periodicals which are to be found in the British Museum Newspaper Library at Colindale, rather than at the British Museum in London, are so noted. As the two libraries are separated by some twenty miles I think that the use of the BM-N symbol for magazines at the Newspaper Library will save scholars hours of wasted effort. 2) A number of periodicals which were listed at the British Museum, but which were actually destroyed in the Second World War, are so noted. 3) Additional library locations are given for a number of the periodicals. 4) Names of editors for some magazines have been added. 5) A number of additional title changes are noted. 6) Some dates have been changed. 7) Frequency of issue for several periodicals not noted in the first edition are given. 8) Complete titles are given for those periodicals whose titles, for one reason or another, do not appear in the first edition. 9) Locations are noted for some periodicals for which no library was specified previously. 10) About 260 magazines which are now on microfilm at Loyola University, Chicago, Illinois, are so noted, for the convenience of scholars in the vicinity. In all, approximately 370 changes of one kind or another have been incorporated into the original 674 entries.

The compiler wishes to express his gratitude, first to the librarians in the United States, who allowed him not only to use the catalogues of their libraries, but also to visit stacks and rare book rooms to check the periodicals personally. Further, when it became necessary to verify some of the information by letter, librarians at the following institutions were most generous in their cooperation: Boston Public Library, Harvard University, Folger Shakespeare Library, the Library of Congress, the Library Company of Philadelphia, The New York Public Library, Princeton University, Rutgers University, the University of California, the University of Illinois, and Yale University.

Second, a most sincere word of appreciation is due to the many librarians in England, Scotland, and Ireland who responded generously to the compiler's letters of enquiry. He particularly wishes to express his gratitude to Miss Mary Flower, who checked some two hundred periodicals at the British Museum; to C. S. Minto of the City Library of Edinburgh, who went to the trouble of compiling a list of all Edinburgh dramatic periodicals which he was able to trace in his library, and some at the National Library of Scotland; to Victor H. Woods, F.L.A., City Librarian of the Reference Library, Birmingham, England, who compiled a list of Birmingham periodicals in the Birmingham Public Library; and to Marion P. Linton, Assistant Keeper at the National Library of Scotland. A deep debt of gratitude is also owed to the librarians of the following libraries, some of whom answered as many as three of my letters of enquiry: Birmingham Public Library, Bodleian Library, Brighton Public Library, Cambridge University, Coventry Public Library, Darlington Public Library, Glasgow University, Gloucester Public Library, Leeds Public Library, Liverpool Public Library, Manchester Public Library, National Library of Ireland, Newcastle-upon-Tyne Public Library, Shakespeare Memorial Library, Sheffield Public Library, and Southampton Public Library. Such wholehearted cooperation from these unrecognized heroes of scholarly research helped to lighten the task of this compiler, and helped to make the work more accurate.

Finally, my greatest debt of gratitude and heartfelt appreciation goes to the numerous members of the staff of the British Museum, who gave so unselfishly of their time in helping me to track down scores of elusive items. Of the many persons to whom I owe so much I wish to single out Mr Ian Willison, Superintendent of the North Library, who not only gave moral support, but also seemed to know the right person to consult for solving each problem.

Thus, if this work has any value it is due to the assistance and cooperation of so many.

Library Symbols[1]

*AAP	Auburn University, Auburn, Alabama
*AU	University of Alabama, University, Alabama
BEDD	Beddington and Wallington Public Libraries
BM	British Museum, London
BM-N	British Museum Newspaper Library, Colindale
BP	Birmingham Public Library, Birmingham
BU	Birmingham University Library, Birmingham
BdP	Bradford Public Library, Bradford
BiP	Brighton Public Library, Brighton
BiR	Birmingham Repertory Theatre Library, Birmingham
BnU	University College of North Wales Library, Bangor, Wales
BrP	Bristol Public Library, Bristol
BrU	University of Bristol Library, Bristol
C	Cambridge University Library, Cambridge
*CLSU	University of Southern California, Los Angeles, California
*CLU	University of California at Los Angeles, Los Angeles, California
CROY	Croydon Public Library, Croydon
*CSmH	Henry E. Huntington Library, San Marino, California
*CSt	Stanford University, Stanford, California
*CU	University of California, Berkeley, California
CaB	University of British Columbia, Vancouver, B. C., Canada
CaL	University of Western Ontario, London, Ontario, Canada
CaOTP	Toronto Public Library, Toronto, Ontario, Canada
CaOTU	University of Toronto, Toronto, Ontario, Canada
CaOOP	Library of Parliament, Ottawa, Ontario, Canada
CaQMM	McGill University, Montreal, Quebec, Canada
*CoU	University of Colorado, Boulder, Colorado

[1] Symbols which are preceded by an asterisk indicate that the library is located in the United States. Unless otherwise indicated all other libraries are located in England.

[xix]

*CtHT-W	Trinity College, Hartford, Connecticut
*CtY	Yale University, New Haven, Connecticut
CvP	Coventry Public Library, Coventry
D	Trinity College, Dublin, Ireland
*DCU	Catholic University of America, Washington, D.C.
*DFo	Folger Shakespeare Library, Washington, D.C.
*DLC	Library of Congress, Washington, D.C.
*DP	United States Patent Office Library, Washington, D.C.
DaP	Darlington Public Library, Darlington
*DeU	University of Delaware, Newark, Delaware
DnP	Dundee Public Libraries, Albert Institute, Dundee, Scotland
DuC	Durham County Library, Durham
E	National Library of Scotland, Edinburgh, Scotland
EALG	Ealing Public Libraries, Ealing
EP	Edinburgh Public Library, Edinburgh, Scotland
ERIT	Erith Public Library, Erith
EdP	Edmonton Public Library, Edmonton, Canada
*FU	University of Florida, Gainesville, Florida
FiP	Finsbury Public Library, London
GM	Mitchell Library, Glasgow, Scotland
GU	Glasgow University Library, Glasgow, Scotland
GaU	University College, Galway, Ireland
HLU	University of Hull, Hull
*IC	Chicago Public Library, Chicago, Illinois
*ICLoy	Loyola University Library, Chicago, Illinois
*ICN	Newberry Library, Chicago, Illinois
*ICU	University of Chicago Library, Chicago, Illinois
*IEN	Northwestern University, Evanston, Illinois
*IU	University of Illinois, Urbana, Illinois
*IaU	University of Iowa Library, Iowa City, Iowa
*InU	Indiana University Library, Bloomington, Indiana

*KU	University of Kansas Library, Lawrence, Kansas
KeP	Kensington Public Library, Kensington
*KyU	University of Kentucky Library, Lexington, Kentucky
LCM	Royal College of Music, London
LGU	Guildhall Library, London
LIE	Institute of Education, University of London, London
LU	London University Library, London
LU-BTM	London University, British Theatre Museum Collection, London
LU-C	University College Library, London
LU-MM	London University, Malcolm Morley Collection, London
LU-TR	Society for Theatre Research Collection, London University, London
LVA	Victoria and Albert Museum Library, London
LdP	Leeds Public Library, Leeds
LdU	Leeds University Library, Leeds
LvP	Liverpool Public Library, Liverpool
LvU	University of Liverpool Library, Liverpool
*MB	Boston Public Library, Boston, Massachusetts
*MBAt	Boston Athenaeum, Boston, Massachusetts
*MBU	Boston University, Boston, Massachusetts
*MH	Harvard University Library, Cambridge, Massachusetts
MP	Manchester Public Library, Manchester
*MdBE	Enoch Pratt Library, Baltimore, Maryland
*MdBP	Peabody Institute, Baltimore, Maryland
*MiD	Detroit Public Library, Detroit, Michigan
*MiDW	Wayne State University, Detroit, Michigan
*MiU	University of Michigan Library, Ann Arbor, Michigan
*MnS	St Paul Public Library, St Paul, Minnesota
*MnU	University of Minnesota Library, Minneapolis, Minnesota
*MoS	St Louis Public Library, St Louis, Missouri
*MoU	University of Missouri Library, Columbia, Missouri
*NB	Brooklyn Public Library, Brooklyn, New York

*NBuG	Grosvenor Library, Buffalo, New York
*NCH	Hamilton College Library, Clinton, New York
*NFQC	Queen's College Library, Flushing, New York
*NIC	Cornell University Library, Ithaca, New York
NLD	National Library of Ireland, Dublin, Ireland
*NN	New York Public Library, New York, New York
*NNC	Columbia University, New York, New York
*NNF	Fordham University Library, Bronx, New York
*NNFr	Frick Art Reference Library, New York, New York
*NNHi	New York Historical Society, New York, New York
*NNU	New York University Libraries, New York, New York
*NNWH	Walter Hampden Memorial Library, New York, New York
NP	Nottingham Public Library, Nottingham
*NPV	Vassar College, Poughkeepsie, New York
*NRU	University of Rochester, Rochester, New York
NU	Nottingham University, Nottingham
*NbU	University of Nebraska Library, Lincoln, Nebraska
*NcD	Duke University Library, Durham, North Carolina
*NcGW	Women's College of the University of North Carolina, Greensboro, North Carolina
*NcU	University of North Carolina, Chapel Hill, North Carolina
*NhD	Dartmouth College, Hanover, New Hampshire
*NhU	University of New Hampshire, Durham, New Hampshire
*NjP	Princeton University Library, Princeton, New Jersey
*NjR	Rutgers University Library, New Brunswick, New Jersey
NwP	Newcastle-upon-Tyne Public Library, Newcastle-upon-Tyne
O	Bodleian Library, Oxford
*OC	Cincinnati Public Library, Cincinnati, Ohio
*OCU	University of Cincinnati Library, Cincinnati, Ohio
*OCl	Cleveland Public Library, Cleveland, Ohio
*OClW	Western Reserve University, Cleveland, Ohio

*OO	Oberlin College, Oberlin, Ohio
*OU	Ohio State University Library, Columbus, Ohio
*PBL	Lehigh University, Bethlehem, Pennsylvania
*PBm	Bryn Mawr College Library, Bryn Mawr, Pennsylvania
*PHC	Haverford College Library, Haverford, Pennsylvania
*PP	Free Library, Philadelphia, Pennsylvania
*PPC	College of Physicians, Philadelphia, Pennsylvania
*PPL-R	Library Company of Philadelphia, Ridgeway Branch, Philadelphia, Pennsylvania
*PSt	Pennsylvania State College Library, University Park, Pennsylvania
*PU	University of Pennsylvania Library, Philadelphia, Pennsylvania
*PV	Villanova University Library, Villanova, Pennsylvania
*PVC	Villanova College, Philadelphia, Pennsylvania
PmP	Portsmouth Public Libraries, Portsmouth, Hants
*RPB	Brown University Library, Providence, Rhode Island
SP	Sheffield Public Library, Sheffield
SU	Sheffield University, Sheffield
SaU	St Andrews University Library, St Andrews, Fife, Scotland
SoP	Southampton Public Libraries, Southampton
SptP	Southport Public Library, Southport, Lancashire
SwC	Swindon Central Library, Swindon
SwP	Swansea Public Library, Swansea
*TU	University of Tennessee, Knoxville, Tennessee
*TxHR	Rice University, Houston, Texas
*TxU	University of Texas Library, Austin, Texas
*ViU	University of Virginia, Charlottesville, Virginia
*ViW	College of William and Mary Library, Williamsburg, Virginia
*WHi	State Historical Society of Wisconsin Library, Madison, Wisconsin
*WM	Milwaukee Public Library, Milwaukee, Wisconsin

*WU	University of Wisconsin, Madison, Wisconsin
WEST	Westminster Public Library, London
*WaU	University of Washington Library, Seattle, Washington
WiM	Wigan Mining and Technical Company, Wigan
WmP	Westminster Public Library, London

Britain's Theatrical Periodicals

Chronological List

1720

The Anti-Theatre. By Sir John Falstaffe, pseud [Sir Richard Steele?] London. Nos 1–15. 15 Feb – 4 Apr 1720. Semiweekly.   ***1***
    CtY, ICLoy (microfilm), MB, MH, O

The Theatre. By Sir John Edgar, pseud [Sir Richard Steele] London: Printed for W. Chetwood. Nos 1–28. 2 Jan – 5 Apr 1720. Semiweekly. [Other editions printed in 1720, and in 1791]   ***2***
    BM, DFo (missing Nos 27–28), ICLoy (microfilm), MB, MH, O, TxU

1734

Cote's Weekly Journal; or, The English Stage-Player. London: Printed by J. Taylor, at T. Edlin's. Nos 1–9. 11 May – 6 July 1734. Weekly.   ***3***
    ICLoy (microfilm), O

The Prompter, a Theatrical Paper. [By Aaron Hill and William Popple] London. Nos 1–173. 12 Nov 1734 – 2 July 1736. Semiweekly.   ***4***
    CtY (missing Nos 24, 84, 93, 116, 138, 152), ICLoy (microfilm), O

1739

Country Correspondent; or, The Stage Monitor. To be continued occasionally. By Tho. Earl, Esq. London: Printed for Charles Corbet, over-against St. Dunston's Church in Fleet-street, and Sold by the Booksellers of London and Westminster, and at several Coffee-Houses, &c. No 4. 14 Aug 1739. [This is signed from Tom's Coffee-House, Covent-Garden. A second paper in this volume is: *The Country Correspondent: Humbly address'd to Gustavus Vasa, Esq.* It is dated, 26 May 1739] Irregular.   ***5***
    DFo

1749

The Play-house Journal. Dublin. No 1. 18 Jan 1749/50. [Single sheet]   ***6***
    BM, ICLoy (microfilm)

1751

The Nettle. Dublin. No 1. 24 Oct 1751.   ***7***
    BM, ICLoy (microfilm)

1752

The Covent-Garden Journal. Dublin. Vols 1–2. Nos 1–76. 23 Jan 1752 – 7 June 1753. then, *The Covent-Garden Journal; or, the Censor.* Vol 2. Nos 77–82. 14 June – 19 July 1753. then, *The Censor; or, Covent Garden Journal.* Vol 2. Nos 83–100. 26 July – 22 Nov 1753. Irregular.   ***8***
    BM-N, CSmH, CtY, ICLoy (microfilm), MH, NjP, O (incomplete)

The Dramatic Censor. Being remarks upon the conduct, character, and catastrophe of our most celebrated plays. By several hands. London: Printed for

Richard Manby, and H. S. Cox. No 1. 1752. [In No 1, which treats of Otway's *Venice Preserved* BY MR. DERRICK, the publisher announces that No 2 will be remarks upon the play of *Richard the Third*, as it is altered from Shakespeare by Mr. Cibber . . . by Mr. Gentleman. I can find no record of a second number of this periodical but, in 1770, *The Dramatic Censor*, by Francis Gentleman, contained as its first article, *Richard the Third*, as altered from Shakespeare by Cibber]   9

BM, CtY, DFo, ICLoy (microfilm), MH, NjP, O

Have At You All; or, The Drury-Lane Journal. By Madam Roxana Termagant [i.e., Bonnel Thornton] Address'd to Sir Alexander Drawcansir [pseud] Author of the Covent Garden Journal. Continued every Thursday. London: Printed: and sold at the Publick Register Office in King Street, Covent Garden. Where Letters to the Authoress are taken in. Nos 1–13 [i.e., 12] 16 Jan – 9 Apr 1752. Weekly. [No 12 is omitted in the numbering, and printed as No 13. This error accounts for the mistakes by some libraries which indicate a total of 13 issues instead of 12]   10

BM, CSmH, CtY, DFo, MH, NIC, O

1754

The Tuner.   Letter the [1st]–5th. To be occasionally continu'd. London: Printed for M. Cooper, and sold by Mr. Lewis, Mrs. Kingman, and G. Woodfall. 21 Jan 1754 – 5 Nov 1755. Irregular. [The periodical has been attributed to Paul Hiffernan]   11

CtY, ICLoy (microfilm), O

1758

Theatrical Review: for the year 1757, and Beginning of 1758.   Containing critical remarks on the principal performers of both the theatres. Together with observations on the dramatic pieces, new or revived; that have been performed at either house within that period. To which is added, a scale of the comparative merit of the above performers. London: Printed for J. Coote. 1758. Annual. [On Drury Lane, and Covent Garden theatres. For 1757 and beginning of 1758]   12

CSmH, CtY, ICLoy (microfilm), InU, IU, MB, MH, NN, O, PPL-R, Garrick Club

1763

The Theatrical Review; or, Annals of the Drama.   London: Printed for Mess. Wilson and Fell, and S. Williams. Nos 1–6. 1 Jan – 1 June 1763. Monthly. [Imitates the *Thespian.* The two periodicals were bitter rivals]   13

BM, CLU, DFo, DLC, ICLoy (microfilm), ICU, MB, MH, O

1767

The Monitor; or, Green-Room Laid Open.   London: Printed for W. Bingley. No 1. 17 Oct 1767. then, *The Theatrical Monitor; or, Stage Management and Green-Room Laid Open.* Nos 2–18. 24 Oct 1767 – 16 Apr 1768. Weekly [The British Museum has another edition of the work. The title page for the volume reads: *The Monitor; or Green-Room Laid Open; With Remarks Thereon, Which occasioned the Letters to Mr. Spatter*]   14

BM (No 1), DFo (17 Oct 1767 – 27 Feb 1768), O (Nos 1–9, to 19 Dec 1767)

1768

Covent Garden Chronicle. London: Printed for H. Gardner, opposite St. Clement's Church, Strand. No 2. 9 Mar 1768. [There is no indication of frequency. This is the only number of the periodical which I have been able to locate. It is critical of plays and players, in opposition to the *Theatrical Monitor*]   **14a**
  O

1770

The Dramatic Censor; or, Critical Companion. [By Francis Gentleman] London: Printed for J. Bell, near Exeter-Change, in the Strand; and C. Etherington, at York. Vols 1–2. 1770 [The individual essays are not dated]   **15**
  BM, BP, CSmH, CtY, DLC, ICN, ICU, IU, LU, MB, NcU, NIC, NN, NNC, O

1772

The Macaroni, Scavoir Vivre, and Theatrical Magazine. London: Printed for the Authors and sold by J. Williams. Vols 1–2. [Nos 1–24] Oct 1772 – Sept 1774. then, *The Macaroni, Savoir Vivre, and Theatrical Magazine; or, Monthly Register of Taste, Fashions, and Amusements.* Vol 3. [No 25] Oct 1774. Monthly [There are slight variations in the title]   **16**
  BM (missing p 481–488 of the issue for Aug 1773 and p 567–568 of the issue for Sept 1773), MB (missing all after Dec 1773)

The Theatrical Review; or, New Companion to the Play-House. Containing a critical and historical account of every tragedy, comedy, opera, farce, &c. exhibited at the theatres during the last season; with remarks on the actors who performed the principal characters. The whole interspersed with occasional reflections on dramatic poetry in general; the characters of the best English dramatic authors; and observations on the conduct of the Managers. Calculated for the lover of theatrical amusements. By a society of gentlemen, independent of managerial influence. [Ed by J. Potter] London: Printed for S. Crowder, in Pater-noster Row; J. Wilkie, No 71, St. Paul's Church-yard and J. Walter, at Charing Cross. Vols 1–2. 1772. [A reprint of articles which first appeared in the *Public Ledger*, reissued in two volumes with corrections and additions. The first review was dated 21 Sept [1771], and the last, 10 Apr [1772] Index]   **17**
  BM, CSmH, CtY, ICLoy (microfilm), MB, MH, Garrick Club

1774

Public Advertiser; or, The Theatrical Chronicle. Dublin. Nos 67–68. 11/14 – 16 Feb 1774. [I have not been able to discover any other issues]   **18**
  BM (missing all before No 67)

1776

The Monthly Museum, Comprehending a Political and Parliamentary Remembrance; a Classical Miscellany, a Poetical Kalendar, a Critical Catalogue, a Theatrical Diary, and an Historical Register for the Year. London: Printed for Wallis and Stonehouse, Ludgate Street. [No 1] 1776. Monthly. [*The Theatrical*

Diary is for the month of January at the Theatre Royal, Drury Lane, and Covent Garden]   *19*
ICLoy (microfilm), ICN (missing p 25–30)

1784

The Edile; or, A Review of the Dublin Stage.   Dublin. Nos 1–5. Nov 1784.   *20*
Not located (O'Neill p 86; Loewenberg p 23)

1786

The Dramatic Magazine; or, Tragic, Comic and Operatical Library.   London: G. Lister. Nos 1–12 [Dec] 1786 – 1787 [A note in No 2 reads, "To be continued monthly"] Monthly.   *21*
C, ICLoy (microfilm), MnU (1, 3–[6, 10–12])

1788

The Theatrical Register.   Containing candid and impartial strictures on the various performances at the Theatre-Royal, York, interspersed with occasional remarks by obliging correspondents. York: Printed by L. Lund. Vol 1. Nos 1–18. [4 Feb – 27 May?] 1788. Weekly. [The issues are not dated]   *22*
BM, DLC, ICLoy (microfilm), MH (missing Nos 1, 9–18), PU

1789

The Prompter, a Theatrical Paper.   [By James Fennell] London: Nos 1–19. 24 Oct – 10 Dec 1789. Daily (irregular)   *23*
BM, ICLoy (microfilm), O

1790

The Lives and Traits of the Bon Ton Theatricals.   (To be continued weekly). Together with the managers and performers of all the principal theatres in the Three Kingdoms. London: Printed for the Authors, and sold by J. Southern, St. James's-street; W. Nicol Jun. No 1. 14 June 1790. Weekly.   *24*
DFo

1791

The Conjuror's Magazine; or, Magical and Physiognomical Mirror, Including a superb edition of Lavater's Essays on Physiognomy.   London. Vols 1–2. Aug 1791 – July 1793. then, *The Astrologer's Magazine; and Philosophical Miscellany*. With a monthly portion of Lavater's Physiognomy, etc. Aug 1793 – Jan 1794. Monthly.   *25*
BM (two copies; imperfect), NN, O

Theatrical Guardian.   [Ed by James Fennell] London: Printed for the Author, and sold by E. and T. Williams. Nos 1–6. 5 Mar – 9 Apr 1791. Weekly.   *26*
BM (missing Nos 5–6), CU, DFo, ICLoy (microfilm), MB, MH (Nos 1–5), NIC, O

1792

The Thespian Magazine and Literary Repository. London: Printed by T. Wilkins. Vols 1–3. [Nos 1–24] June 1792 – Sept 1794. Monthly [except for Aug and Sept 1793, and May and Aug 1794, when no issues were printed. Each volume has an index]   27

     CSmH, CtY, DFo, DLC, ICLoy (microfilm), ICU, MB, MBAt, MH, MiU, NN, NNHi, O (incomplete), PU, Garrick Club

1795

Dramatic Review; or, Mirror of the Stage. London. 1795.   28

     Not located (Crane No 1206)

The Magic and Conjuring Magazine and Wonderful Chronicle. London. Vol 1. Nos 1–4. 1795. [I have been unable to determine the dates of the first and last issues, or frequency]   29

     BM (destroyed)

The Monthly Mirror. Reflecting men and manners; with strictures on their epitome, the stage. London: T. Bellamy. Vols 1–22. Dec 1795 – Dec 1806. New Series, Vols 1–9. Jan 1807 – Feb 1811. Monthly.   30

     BM, CtY, ICLoy (microfilm), ICN (missing new series, Vols 1–2), ICU, LU (missing Vol 31), MB (missing new series, Vol 9), MH, NIC, NcU, O, TxHR, Garrick Club

1796

The Thespian Telegraph; or, Dramatic Mirror. London: Printed and Published (for the editors) by J. Hammond, No 12, St. Martin's Lane, Charing Cross. And Sold by H. D. Symonds, No. 20, Paternoster Row, J. Aldrich, Great Piazza, Covent Garden, T. Woodham, No 34, High Holborn, Allin, Ann Street, Birmingham, and all Booksellers and Newsmen in Town and Country. No 1. [June] 1796. [See *Notes and Queries* 11th Series IV (19 Aug 1911) 149] Monthly.   31

     DFo, ICLoy (microfilm)

1800

British Theatre. London. 1800.   32

     Not located (Crane No 1082)

The Dramatic Censor; or, Weekly Theatrical Report. Comprising a complete chronicle of the British Stage, and a regular series of theatrical criticism in every department of the drama. By Thomas Dutton. London: J. Roch. Vols 1–5. Nos 1–52. 4 Jan 1800 – Dec 1801. Weekly [4 Jan – 21 June 1800] Monthly [July 1800 – Dec 1801]   33

     BM, CSmH, CtY (missing Vols 3–4), DLC, ICN, MB, MH, NIC, O

1801

Authentic Memoirs of the Green-Room. Evolving Sketches, Biographical, Critical, and Characteristic, of the Performers of the Theatres-Royal, Drury-Lane, Covent-Garden, and the Hay-Market. London: Printed by and for J. Roache. Vols 1–4. [1801]–1804. Annual.   34

     BM (destroyed), CtY, MB (missing Vol 4)

The Theatrical Repertory.   Containing criticism on the performances which were represented at Drury-Lane and Covent-Garden theatres, during the season 1801–02. With occasional observations on other places of public entertainment. London: Printed by T. Woodfall, No 2, Little Russel-Street, Covent-Garden, and may be had of all the Booksellers. Nos 1–28. 19 Sept 1801 – 28 June 1802. Weekly.   **35**
> BM, CSmH, (1–15), CtY, DFo, DLC, ICLoy (microfilm), MB (missing Nos 27–28), MH, NhD, (1–26), NIC, NN

1803

The Edinburgh Theatrical Censor.   Edinburgh: J. Buchanan. Nos 1–12. 21 Mar – 28 July 1803. Weekly (irregular).   **36**
> CtY, ICLoy (microfilm), MB

The Glasgow Theatrical Register, from Nov 16 to Dec 8, 1803, Inclusive.   Containing cursory remarks on the performances at the theatre. Glasgow: W. Falconer. 1803. [Covers a three week season under Jackson's management]   **37**
> CtY

The Man in the Moon, Consisting of Essays and Critiques on the Politics, Morals, Manners, Drama, etc., of the Present Day.   Ed by Geo. Brewer. London. Nos 1–24. 12 Nov 1803 – 28 Jan 1804. Biweekly and weekly [Hope, No 564, says this periodical is by Will. Smelly, and not George Brewer]   **38**
> BM, CtY, DLC, ICLoy (microfilm), ICU, MB, MH, MnU, NjP, NN, O

The Townsman, Addressed to the Inhabitants of Manchester on Theatricals.   [By James Watson] Manchester: G. Banks. Nos 1–24. 8 Dec 1803 – 12 Jan 1805. Triweekly, weekly, triweekly.   **39**
> BM, CSmH (missing Nos 19–24), ICLoy (microfilm), MB, MH (1–20)

1804

Argus; or, The Theatrical Observer.   Containing critical, yet impartial strictures, on the merits and demerits of the principal performers of the Theatre Royal, Manchester. Manchester. Nos 1–7. 24 Nov 1804 – 30 Mar 1805. Irregular. [No 6 is dated 9 Feb 1805]   **40**
> BM (destroyed), MB (missing No 7), MH (missing all after No 4)

1805

Argus Corrected; Containing an Analytical Enquiry into His Qualifications as a Theatrical Observer; and a Detection of His Numerous Errors. Manchester. Nos 1–2. 5–19 Jan 1805. Biweekly.   **41**
> BM (destroyed)

Glasgow Theatrical Register.   Glasgow. Pt. IV. Nos 1–2; supplement, Nos 1–3. 1 May – 5 Oct 1805. Irregular. [I have been unable to determine the extent of the issue]   **42**
> MH

Stage; or, Theatrical Touchstone.   To be continued every fortnight. By Pertinax Probe, Esq. London: G. Hayden and A. MacPherson. Vol 1. [Nos 1–4] 20 July – 28 Sept 1805. Biweekly (irregular).   **43**
> ICLoy (microfilm), ICN

Theatric Magazine; or, General Repository. Dublin. Nos 1–2. 30 Dec 1805 – 13 Jan 1806. Biweekly.   **44**
    I, ICLoy (microfilm)

The Theatrical Recorder. Ed by Thomas Holcroft. London: Printed by C. Mercier & Co. Vols 1–2. Nos 1–12. Jan – Dec 1805. Monthly. [There is an added issue following No 12 called "Supplement to Vol 2."]   **45**
    CtY, CLU, ICLoy (microfilm), ICN, ICU, LU, MB, MH, NIC, NN, O (missing Vol 1)

1806

Authentic Memoirs of the Green Room (For 1806). Involving Sketches, Biographical, Critical & Characteristic, of the Performers of the Theatres Royal, Drury-Lane, Covent-Garden, and the Haymarket. London: Printed by and for J. Roach, at The Britannia Printing Office. Vols 1–2. 1806. [This is another edition, with new title pages, of parts 2–4 of the 1801–1804 edition, with the addition of a new part] Annual.   **46**
    BM, MB (dates the work 1814?)

The Liverpool Dramatic Censor; or, Theatrical Recorder. Containing strictures on actors and actresses, and a critical analysis of every popular dramatic composition represented at the Theatre Royal in this town during the season. With biographical sketches of celebrated dramatists. Liverpool. Vol 1. Nos 1–4. 8 June – 1 July 1806. Weekly.   **47**
    BM (missing all after No 1), LvP, MB, NIC

The Public Reporter; or, Monthly Register of Events. Containing a faithfull record of public and domestic occurrences: an impartial review of the drama; and an ample detail of our police, courts of law, the funds, markets, etc. London. Jan 1806. Monthly. [I have been unable to discover whether there were additional issues of this periodical]   **48**
    BM (destroyed)

The Thespian Review. An examination of the merits and demerits of the performers on the Manchester stage. Pro and con. Manchester. Nos 1–7. 1 Feb – 15 Mar 1806. Weekly.   **49**
    BM, ICLoy (microfilm)

1807

The Artist. A collection of essays relative to painting, poetry, sculpture, architecture, the drama, discoveries of science, and various other subjects. Ed by Prince Hoare. London. Vol 1. Nos 1–21. 14 Mar – 1 Aug 1807. Vol 2. Nos 1–20. 1809. Weekly (in Vol 1). [The issues are undated in Vol 2. The work was reprinted in 1810]   **50**
    BM, ICLoy (microfilm), MB, NN, NjP, O

The Censor; or, Theatrical Review. By a Candid Hearer. To be continued occasionally. Manchester. 1807. Irregular.   **51**
    Not located (Loewenberg p 45)

The Theatrical Review. [Ed by Thomas Holcroft?] London: Printed by D. N. Shury. Nos 1–3. 1 Jan – 1 Mar 1807. Monthly [The Folger Shakespeare Library copy attributes the periodical to Thomas Holcroft]   **52**
    DFo, ICLoy (microfilm), MB

1808

Examiner. A Sunday paper on politics, domestic economy, and theatricals. London. [Nos 1–1508] 3 Jan 1808 – 25 Dec 1836. Weekly. [Successively edited by such men as Leigh Hunt and A. Fonblanque]   **53**
  BM, CtY, DLC, MB, MH, NN

1809

Lincoln Dramatic Censor. Lincoln. Nos 1–4. 21 Oct – 18 Nov 1809. Weekly. **54**
  MB, MH

1810

The Covent Garden Journal. Published for J. Stockdale, London, 1810. [Not considered as a periodical because I have not been able to find proof that the work was published in individual numbers. The postscript, p 815, although it states that "this Work was published in Weekly Numbers," does not indicate where these weekly numbers appeared as a separate work]   **54a**

1811

The Dramatic Censor; or, Critical and Biographical Illustration of the British Stage. For the year 1811. Involving a correct register of every night's performances at our metropolitan theatres, and published with a view to sustain the morality and dignity of the drama. Ed by J. M. Williams. London: Printed by G. Brimmer. 1811. Monthly. [Published in monthly parts]   **55**
  BM, BP, CSmH, CtY, DFo, DLC, IaU, ICLoy (microfilm), ICN, MB, MH, MiU, NIC, NcU, O, OC, WU

The Irish Dramatic Censor. Dublin. Nos 1–6. 1811 – 1812. [The issues are not dated]   **56**
  BM, ICLoy (microfilm), MH

The Scourge; or, Monthly Expositor of Imposture and Folly. London. [Nos 1–40] Jan 1811 – Apr 1814. then, *The Scourge; or, Literary Theatrical and Miscellaneous Magazine.* [Nos 1–26] May 1814 – June 1816. then, *The Scourge and Satirist; or, Literary Theatrical and Miscellaneous Magazine.* [Nos 1–4] 1 July – 1 Oct 1816. Monthly. [Contains colored illustrations by G. Cruikshank]   **57**
  DLC (Vols 1–9), MH, NjP, O

1812

The Harmonic Olio, Embracing All the New Songs As They Come Out at Different Theatres. Hampstead. Nos 1–7. 1812. Biweekly. [Words only]   **58**
  LGU (missing Nos 2, 6)

The Theatrical Inquisitor; or, Literary Mirror. London: Printed and published by W. Oxberry. [Later, Published by Sherwood, Neely, and Jones] Vol 1. Sept 1812 – Jan 1813. then, *The Theatrical Inquisitor; or, Monthly Mirror.* Vols 2–14. Feb 1813 – June 1819. then, *The Theatrical Inquisitor.* Vol 15. July – Dec 1819. then, *The Theatrical Inquisitor and Monthly Mirror.* Vol. 16. Jan – June 1820. then, *The Theatrical Inquisitor.* Vol 17. June – Nov 1820. Monthly. [Merged into, *The London Magazine* and *Monthly Critical and Dramatic Review*]   **59**
  BM (missing all before Aug 1813), CSmH (1–16), DLC, ICLoy (microfilm), IU (1–16), MB (Sept 1812 – June 1814), MH, MiU, NB, O, Garrick Club (Vols 1–16)

1813

Theatre. By Edward Range, Esq. Edinburgh. Nos 1–[8]. 17 Nov 1813 – 5 [Jan 1814] Weekly   **60**
    BM, ICLoy (microfilm), EP

Theatrical Gazette. London. No 1. 30 Nov 1813. [I have been unable to learn any other details about this periodical]   **61**
    BM (destroyed)

1814

Dramatic Review, and Register of the Fine Arts. London. Nos 1–3. 12 – 26 Feb 1814. Weekly.   **62**
    ICLoy (microfilm), ICU

The Monthly Theatrical Reporter; or, Literary Mirror. By Tho. Dutton. London: Printed and Published by J. Roach. Vol 1. [Nos 1–10] Oct 1814 – July 1815. Monthly. [Only the first four issues are numbered. Nos 1–4 lack subtitle. Nos 5–10 are by Thomas Dutton. Contains plates by G. and I. R. Cruikshank]   **63**
    BM, C, ICLoy (microfilm), MH, O, SaU

The Stage. London: Printed and Published by D. Deans, at the Stage Office, Catherine Street, Strand. Vol 1. Nos 1–22. 17 Nov 1814 – 13 Apr 1815. Vol 2. Nos 1–21. 20 Apr – 11 Sept 1815. Vol 3. Nos 1–20. 16 Sept 1815 – 23 Dec 1815. New Series. Vol 1. Nos 1–47. 30 Dec 1815 – 16 Nov 1816. Weekly. [Index in each volume]   **64**
    BM, DLC, ICN (1–[2]), ICLoy (microfilm), O

1815

The Prompter; or, Theatrical Investigator. Manchester: Printed and published by M. Willson. Nos 1–19. [Nov] 1815 – [Mar] 1816. Weekly. [No 2 criticises the productions for the week of 28 Nov – 1 Dec 1815. No 19 criticises productions as late as 27 Mar 1816. A second edition was also published in 1816]   **65**
    BM, CtY, ICLoy (microfilm), MB

Theatrical Gazette. London. No 1. 30 Nov 1815. Daily.   **66**
    BM (destroyed), ICLoy (microfilm), MH, NN

1816

The Corrector; or, Dramatic Intelligence. Containing original criticisms on the performances and performers at the Theatre-Royal, Liverpool, for the summer season, 1816. Liverpool. Nos 1–8. [May – June] 1816. Weekly [?] [The numbers are undated, but No 2 criticises productions from 13 May to 17 May 1816. No 8 mentions a performance for 28 June 1816]   **67**
    BM (destroyed), MH

Covent-Garden Theatrical Gazette. A complete analysis of the evening's entertainments, with the names of characters, performers, etc. Ed by W. Leggett. London: J. Fairburn. Nos 1–148. 9 Sept 1816 – 9 Apr 1817. Triweekly [Nos 1–11]; daily [Nos 12–13]; five days a week [Nos 14–22]; six days a week [Nos 23–148]   **68**
    BM (Nos 1–140), DFo, ICLoy (microfilm), MH

Drury-lane Theatrical Gazette.   London: Published by John Fairburn. Nos 1–
148. 7 Sept 1816 – 9 Apr 1817. Three days a week [in 1816]; six days a week
[in 1817] [There are some irregularities in frequency of publication]   **69**
   BM (missing Nos 141–148), DFo, ICLoy (microfilm)

The Prompter Prompted; or, The Theatrical Investigator Dissected.   By Jeremy
Collier, Jun. Manchester. Nos 1-5. 1816. [The issues are not dated]   **70**
   BM (destroyed), ICLoy (microfilm), NIC

The Thespian Critique.   Inscribed (without permission) to William Murray, of
the Theatre Royal, Edinburgh, by Patrick Pit, Esq. Edinburgh. Nos 1–5. Oct –
Nov 1816. Weekly.   **71**
   EP, ICLoy (microfilm), MB (Nos 1–4)

1817

The British Stage and Literary Cabinet.   By J. Broughton, and J. Pulham, Esqs.
London: Printed by F. Marshall, Kenton Street, Brunswick Square. Published
for the Proprietors, by Chappell, Royal Exchange. Vols 1–6. Nos 1–62. Jan
1817 – Feb 1822. Monthly. [Thomas Kenrick, Esq. edited Vol 5. The first three
volumes have indexes. This periodical is a rival of *The Theatrical Inquisitor*] **72**
   BM (missing all after 1820), ICLoy (microfilm), MH, NIC (Nos 1–61), Garrick Club
   (Vols 1–5, Nos 1–60. Dec 1821)

The Knight Errant.   A literary miscellany, consisting of original prose and verse,
with occasional notices of new books, the drama, etc., etc., by Sir Hercules
Quixote, R. E.   London. Vol 1. Nos 1–5. 5 July – 16 Aug 1817. Weekly (irregular).   **73**
   BM, ICLoy (microfilm)

1818

*The Theatrical Gazette; or, Nightly Reflector of the Theatres Royal, Covent Gar-
den, and Drury Lane.*   London. No 1. 7 Sept 1818. [The first theatrical notice
in the periodical is dated, 7 Sept 1818] Daily.   **74**
   BM (destroyed)

The Thespian Censor; or, Weekly Dramatic Journal.   Edinburgh. Nos 1–3.
19 Jan – 2 Feb 1818. Weekly.   **75**
   EP, ICLoy (microfilm)

1819

Dramatic Inspector.   Dublin. No 1. 20 May 1819.   **76**
   Not located (O'Neill, p 86)

The Inspector — a Weekly Dramatic Paper.   Ed by J. B. Collis. London. Nos 1–4.
2 – 23 Jan 1819. Weekly.   **77**
   BM (destroyed), O (missing Nos 2–4)

Proceedings of the Sheffield Shakespeare Club.   Sheffield. Nov 1819 – Jan 1829.
[A reprint of the accounts of the annual dinners of the Club, as printed in the
local newspaper. This reprint was published in 1829]   **78**
   BP, ICLoy (microfilm), LdP, SP

The Theatre; or, Dramatic and Literary Mirror.   Containing theatrical essays —
literary reviews — theatrical criticisms — original and selected poetry — the-

atrical anecdotes — provincial theatres, etc. London. Vol 1. Nos 1–23. 20 Feb – 30 Oct 1819. Weekly and biweekly [Hope, No 654, says that it was extended to 28 numbers]   **79**

MB, MH (incomplete), NN (missing Nos 15–23), O (Nos 1–23)

1820

The Cornucopia; or, Literary and Dramatic Mirror. Containing a variety of interesting subjects under the head of miscellanies. Embellished with coloured engravings, illustrative of interesting dramatic incidents, designed and engraved by J. Findlay. London: J. Jameson. Vol 1. Nos 1–13. Sept 1820 – Sept 1821. Monthly.   *80*

BM, BP, ICLoy (microfilm), ICN, MB, MH

The Critic; or, Weekly Theatrical Reporter. London: Printed for the Proprietors by W. Molineux. Nos 1–7. 22 July – 2 Sept 1820. Weekly.   *81*

CtY, ICLoy (microfilm)

Dramatic Miscellany and Medley of Literature. London. No 1. 8 Apr 1820. [I have been unable to discover any other information concerning this periodical]
BM (destroyed)   *82*

Keene's Theatrical Evening Mirror. London: Printed by W. Keene. Vol 1. Nos 1–25. 18 June – 24 Oct 1820. Irregular. [The second number was published three months after the first issue, on Sept 20. In No 25, 24 Oct, the editor says that he is giving up publication of the magazine]   *83*

BM (missing No 7)

The London Magazine; and Monthly Critical and Dramatic Review. London: Published by Gold and Northhouse, No 19, Great Russell-Street, Covent-Garden; and Sold by John Chappell and Son, 98, Royal Exchange, and by All Booksellers Throughout the United Kingdom. Vols 1–3, [No 13] Jan 1820 – Jan 1821. then, *Gold's London Magazine, and Theatrical Inquisitor.* Vol 3, No 14 – Vol 10. Feb 1821 – 1824. New Series, Vols 1–10. 1825 – 1829. Monthly. [The title varies. Absorbed, *The Theatrical Inquisitor*]   *84*

BM (missing Vol 1 [Nos 1–6], and Vol 4, No 1), ICLoy (microfilm), IU (incomplete), MH (incomplete)

Theatrical Observer; or, Thespian Critique. Glasgow. No 1. 22 July 1820.   *85*

BP, ICLoy (microfilm)

1821

The Censor; or, Review of Public Amusements in Liverpool. Liverpool. Nos 1–11. Dec 1821 – Feb 1822. Monthly.   *86*

Not located (Loewenberg p 47)

The Drama, a Daily Register of Histrionic Performances on the Dublin Stage. And critical review of general dramatic literature. By two gentlemen of the Dublin University. Dublin: Printed by W. Underwood. Vol 1. Nos 1–42. 23 Oct – 10 Dec 1821. Six days a week. [Index]   *87*

DLC (missing p 49–50, and Nos 34–42), ICLoy (microfilm), MB, MH, NIC, NN 1[2]

The Drama; or, Theatrical Pocket Magazine. Wholly dedicated to the stage, and containing original, dramatic biography, essays, criticisms, poetry, reviews, anecdotes, bon mots, chit chat, with occasional notices of the country theatres. The whole forming a complete critical and biographical illustration of the British stage. London: Published by T. and J. Elvey. Vols 1–7. May 1821 – Apr 1825. New Series. Vols 1–2. Nos 1–18. 1825–1826. Monthly. **88**

   BM (missing New Series), C, CtY, DFo, MB, MH, NjP (missing New Series), O, PU (missing New Series), Garrick Club (missing New Series Vol 2)

The Dramatic Review. Dublin. Nos 1–17. 19 Apr – 11 May 1821. Five days a week. **89**

   Not located (Crane No 1206; Powers (p 10) says that he copied it from the Catalogue of the Dublin Library.)

The Liverpool Theatrical Investigator, and Review of Amusements. Liverpool: T. B. Johnson, printer, Manlety Lane. Vol 1. Nos 1–129. 29 May – Dec 1821. Daily (irregular). Vol 2. Nos 1–26. 5 June – 23 Nov 1822. Weekly (irregular). **90**

   BM (missing Vol 2), ICLoy (microfilm), ICN, MB (missing Vol 1, Nos 1–2, 6, 16–17, 19–20, 22–23, 29, 80–102, 105–125, 127–129; Vol 2, No 21)

Original Theatrical Observer. Dublin. Vols 1–13. 19 July 1821 – 13 Aug 1822. Six days a week. [The title, until 4 Dec 1821, was, *The Theatrical Observer.* When the editor learned that another periodical was using the same name he changed the title] **91**

   ICLoy (microfilm), MB (Vols 10, 12–13), MH (Vols 6–11), MiU (Vols 1–10)

The Stage. A theatrical paper published daily. [Ed by F. W. Conway, and J. T. Haydn] Dublin. Vol 1. Nos 1–30. 9 Apr – 12 May 1821. Daily. **92**

   BM (missing No 22; title page mutilated), ICLoy (microfilm), MH, NLD

Thalia's Tablet and Melpomene's Memorandum Book. London. No 1. 8 Dec 1821.

   ICLoy (microfilm), MH (two editions) **93**

The Theatrical Observer. Dublin: Printed by J. J. Nolan. Vols 1–8. 19 Jan 1821 – 28 Jan 1822. then, *Nolan's Theatrical Observer.* Vols 9–19. 5 Feb 1822 – 1825. Six days a week. **94**

   BM (3rd ed 4 vols. 1821), CtY (Vols 1–10), IU (Vols 1 [2]–[5–6]–14–[17]), MB (Vols 1–4), MH (Vols 1–[7]–[10]–[14–19])

The Theatrical Observer: and Daily Bill of the Play. London: Printed by E. Thomas, Denmark-Court, Strand. Published by C. Harris, 25, Bow Street. Vols 1–53. Nos 1–16,897. 24 Sept 1821 – 31 Aug 1876. Six days a week (with some irregularities). [The title varies] **95**

   BM (destroyed), ICU (incomplete), LVA (1821–1831), MB (3 Nov 1821 – 30 June 1876), MH (incomplete), NN (1821–1857), O (Vols 1–10)

Theatrical Spectator. London. Nos 1–11. 7 Apr – 23 June 1821. Weekly. **96**

   ICLoy (microfilm), MH (Nos 1–2, 4–11)

Thespian. A series of essays on the drama, applicable chiefly to the theatricals of Liverpool. Liverpool: Printed by Smith and Melling. Nos 1–91. 1 Aug – 1 Dec 1821. Six days a week. **97**

   CSmH, DLC, ICLoy (microfilm), MH, O (missing No 91)

1822

The Bath Theatrical Review. A series of criticisms on the performers and drama in general, for the season 1822–23. Bath: Printed and published for the Proprietors, at Keenes' Bath Journal and General Printing Office, No 7, Kingsmead-street. Vol 1. Nos 1–25. 12 Oct 1822 – 30 Oct 1823. New Series, Vol 1. Nos 1–2. 6–8 Dec 1824. Weekly (from No 11. Irregular before). **98**
BM, DFo, MH, NIC, NjP, O

The Edinburgh Dramatic Review. Edinburgh: Printed for James L. Huie. Vols 1–9. Nos 1–441. 7 Oct 1822 – 6 July 1824. New Series, Vols 1–5. Nos 1–245. 15 Nov 1824 – 24 Dec 1825. Six days a week. **99**
DFo (missing all after Vol 8), E (missing all after New Series, Vol 3), MB (missing New Series), MH, NN (missing all after Vol 7)

Independent Theatrical Observer. Dublin. Vols 10–11. [Nos 1–50] 17 June – 14 Aug 1822. Six days a week. [Numbering begins with Vol 10 as this was to supersede the *Original Theatrical Observer* which, however, did not cease] **100**
MB (Vol 10, No 33; Vol 11, Nos 2, 8), MH

The Mirror of the Stage; or, New Dramatic Censor; Consisting of Original Memoirs of the Principal Actors, Criticisms on the New Pieces and Performers As They Appear, Anecdotes, Original Essays, etc. London: Published for the Proprietors by E. Duncombe, at his Theatrical Repository. Vols 1–5, No 2. Nos 1–24. 12 Aug 1822 – 11 Oct 1824. Biweekly (then once every three weeks). [The subtitle varies] **101**
BM, CLU (Vols 1–4), ICLoy (microfilm, Vols 1–4), MB (Vol 3, Nos 2–12; Vol 4, No 20), NBuG (Vols 1–4)

The Museum; or, Record of Literature, Fine Arts, Sciences, Antiquities, The Drama, &c. London: Printed by A. J. Valpy. Vol 1. Nos 1–36. 27 Apr 1822 – 28 Dec 1822. Vol 2. Nos 37–66. 4 Jan – 26 July 1823. then, *The Literary Museum, and Register of Arts, Sciences, Belles-Lettres, &c.* Vol 2. Nos 67–88. 2 Aug – 27 Dec 1823. Weekly. [Ed by W. J. Graham. Index] **102**
DLC, ICN (missing New Series), MH

The Stage. London: Printed by W. Molineux, Breams Building, Chancery Lane. No 2. 1 May 1822. [I have not been able to discover any other issue of this periodical which, in its four pages, is devoted to Drury Lane and Covent Garden. There is no indication of its frequency] **102a**
O

The Theatre; or, Daily Miscellany of Fashion. Dublin. Nos 1–13. 16 – 30 Nov 1822. New Series, Nos 1–25. 2 – 31 Dec 1822. New Series, Nos 1–18. 4 – 22 Jan 1823. Daily. [Title changes slightly] **103**
BM (destroyed), CtY (Series 2, Vols 1–2), MH (Series 2, Vols [1–2])

Theatrical Guide; or, Daily Chronicle of Public Amusements. London. Nos 1–4. 1822. Daily. [I have not been able to determine the exact dates of the issues] **104**
BM (destroyed)

The Theatrical Looker-on at the Birmingham Theatre. [Edited by Francis Lloyd] Birmingham: [Printed by James Drake] Vols 1–2 [Nos 1–50] 27 May 1822 – 21 Nov 1823. Weekly (irregular). **105**
BM (Vol 1 only), BP, CtY, DFo, ICLoy (microfilm, Nos 1–25), MB (missing No 1), MH, NIC, OU

1823

The Birmingham Reporter, and Theatrical Review; or, The Opinions, Doubts, and Perplexities of Humphrey Digbeth, Manufacturer and Others. Birmingham: Printed and sold by C. Buckton. Vol 1. Nos 1–14. 19 June – 18 Sept 1823. Weekly.
    BP (missing Nos 4, 8–9, 13–18), MB (missing Nos 13–14), MH   **106**

British Stage. London: Onwhyn. Nos 1–7. 1–8 Jan 1823. Daily. [Includes a registration number dated, Nov 1822]   **107**
    CtY, ICLoy (microfilm)

Dramatic Observer and Musical Review. London: Published at 56, Fleet-street. Vol 1. No 1. 14 Apr 1823; No 6. 19 Apr 1823. Daily. [I have not been able to locate any other issues of the periodical]   **108**
    ICLoy (microfilm of No 1), MH (No 1), O (No 6)

The Dramatical and Musical Magazine. London. [Nos 1–8] Jan – Aug 1823. Monthly.   **109**
    ICLoy (microfilm), MH

The Edinburgh Theatrical Observer and Musical Review. Edinburgh. Vols 1–2. [Nos 1–55] 15 June 1823 – 30 Mar 1824. Irregular.   **110**
    BM (incomplete), MB (15 July – 31 Dec 1823), MH

Genuine Theatrical Observer. Dublin: T. Flanagan. Vol 1. Nos 1–11. 30 Oct – 12 Nov 1823. Daily.   **111**
    ICLoy (microfilm), MH (Nos 2, 10, 11)

Journal of Music and the Drama. London. Nos 1–9. 15 Feb – 19 Apr 1823. Weekly.
    ICLoy (microfilm), ICN, Garrick Club (No 1)   **112**

The London Theatrical Observer. London. 1823–1840.   **113**
    Not located (Lowe p 219)

The Theatrical Examiner; or, Critical Remarks on the Daily Performances, with the Bills of the Plays. London: Printed by J. H. Cox. Published by T. Holt, J. Fitzwilliam & Co., and W. Barrow. Vols 1–9. 24 July 1823 – 3 Mar 1831. Daily. [Because of the incompleteness of the holdings at the various libraries it is difficult to know the date that the periodical actually began publication. The 24 July date is for No 82]   **114**
    BM (incomplete), DFo (incomplete), ICLoy (microfilm), MB ([6–8]), MH ([1–9], NN ([1–7])

Theatrical Record. Edinburgh. No 1. 1 June 1823.   **115**
    EP

The Thespian. Bristol. Vol 1. Nos 1–15. 6 Jan – 14 Apr 1823. Weekly.   **116**
    BM (destroyed), MB (Vol 1, No 2. 13 Jan 1823)

The Vauxhall Observer; or, Critical Remarks on the Amusements at the Gardens, with an Account of the Songs, etc. London. Nos 1–51. 19 May – 8 Nov 1823. Three days a week.   **117**
    BM (destroyed), Garrick Club (No 8. 4 June 1823), O (No 21. 4 July 1823; No 34. 1 Aug 1823; No 41. 15 Aug 1823; No 47. 29 Aug 1823)

The Weekly Magazine; or, Literary Observer, Containing Original Reviews of New Publications! Original poetry, notice of Old English and other Authors; theatrical intelligence; female fashions; trite sayings, curious anecdotes, etc. London. Vol 1. Nos 1–16. 15 Nov 1823 – 6 Mar 1824. Weekly.   *118*
>BM (destroyed)

1824

The Birmingham Spectator. A miscellany of literature and of dramatic criticism [Edited by W. Hawkes Smith] Birmingham: Printed and published by J. Drake. Nos 1–24. 29 May – 6 Nov 1824. Weekly. [Succeeds *The Theatrical Looker-On*]
>BM, BP, CtY, DFo, ICLoy (microfilm), ICN, ICU, MB, MiU, O   *119*

The Dramatic Argus. Dublin. Vols 1–2. 18 Nov 1824 – 10 Feb 1825. Daily.   *120*
>BM (destroyed), IU

The Glasgow Theatrical Observer. Glasgow. Nos 1–16. 20 Apr – 4 Nov 1824. Weekly (to 25 May, then irregular).   *121*
>GU, ICLoy (microfilm)

The Literary Cynosure. [Edinburgh] No 1. 22 Jan 1824. Weekly.   *122*
>E, ICLoy (microfilm)

The Newcastle Theatrical Observer. Newcastle: R. T. Edgar. Nos 1–6. 24 Jan – 14 Feb 1824. Two days a week.   *123*
>ICLoy (microfilm), NNC

The News of Literature and Fashion; or, Journal of Manners and Society, the Drama, the Fine Arts, Literature, Science, etc. London. Vols 1–4. Nos 1–113. 12 June 1824 – 19 Aug 1826. Weekly.   *124*
>BM (destroyed), CaL (missing all after Vol 1), O

The Prompter; or, Theatrical Review. London. 1824.   *125*
>Not located (Lowe p 271)

The Theatrical Examiner for Sheffield. Sheffield: Howlden. Nos 1–20. 28 Oct 1824 – 24 Jan 1825. Irregular (to 13 Dec 1824); Weekly (after 13 Dec).   *126*
>BM (incomplete), ICLoy (microfilm), LdP, MB, SP

Theatrical John Bull [Edited by Joseph Allday] Birmingham: W. Cooper. Nos 1–21. 29 May – 16 Oct 1824; Nos 1–19. 28 May – 31 Sept 1825. Weekly (during the theatrical season).   *127*
>BM (Nos 1–21), BP, ICLoy (microfilm, Nos 1–21), MB, MH, NIC (missing all after No 19), O

The Theatrical Note-Book. Birmingham: [Printed by James Drake] Vol 1. No 1. 28 June 1824. [There is no indication of intended frequency]   *128*
>BM, BP, ICLoy (microfilm), MH

The Weekly Dramatic Chronicle and Entertaining Miscellany. London: J. Dunbar. [No 1 was published by J. Loundes] Nos 1–10. 27 Nov 1824 – 29 Jan 1825. Weekly.   *129*
>BM (destroyed), CtY (incomplete)

1825

The Edinburgh Dramatic Recorder.   Edinburgh. Nos 1–12. 29 Jan/ 5 Feb – [23/ 30 Apr 1825] Weekly.   **130**
> CtY, E, ICLoy (microfilm), MH

Oxberry's Dramatic Biography and Histrionic Anecdotes.   London. Vols 1–7. Nos 1–108. 1 Jan 1825 – 12 Aug 1827. Weekly. [Vols 6–7 also called New Series, Vols 1–2 (Nos 1–27). Vols 6–7 mostly unnumbered]   **131**
> BM, BP (1–5), DFo, ICLoy (microfilm), MB, MH

The Roscius, Consisting of Original Memoirs of the Principal Actors and Actresses.   Strictures on the drama, and its interests; original essays, green-room gossips, anecdotes, &c. London: Printed and Published by Duncombe, 19, Little Queen Street. Nos 1–7. 4 Jan – 9 Aug 1825. Monthly.   **132**
> DFo, MB (missing No 6), MH, MiU

The Theatrical Mince Pie.   London: J. Holt. Vol 1. Nos 1–8. 1 Jan – 19 Feb 1825. Weekly.   **133**
> ICLoy (microfilm), ICU, MB, MH

The Thespian Sentinel; or, Theatrical Vademecum.   London: T. and J. Allman. Vol 1. Nos 1–48. 27 Sept – 19 Nov 1825. Vol 2. Nos 1–47. 21 Nov 1825 – 14 Jan 1826. Vol 3. Nos 1–53. 16 Jan – 18 Mar 1826. Six days a week.   **134**
> ICLoy (microfilm), ICN, MB (missing all after Vol 1, No 40), MH

The Weekly Dramatic Register, A Concise History of the London Stage . . . Compiled from the *Theatrical Observer.*   London: Printed and Published by E. Thomas. Vols 1–3. Nos 1–156. 1 Jan 1825 – 29 Dec 1827. Weekly.   **135**
> BM (destroyed), DFo, ICLoy (microfilm), MB, MH, NIC, O (Nos 4–58)

1826

The Dramatic Speculum.   Liverpool. Nos 1–5. 21 June – 5 July 1826. Semi-weekly. [None of the standard sources seem to indicate that there was more than one issue]   **136**
> BM (missing all after No 1), DFo, ICLoy (microfilm)

The Dundee Theatrical Review.   Dundee: Printed and Published by J. Chalmers. No 1. 6 Oct 1826.   **137**
> CtY, ICLoy (microfilm)

The Glasgow Dramatic Review.   Glasgow. Nos 1–6. 9 Dec 1826 – 13 Jan 1827. Weekly.   **138**
> GU, ICLoy (microfilm)

The Hull Dramatic Censor: Containing Remarks and Criticisms on the Various Productions and Performances, As Brought Forward at the Theatre Royal, Hull, During the Present Season.   Hull. Vol 1. Nos 1–15. [9 Dec 1826] – 17 Mar 1827. Weekly. [Dating begins with No 2, 16 Dec 1826]   **139**
> BM (has two editions of No 1)

The Opera Glass, for Peeping into the Microcosm of the Fine Arts, and More Specially of the Drama. London: T. Dolby. Nos 1–26. 2 Oct 1826 – 24 Mar 1827. Weekly.   **140**

CtY, DLC, ICLoy (microfilm), MB, MH, O (Nos 1–16)

The Wasp. A literary satire. Containing an exposé of some of the most notorious literary and theatrical quacks of the day. London: W. Jeffreys. Vol 1. Nos 1–12. 30 Sept – 16 Dec 1826. Weekly.   **141**

BM, CtY, DLC, ICLoy (microfilm), IaU (Nos 1–11), MH (Nos 1–7), NIC, PHC

1827

The Beauties of the Magazines and Spirit of the Times. Containing choice selections from the whole of the periodical literature, etc., and also dramatic criticisms. London. New Series. Vol 1. Nos 1–24. 8 Sept 1827 – 16 Feb 1828. Weekly.   **142**

BM, ICLoy (microfilm)

The Edinburgh Dramatic and Musical Magazine. Edinburgh. Nos 1–3. 19 Nov – 3 Dec 1827. Weekly.   **143**

ICLoy (microfilm), MH

The Edinburgh Dramatic Review, and Thespian Inquisitor. Ed by Hanibal Hallucinate, Esq. Edinburgh: D. Speare. Nos 1–50. 22 Oct – 31 Dec 1827. Six days a week. [No 44 omitted in the numbering]   **144**

CtY, DP, ICLoy (microfilm)

The Glasgow Theatrical Review. Glasgow. Nos 1–5. 22 Sept – 3 Nov 1827. Weekly (except that three weeks intervene between Nos 3 and 4)   **145**

GU, ICLoy (microfilm)

The Literary Cabinet and Journal of Belles Lettres, Fine Arts, Drama. London. Nos 1–3. 17 Feb – 3 Mar 1827. Weekly.   **146**

BM, ICLoy (microfilm)

The North Shields Dramatic Censor. North Shields. Nos 1–15. 27 Oct 1827 – 29 Jan 1828. Weekly.   **147**

ICLoy (microfilm), NwP (Nos 2–15)

The Norwich Theatrical Observer, and Dramatic Review. Ed by Dr. A. T. Fayerman, M.D. Norwich: Printed and sold by P. Cranefield. Nos 1–42. 10 Feb – 3 Oct 1827. Weekly (irregular). [The title varies in Nos 38–42 to, *The Norwich Theatrical Observer and Ranelagh Spectator.* It seems that No 37 was never published]   **148**

BM (destroyed), ICU (missing Nos 2, 18, 37), O (missing No 37)

Paul Pry. A weekly review of theatrical performances. North Shields. Nos 1–7. 5 Nov 1827 – 9 Jan 1828. Weekly (to 10 Dec 1827, then one extra number).   **149**

ICLoy (microfilm), NwP

Stratford Theatrical Review and Stage Reporter. Stratford-upon-Avon. Nos 1–10. 10 Dec 1827 – 8 Feb 1828. Weekly.   **150**

BM, ICLoy (microfilm)

The Surrey Dramatic Spectator; or, Critical Remarks on the Daily Performances, with the Bills of the Play. [London] Vol 1. Nos 1–113. 1827 – 1828. [I have not been able to discover the dates of the first and last issues]   *151*
  BM (destroyed), MB (No 79. 30 Jan 1828), MH (very incomplete)

The Theatrical Examiner. [Newcastle-on-Tyne] 26 Nov – 24 Dec 1827. Weekly.
  Not located (Loewenberg p 48)   *152*

The Theatrical Mirror; or, Daily Bills of the Performances.   London. Vol 1. Nos 1–36. 1 Oct – 10 Nov 1827. Daily.   *153*
  MB (incomplete), MH (Nos 5, 16)

1828

The Athenaeum.   A journal of literature, science, the fine arts, music, and the drama. London: J. Francis. Nos 1–4737. 2 Jan 1828 – 11 Feb 1921. Weekly [Jan 1828 – Dec 1915]; monthly [Jan 1916 – Mar 1919]; weekly [Apr 1919 – Feb 1921]   *154*
  BM, DLC, ICN, ICU, IU, MB, MH, MiU, NN, NNC, TxU

The Censor.   An entirely original work, devoted to literature, poetry, and the drama. Complete in one volume. [By Gilbert Abbott à Beckett, assisted by his brothers Thomas Turner, and William à Beckett] London: J. Clements; Cowie and Strange. Nos 1–16. 6 Sept 1828 – 4 Apr 1829. Biweekly. [Index]   *155*
  BM, CSmH, DLC, IaU, ICLoy (microfilm), MH, TxHR

The Dramatic Correspondent and Amateur's Place Book.   London. Nos 1–21. 26 July 1828 – 31 Jan 1829. Weekly.   *156*
  DLC (missing Nos 14–21), ICLoy (microfilm), MB (missing Nos 1–12), MH (missing Nos 1–12)

The Dramatic Register.   Newcastle Upon Tyne. Nos 1–10. 27 Dec 1828 – 28 Feb 1829. Weekly.   *157*
  NwP (No 1)

Edinburgh Dramatic Journal; or, Theatrical Observer.   Edinburgh: Printed and published by T. Colquhoun. Nos 1–11. 11 Oct – 29 Nov 1828. Irregular. [Nos 4–9, twice a week; Nos 10–11, twice a week; Nos 1–3, weekly]   *158*
  CtY, DFo, DP, ICLoy (microfilm), MH

Edinburgh Dramatic Tête-à-tête; or, Companion to the Theatre.   Edinburgh. Nos 1–42. 20 Mar – 7 May 1828. Daily.   *159*
  ICLoy (microfilm), MH, NIC

The Manchester Theatrical Censor.   Manchester. Nos 1–6. 24 May – 28 June 1828. Weekly.   *160*
  MP

Oxberry's Dramatic Mirror.   London. Nos 1–24. 1828.   *161*
  CtHT-W

Oxberry's Theatrical Inquisitor; or, Monthly Mirror of the Drama.   By the Editors of *Oxberry's Dramatic Biography.* [Ed by Catherine Elizabeth Oxberry] London: Published by George Virtue, 26, Ivy Lane, Paternoster Row, Bath Street, Bristol, & St. Vincent Street, Liverpool. Vol 1. Nos 1–[6] Feb – July 1828.

Monthly. [Superseded by, *Stage; or, Theatrical Inquisitor.* Only the first issue
has a date and a number]   **162**
   CtY, DFo, ICLoy (microfilm), ICU, MB, MH, NIC

Plymouth Theatrical Spy.   Plymouth. Nos 1–8. 5 Jan – 23 Feb 1828. Weekly. **163**
   ICLoy (microfilm), MH

Spectator, a Weekly Review of Politics, Literature, Theology, Drama, and Art.
   London. Nos 1–1696. 5 July 1828 – 29 Dec 1860. Weekly.   **164**
   BM, MB, MdBE

The Stage; or, Theatrical Inquisitor.   London: W. A. Wright. Vols 1–2. Nos 1–11.
   Aug 1828 – Feb 1829. Monthly (Aug – Oct 1828); Semimonthly (Nov 1828 –
   Feb 1829). [Supersedes *Oxberry's Theatrical Inquisitor*]   **165**
   BM (missing Nos 1, 7), BP (missing No 11), DLC, MH, NN

The Theatre.   London: C. Baynes. Nos 1–13. 4 Oct – 27 Dec 1828. Weekly. [The
   editor says that the magazine is intended exclusively as a history of the stage] **166**
   BM (destroyed), MB (missing all after No 4), NN

Theatrical Censor.   Manchester. Nos 1–6. 24 May – 28 June 1828. Weekly. (**167**)
   ICLoy (microfilm), MB, MP

The Theatrical Tickler.   By Barnaby Brother. Norwich. No 2. 23 Jan 1828. [The
   Norwich Theatre]   **168**
   DFo, ICLoy (microfilm)

Weekly Dramatic Review.   Edinburgh. Nos 1–6. 7 July – 11 Aug 1828. Weekly. **169**
   EP, ICLoy (microfilm)

1829

The Apollo: Containing selections from the pens of Dibdin, Moore, Moncrieff,
   W. H. Freeman, Hudson, Beuler, Ball, &c.   Besides Many Excellent Originals,
   With All the Popular Songs, Glees, Duets, &c. As they are brought out at the
   Theatres and Metropolitan Concerts; Together with one of the most Popular
   Recitations of the Day. London: H. Arliss. [1829?] Irregular. [A reissue in 3
   volumes appeared in 1830. This is to be found complete at the BM. The [1829?]
   date appears in the BM catalogue. Nos 11, 14, 27, 28, 30, 31, 34, 40. Nos 11, 14,
   27, 30 are renumbered in manuscript as, 19, 10, 16, 13, respectively. Nos 11 and
   28 are numbered in manuscript only]   **170**
   BM (Nos 11, 14, 27, 28, 30, 31, 34, 40)

*The Columbine and Weekly Review of Literature, the Sciences, Fine Arts, The-
   atricals,* etc., etc.   London: Sparkes and Jones. Nos 1–19. 4 July 1829 – 17 Apr
   1830. Irregular. then, *The Columbine; or, Dramatic Mirror.* New Series. Nos
   1–23. 24 Apr – 25 Sept 1830. Weekly. [The Boston Public Library has a No 27,
   dated 18 June 1831]   **171**
   MB (missing Nos 1–19; New Series, Nos 3, 4, 6, 8–23), MH

The Court Journal [and fashionable gazette; court circular and fashionable gazette]
   London: Printed for H. Colborn; and published by W. Thomas, at the Office, 12,
   Catherine-Street, Strand. Nos 1–4950. 2 May 1829 – 13 Mar 1925. Weekly. [The
   title varies]   **172**
   BM-N, CtY (1–922), DLC (1–2, 33–483, 506–620, 1127–4950), MH (193–1631)

The Dramatic Censor. By Proteus Porcupine, Esq. Edinburgh. Nos 1–38. 23 Sept –
12 Dec 1829. Daily (23 Sept – 20 Oct); semiweekly (21 Oct – 12 Dec).   *173*
> EP (missing Nos 30, 35), ICLoy (microfilm)

The Dramatic Magazine. Embellished with numerous engravings of the principal
performers. London. Vols 1–3. Mar 1829 – Apr 1831. Monthly.   *174*
> BM, CtY, DFo, ICLoy (microfilm), MB (missing Mar – Apr 1831), MH, NN, O (to Jan
> 1831)

Dramatic Tatler; or, Companion to the Theatre. From Monday, March 30, till
Saturday, April 18, 1829. Edinburgh: C. M' Kenzie. Nos 1–17. 30 Mar – 18 Apr
1829. Daily.   *175*
> ICLoy (microfilm), MH

The Harlequin. A journal of the drama. Conducted by the editor [John Timbs]
of the "Companion to the Theatres." London: Printed for Edward Philip Sanger.
Nos 1–9. 16 May – 11 July 1829. Weekly. [Index]   *176*
> BM (destroyed), DFo, DLC, ICLoy (microfilm), MB, MH, MiU, MnU, NB, OO

Monthly Theatrical Review. London. Nos 1–4. Sept – Dec 1829. Monthly   *177*
> ICLoy (microfilm), MH

The Opera Glass. A series of criticisms on the performances of the Glasgow stage;
notices of musical and rhetorical exhibitions; and in the shape of "Green room
chat." A record of those occurrences of interest, which have taken place on the
London and Provincial boards. Glasgow: J. Mitchell. Nos 1–27. 19 Dec 1829 –
5 June 1830. Weekly.   *178*
> GM, ICLoy (microfilm), MB

*Pierce Egan's Weekly Courier, To the Sporting, Theatrical, Literary, and Fash-
ionable World.* London: Printed and Published by Pierce Egan. Published at
No 113, Strand. Vol 1. Nos 1–17. 4 Jan – 26 Apr 1829. Weekly.   *179*
> BM-N

Theatrical Critique. Newcastle. [Nos 1–2] 7 Nov – 10 Dec 1829.   *180*
> MB

Thistle; or, Literary, Theatrical, and Police Reporter. Glasgow. Vols 1–3. 1829–
1832.   *181*
> GM, ICLoy (microfilm)

The Weekly Theatrical Reporter. [Dublin]: Byrne, 16, College-Green, by Wise-
heart, 6, Suffolk-st. and Hanlan, 50, Mary-st. J. Scott, Printer, 13, Fownes's-Street.
Nos 1–8. 25 Apr – 13 June 1829. Weekly.   *182*
> NNWH

1830

Chat of the Week and Gazette of Literature, Fine Arts, and Theatricals. [Ed by
Leigh Hunt] London. Nos 1–13. 5 June – 28 Aug 1830. Weekly.   *183*
> MB, NN

*The Dramatic Gazette; or, Weekly Record of the Stage, Music, Public Exhibi-
tions, etc.* London. Vol 1. Nos 1–12. 9 Oct 1830 – 1 Jan 1831. Weekly. [Page

129 is incorrectly numbered 149. This twenty-page error in numbering is continued throughout the remainder of the volume]   *184*
    BM (destroyed), MB, NIC

New Evening Theatrical Observer. With bills of the play. [London] No 10. 1 Jan 1830. Daily. [I have not been able to discover any other issues]   *185*
    MB

The New Opera Glass; or, Theatrical Tribunal. Glasgow. Nos 1–8. 19 Nov 1830 – 8 Jan 1831. Weekly.   *186*
    GU, ICLoy (microfilm)

Philo-Danmonion. A western magazine, of matter chiefly original, comprising essays literary, scientific, and antiquarian; poetry and criticisms; notices of the fine arts, drama, &c., with miscellaneous information on subjects more immediately connected with Devon and Cornwall. Plymouth: Published by W. Curtis, and sold by Longman and Co., Paternoster Row, and Ridgway, Piccadilly, London. T. J. Bond, Printer. Vol 1. [Nos 1–6] Jan – 15 June 1830. Monthly.   *187*
    ICLoy (microfilm), ICN

The Prompter. [Ed by R. Carlile] London. Vol 1. Nos 1–53. 13 Nov 1830 – 12 Nov 1831. Weekly.   *188*
    BM, CSmH, CtY, ICLoy (microfilm), NcD

The Tatler. A daily journal of literature and the stage. London: Published by J. Onwhyn, At the Office, 4 Catherine Street, Strand. Vols 1–4. Nos 1–493. 4 Sept 1830 – 31 Mar 1832. Daily. New Series. Ed by R. Seton. Nos 1–59. 2 Apr – 6 Oct 1832. Triweekly. [Index]   *189*
    BM (missing Nos 40–59), ICLoy (microfilm), ICN (missing New Series), MB (missing Vols 1–4), MiU (missing New Series), O

Theatrical Argus, and Stage Reporter. Birmingham. Printed by Chidlow. No 1. 3 May 1830.   *190*
    BP, ICLoy (microfilm)

The Theatrical Observer. Birmingham: Printed and Published by J. C. Barlow. 1830. [Asa Briggs (p 28) gives the above information. The periodical is not at the Birmingham Public Library, nor have I been able to find any other mention of the periodical]   *190a*

The Theatrical Tattler. Birmingham: Printed by James Drake. Nos 1–3. 17 Apr – 1 May 1830. Weekly.   *191*
    BP (missing No 1), ICLoy (microfilm, Nos 2–3), MB (missing Nos 1–2)

1831

The Acting Manager; or, The Minor Spy. A weekly review of the public and private stage. London. Nos 1–4. 14 May – 18 June 1831. Weekly [Nos 1–2]; biweekly [Nos 3–4]   *192*
    BM, ICLoy (microfilm), MH

The British Stage; or, Dramatic Censor. London. Vol 1. Nos 1–3. Apr – June 1831. Monthly.   *193*
    BM, ICLoy (microfilm), MH

The Dramatic Annual.   A playwright's adventures. By F. Reynolds. London.
1831. Annual. [The collective title occurs only in the dedication]   ***194***
   BM, ICLoy (microfilm), O, SaU

Figaro in London.   London: W. Strange. Vols 1–8. Nos 1–402. 10 Dec 1831 – 17
Aug 1839. Weekly. [Vols 7 and 8 are without a title page]   ***195***
   BM, CLU, CU (1–3), ICN (1, 3–7), ICU (1–6), MH, NN (1–7), PU (1–5), TxU (1–7)

The Literary Beacon.   A guide to books, the drama, music and the fine arts.
London. Nos 1–12. 18 June – 3 Sept 1831. New Series. Nos 1–3. 10 – 24 Sept
1831. Weekly.   ***196***
   BM, MB

The Literary Guardian and Spectator of Books, Science, Fine Arts, the Drama,
etc.   (Ed by Messrs. Book-worm, Glowworm and Silkworm). London: Published by William Tindall, at the Literary Guardian Office, 3, Wellington
Street, Strand. Vols 1–2. Nos 1–45. 1 Oct 1831 – [4 Aug 1832] Weekly. [The
subtitle varies. Index]   ***197***
   BM (destroyed), ICLoy (microfilm), ICN (missing Vol 2), O (Nos 1–44)

The National Omnibus; and Entertaining Advertiser.   London. Vol 1. No 1.
1 Apr 1831. then, *The National Omnibus; and Weekly Advertiser.* A journal of
literature, science, music, theatricals, and the fine arts. Vols 1–2. Nos 2–79.
15 Apr 1831 – 28 Dec 1832. [Missing 13 July 1832] Biweekly (to 30 Sept
1831); Weekly (Oct 1831 – 28 Dec 1832). [*The Union List of Serials* indicates that there are ninety-one issues between 1 Apr 1831 – 22 Mar 1833, and
a New Series, composed of thirty issues, between 29 Mar – 18 Oct 1833]   ***198***
   DLC, ICLoy (microfilm), ICN, MB, NIC

The Owl.   [London] Nos 1–24. 9 Apr – 29 Oct 1831. Weekly.   ***199***
   BM (destroyed), MB

The Play-Goer.   Glasgow. No 1. 5 Feb 1831.   ***200***
   GU, ICLoy (microfilm)

The Theatre.   Containing a review of the performances at the Theatre Royal,
Edinburgh, biographical notices of the principal performers, original essays in
dramatic subjects, provincial intelligence, etc. Edinburgh. No 1. 8 Oct 1831.
   EP, ICLoy (microfilm)   ***201***

The Theatrical Rod.   A weekly journal of the stage, literature and general amusement. London: E. Duncombe. Nos 1–3. [1831] Weekly. [The numbers are not
dated]   ***202***
   ICLoy (microfilm), MB, MH (Nos 1–2)

Theatrical Speculum and Musical Review.   Edinburgh. Nos 1–9. 18 July – 13
Aug 1831. Weekly.   ***203***
   EP, ICLoy (microfilm)

1832

The British Drama and Literary Humourist.   London. Nos 1–2. 1832. [I have
not been able to discover the exact dates of the two issues]   ***204***
   BM (destroyed)

Edinburgh Theatrical Casket.   Edinburgh. No 1. July 1832.   ***205***
   E, ICLoy (microfilm)

Literary Test. A liberal, moral, and independent weekly review of books, the stage, and the fine arts. London. Nos 1–5. 1 – 28 Jan 1832. Weekly. [The sub-title varies]   **206**
  ICLoy (microfilm), LU

The Liverpool Dramatic Journal. Liverpool. No 1. 12 Nov 1832. Weekly.   **207**
  BM, ICLoy (microfilm)

The Looking Glass; or, Daily Theatrical Mirror. Liverpool. Nos 1–3. 15 – 17 Aug 1832. Daily.   **208**
  MB (missing No 1)

New Edinburgh Dramatic Review. Edinburgh. No 1. 9 June 1832.   **209**
  Not located (Loewenberg p 31)

The Opera; or, Cabinet of Songs. Being a selection of songs, duets, glees, etc., from the works of the most esteemed authors. Edinburgh. No 1. 1832.   **210**
  EP, ICLoy (microfilm)

The Wanderer. A weekly journal of literature, science, theatricals, and the fine arts. London. No 1. 1832. Weekly.   **211**
  BM, BP, ICLoy (microfilm), O

1833

The Dramatic Souvenir. Being literary and graphical illustrations of Shake-speare and other celebrated English dramatists. London. 1833. Annual.   **212**
  MH

Figaro in Liverpool. Liverpool: Printed and Published by J. Parnell, 24, Byrom Street. No 1. 14 Jan 1833.   **213**
  BM

The National Standard of Literature, Science, Music, Theatricals, and the Fine Arts. London. Vols 1–3. Nos 1–57. 5 Jan 1833 – 1 Feb 1834. Weekly.   **214**
  BM, GU (missing Vol 3), ICLoy (microfilm)

New Anti-Jacobin. A monthly magazine of politics, commerce, science, litera-ture, art, music and the drama. London. Vol 1. Nos 1–2. Apr – May 1833. Monthly.   **215**
  BM, NIC (No 1), O (No 2), PU (No 1)

New Theatrical Observer. Dublin. 1833.   **216**
  Not located (O'Neill p 86)

The Theatrical Athenaeum. London. No 1. 16 Nov 1833. [Registration issue] **217**
  BM, ICLoy (microfilm)

Theatrical Examiner. Glasgow: W. R. McPhun. Nos 1–10. 23 Nov 1833 – 25 Jan 1834. Weekly.   **218**
  ICLoy (microfilm), MH

1834

Liverpool Dramatic Censor. Liverpool. No 1. 12 July 1834.   **219**
  BM, ICLoy (microfilm)

Paul Pry in Liverpool. Liverpool: Printed by J. Parnell, 24, Byrom Street. Vol 1. No 1. 25 Oct 1834. **220**
BM

The Prompter; or, Theatrical and Concert Guide. London. No 1. 28 June 1834.
BP, ICLoy (microfilm) **221**

Tatler and Theatrical Mirror. Dublin. Nos 1–8. 1 Nov – 22 Dec 1834. Weekly.
BM (missing Nos 1–2) **222**

The Theatrical Critic. London. Nos 1–2. 1834. [I have not been able to determine the dates of the two issues] **223**
BM (destroyed)

1835

The Edinburgh Theatrical and Musical Review. Edinburgh. Vol 1. Nos 1–31. 14 Mar – 19 Sept 1835. Vol 2. Nos 1–3. 17 Nov – 2 Dec 1835. Weekly. [From No 5 to the end, edited by W. H. Logan, aided by Sir Theodore Martin and other friends] **224**
BM (missing Nos 1–4), EP, ICLoy (microfilm), MB (missing Nos 1–12, 17, 21–22, 30, 32), MH (missing Nos 1–4, 8)

Leporello in Liverpool. Liverpool. No 1. 24 Dec 1835. **225**
BM

The London Amusement Guide and Theatrical Reporter. Being a weekly bill of the performances at all the theatres in London, and a guide to every metropolitan exhibition worthy of notice. London. Nos 1–56. 27 July 1835 – 15 Aug 1836. Weekly. **226**
BM-N (missing No 5), ICLoy (microfilm)

The Theatrical Visitor. Glasgow. Nos 1–6. 16 Aug – 19 Sept 1835. Weekly. **227**
GU (missing No 2), ICLoy (microfilm)

1836

The Brighton Theatrical Observer: And Daily Bill of the Play. Bristol. Nos [1]– 51. 30 July – 28 Sept 1836. Six days a week. [The numbering begins with 30 Aug, and is No 26] **228**
LU-BTM (missing eight issues before No 26, and missing No 50)

The Liverpool Thespian Register and Mirror of the Stage. Liverpool. No 1. 15 June 1836. Three issues a week. **229**
BM, ICLoy (microfilm)

The London Amusement Guide. ("The only stamped paper dedicated entirely to the Amusements of London".) London: Published every Sunday morning, at No 7, Catherine Street, Strand. Printed at the Office of Gadsden and Percival, No 2, Upper St. Martin's-lane, by Robert Gadsden. Nos 1–3 [4] 18 Sept – 2 Oct 1836. Weekly. [Number 3 is numbered 2, and No 4 is numbered 3] **230**
BM-N

1837

The Dramatic Review and Weekly Miscellany. Edinburgh. Nos 1–10. 29 July – 30 Sept 1837. Weekly.   **231**
  BM (destroyed), MB, MH

Dramatic Spectator. Ed by Poz, Quiz and Company. Edinburgh: W. Glass. Nos 1–10. 29 July – 30 Sept 1837. Weekly.   **232**
  BM, EP, ICLoy (microfilm), MB, MH, NN

The Idler, and Breakfast-Table Companion. A new and fashionable journal of literature, fine arts, satire and the stage. London. Vols 1–3. Nos 1–114. 13 May 1837 – 4 May 1839. Weekly.   **233**
  BM (missing Vol 3), CtY (1–2), MB (1–3), MnU (1–2), NjP (1–2)

The Tickler, and Dramatic Intelligencer. London. Nos 1–5. 28 Oct – 25 Nov 1837. Weekly.   **234**
  BP (missing Nos 3–4)

1838

Actors by Daylight; or, Pencillings in the Pit. Containing correct memoirs of upwards of forty of the most celebrated London performers; original tales, poetry, and criticisms: the whole forming a faithful account of the London stage for the last twelve months. London: Published for the Proprietors by James Pattie. G. H. Davidson. Vols 1–2. Nos 1–55. 3 Mar 1838 – 16 Mar [1839] Weekly.   **235**
  BM, CLU, CSmH, CtY, DFo, DLC, ICLoy (microfilm), ICN, IaU, MB, MH, NIC, NN, NNC

Actors by Gaslight; or, "Boz" in the Boxes. London: by H. Hetherington; sold by W. Strange. Nos 1–37. 21 Apr – 29 Dec 1838. Weekly.   **236**
  BM, ICLoy (microfilm), MB, MiU, NN

The Brighton Dramatic Miscellany. Published Daily. Brighton. Nos 1–57. 26 July – 29 Sept 1838. Daily [i.e., six days a week]   **237**
  BM (destroyed)

The Call-boy. London. Nos 1–3. 21 Apr – 5 May 1938.   **238**
  Not located (Lowe p 39)

The Era. London. Vols 1–103. Nos 1–5268. 30 Sept 1838 – 21 Sept 1939. [It incorporates the, *Cinematographic Times. The Era* is one of the most important of all theatrical journals]   **239**
  BM-N, BP (missing Vols 7–80, 97–98), WmP (1838–1931), Garrick Club

The London Singer's Magazine. A collection of all the most celebrated and popular songs as sung at the London theatres, public and private concerts, and other places of amusement. [Ed by T. Prest] London: Printed and Published by Cruikshank T. Jones, Findlay &c., John Duncombe & Co. Nos 1–111. [1838–1839] [The dates appear in the British Museum Catalogue] Weekly. [Nos 10, 16–18, 22, 54, are repeated in numbering. Several editions were published, with various editors and subtitles]   **240**
  BM (1–31), MH (1–92, 96–97, 102–108, 111), O, OC (2–7, 9–19 [21–90], 111), PPC (1–61), PPL (1–61)

Theatrical Register and General Amusement Guide.   London. Nos 1–5. 22 Sept – 29
   Oct 1838. Weekly (irregular).   *241*
   BM (missing Nos 1–2, 4, 6), MB

1839

The Theatrical Journal, and Stranger's Guide.   [Ed by H. P. Mills] London. Vols
   1–34. Nos 1–1747. [21 Dec] 1839 – 4 June 1873. Weekly. [The title varies]   *242*
   BM (Vols 1–32), CtY (Vols 1–3, 23–24), FiP (Vols 1–8, 10–16, 18–21, 30–32), MB (Vols
   [3–5], 20, 28), MH (Vols 1–[11–15]–[30–31]–[34]), WEST (Vols 1–8, 10–16, 18–21,
   30–32)

1840

The Musical Journal.   A magazine of information on all subjects connected with
   the science. London. Vol 1. Nos 1–26. 7 Jan – 30 June 1840. Weekly.   *243*
   BM

The Opera Glass.   A weekly musical and theatrical miscellany. Edinburgh. Vols
   1–2. [Nos 1–56] 10 Apr 1840 – 30 Apr 1841. Weekly.   *244*
   EP, ICLoy (microfilm), MB (missing No 27), PVC

The Pepper Box, Containing Criticisms on Theatrical and Other Amusements.
   Glasgow. Nos 1–20. 21 Mar – 1 Aug 1840. Weekly.   *245*
   GU (missing Nos 1–2, 8. No 5 is imperfect), ICLoy (microfilm)

The Psyche.   A magazine of belles lettres, the drama, poetry, music, and the fine
   arts. Ed by the author of "The Czar" [i.e., Edward Smallwood] London. Nos
   1–4. Feb – May 1840. Monthly.   *246*
   BM, C, MB (missing Nos 1–3), MH, MnU, NNC (1–3), O

The Theatrical and Concert Companion.   London. Nos 501–517. 1 June – 14 Sept
   1840. Weekly. [I have not been able to locate the earlier numbers]   *247*
   BM (No 514), LGU (Nos 501, 506, 508, 512, 517)

Theatrical Chronicle and Dramatic Review.   A work devoted exclusively to the
   drama. [Ed by C. T. Fowler] London. Vols 1–4. Nos 1–147. [24 Feb 1840?] – 11
   Feb 1843. Vol 5. Nos 1–16. 23 Sept 1848 – 3 Mar 1849. Weekly. The subtitle
   varies]   *248*
   BM (destroyed), MB (Vols 1–3; New Series, Vol 5, Nos 2–13), MH (New Series, Vol 5)

1841

The Actor's Note-Book.   By James Cooke, Author of *Theatrical Etchings, Shak-
   sperian Gallery,* &c., &c. London. Nos 1–6. 26 Apr – 2 June 1841. Weekly. *249*
   MH

The Lyre.   A Musical and Theatrical Register. [Ed by J. W. Hudson] London:
   Printed by H. Mitchener, of No 3, Edward Street, Hampstead-Road, and Pub-
   lished by him, for the Proprietors, at the "Lyre" Office, No 7, Wellington-Street,
   North Strand. Vol 1. Nos 1–22. 31 July – 27 Dec 1841. Weekly. [From No 6 on,
   Printed by Charles Davies, of 53 Southampton-street, Pentonville; and Pub-
   lished by W. Strange, No 21 Paternoster Row]   *250*
   BM-N (Nos 1–2, to 13 Dec 1841), MB, Garrick Club

1842

The Dramatic and Musical Review. London. Vols 1–11. Nos 1–377. 2 Apr 1842 –
June 1852. Weekly [Vols 1–6, Nos 1–300]; monthly [Vol 7, Nos 301–312]; semimonthly [Vol 8, Nos 313–324. 1 Jan – 15 June 1849]; monthly [Vol 8, Nos 325–
330. July – Dec 1849]; semimonthly [Vol 9, Nos 331–342. 1 Jan – 15 June 1850];
monthly [Vol 9, Nos 343–348. July – Dec 1850]; semimonthly [Vol 10, Nos 349–
360. 1 Jan – 16 June 1851]; monthly [Vol 10, Nos 361–366. July – Dec 1851];
semimonthly [Vol 11, Nos 367–377]   **251**
> BM (missing Nos 145–196, 301–366), BU (missing Vol 11), DLC, ICLoy (microfilm),
> MB (missing Vols 5–11), NIC (missing Vols 9–11), NjP (missing Vols 9–11)

Edinburgh Dramatic Censor, a Weekly Theatrical, Musical and Literary Review.
Edinburgh. Nos 1–8. 12 Nov – 31 Dec 1842. Weekly.   **252**
> EP, ICLoy (microfilm)

Nicholson's Noctes; or, Nights and Sights in London. London. Nos 1–11. 1842. [I
have not been able to discover the dates of the individual issues]   **253**
> BM (destroyed)

The Pandora. A fashionable, theatrical, literary & artistic journal. London. Nos
1–166. 1842 [?] – 1 Mar 1845. then, *The Pandora: A Literary and Artistic Journal.* Nos 167–170. 5 Apr – 5 July 1845. Weekly.   **254**
> BM-N (missing Nos 1–156)

The Prompter and Scottish Dramatic Review. Edinburgh. Vols 1–2. [Nos 1–25]
12 Nov 1842 – 20 May 1843. Weekly.   **255**
> EP, ICLoy (microfilm), MB

1843

The Cicerone. A record of the drama, music and the fine arts. Ed by J. H. Stockqueler, Esq. [His name appears only on the first issue] London: W. W. Barth.
Nos 1–24. 30 Sept 1843 – 9 Mar 1844. Weekly. [In No 24, p 219, there is an
announcement which states that the periodical is now incorporated with the,
Old Oak Chest]   **256**
> BM-N, MB, NN (to 23 Dec 1843)

The Critic. A journal of theatricals, music, and the exhibitions. London. Nos 1–19.
7 Oct 1843 – 10 Feb 1844. Weekly.   **257**
> CtY, ICLoy (microfilm), MB (missing all but No 1), MH

The Critic of Literature, Art, Science and the Drama. London: J. Crockford.
Vol 1. Nos 1–14. Nov 1843 – Aug 1844. then, *The Critic.* Journal of British and
foreign literature and the arts. New Series. Vols 1–25. Nos 1–643. Aug 1844 –
Dec 1863. Irregular. [The title changes several times during the run of the new
series]   **258**
> BM, CtY (New Series, Vols 17–25), DLC (New Series, 2–25), ICLoy (microfilm), MB
> (New Series, Vols 8–17, 19–23, 25), MH (New Series [Vols 11, 15–17, 19–20])

Oxberry's Budget of Plays. Consisting of thirty-nine original dramas, by the most
popular authors of the day. (In one volume.) All of which have been success-
fully performed at the various London theatres. [Ed by W. H. Oxberry] Vol I.
London: Printed by R. Hodson, 90, Holborn Hill. Published by Vickers, Holy-

well-Street, and Cleave, Shoe-Lane, Also By The Proprietor, Three Falcon Court, 145, Fleet Street, 1844. [In this volume dates appear from 12 June, 1843 – 26 Feb 1843 (i.e., 1844). Only Plays appear in this Volume]. then, *Oxberry's Weekly Budget of Plays And Magazines Of Romance, Whim, And Interest.* New & Improved Series. Vol 2. Nos 1–51. 12 June 1843 – 27 [i.e., 20] May 1844. then, *Oxberry's Weekly Budget.* New and Improved Series. Vol 2, No 52. 27 May 1844. then, *Oxberry's Weekly Budget of Plays, And Dramatic Recorder: A Journal Of Theatrical Literature Devoted To The Amateur, And The Play-Going Public.* New And Improved Series. Vol 3. Nos 53–79, 10 June – 7 Dec 1844. Weekly. [The plays are found in Volume I, and the magazine features in Vols 2–3. The printer and publisher vary during the history of the periodical]   **259**

   BM-N (to No 77), MH (missing all before No 53), Garrick Club

The Pictorial Times. A weekly journal of news, literature, fine arts and the drama. London. Vols 1–11. Nos 1–252. 18 Mar 1843 – 8 Jan 1848. Weekly. [Merged into, *Queen; the Lady's Newspaper and Court Chronicle*]   **260**

   CSmH (Vols 1–6), CtY (Vols 1–7), MH (Vols 2, 8–10), NN (Vols 5–6, 8–11)

1844

The Glasgow Dramatic Review. Containing original essays on subjects connected with the drama and the stage. Also critical notices of the performances at the Glasgow theatres. Glasgow: Printed for the Proprietors by W. Gilchrist. Nos 1–54. 13 Nov 1844 – 8 July 1846. Biweekly.   **261**

   E, ICLoy (microfilm), ICU, IU, MB, MH

Scottish Dramatic Mirror and Public Amusement Guide from November to February 1844–45. Edinburgh. Nos 1–31. 9 Nov 1844 – 7 June 1845. Weekly. **262**

   EP (Nos 8, 9, 16, 22, 24, 31), GM, ICLoy (microfilm)

The Stage. A weekly magazine of plays and players. London: Printed for the Proprietors, by H. Quelch, 40, Charlotte Street, Blackfriars Road, and published at the Office of The Stage, by E. Dipple, 42, Holywell Street, Strand; also by J. Allen, 20, Warwick Lane; W. Brittain, 11, Paternoster Row; James Gilbert, 49, Paternoster Row; and W. Jenkinson, 25, Charles Street, Hatton Garden. Nos 1–14, 19 Oct 1844 – 18 Jan 1845. Weekly.   **263**

   BM (destroyed), Garrick Club

1845

The Birmingham Musical Examiner and Dramatic Review. Birmingham. Nos 1–19. 1 Sept 1845 – 3 Jan 1846. Weekly.   **264**

   BM, BP, BU, ICLoy (microfilm), LCM

The Clown of London. At all the theatres, sights, pleasures, and amusements. With fashions for the week, with cuts, humorous numerous right and left . . . Droll things for the passengers on rails and boats, being a weekly collection of locomotive and other wit, from the railway charman's down to that of the humblest stoker on the line. London. Nos 1–39. [1845] Weekly. [The issues are not dated. At the head of the title appears: A friend of Punch's]   **265**

   BM (missing Nos 31–39), MB (missing Nos 15–39), NIC (missing No 38)

The Connoisseur. London. Vols 1–2. Nos 1–17. 19 Apr 1845 – 14 Aug 1846. Monthly. [Vol 2, No 17, 14 Aug 1846, has the title, *The Connoisseur: A Monthly Record of the Fine Arts, Music, and the Drama*]   **266**
  BM (missing all but Vol 2, Nos 10–17)

The Theatrical Critic. Glasgow. Nos 1–2. 13 – 27 Mar 1845. Biweekly.   **267**
  GU, ICLoy (microfilm)

1846

The Drama. A companion to the theatre and concert room. London. Nos 1–7. 10 Oct – 21 Nov 1846. Weekly.   **268**
  ICLoy (microfilm), MB, NjP

Glasgow Theatrical Review. Glasgow. Vols 1–2. Nos 1–58. 25 Feb 1846 – 29 Dec 1847. Weekly.   **269**
  GM, GU

Liverpool Dramatic Argus. Liverpool. Nos 1–6. 20 Apr – 23 May 1846. Weekly.
  ICLoy (microfilm), LvP   **270**

The Manchester Dramatic and Musical Review. Manchester. Nos 1–43. 14 Nov 1846 – 4 Sept 1847. Weekly. [There are also supplements numbered, 12, 16, and 28]   **271**
  BM (missing Nos 3, 17–43), ICLoy (microfilm, missing No 3), MB (missing No 3), MH (missing Nos 17, 40–41), SPtP (missing Nos 5, 10, 13–43)

The Theatrical Times. A weekly magazine of thespian biography, original dramatic essays, provincial, continental, American, metropolitan theatricals; a complete record of public amusements, with original portraits of eminent living actors. London: Published by S. Grieves, Jun. Vols 1–3. Nos 1–143 [i.e., 145]. 13 June 1846 – 17 Mar 1849. New Series [Vol 4] Nos 1–4. 13 Sept – 4 Oct 1851. Weekly. [The publisher changes]   **272**
  BM (missing No 7 of Vol 4), CtY (Vols 1–4), DFo, ICLoy (microfilm, missing the New Series), MB (missing all after Vol 3), MH (Vols 1–4), NN (missing all after Vol 4), NjP (missing all after Vol 3), OClW (missing all after Vol 3), O (Vols 1–3), Garrick Club (Vols 1–3, and No 150. 13 Sept 1851)

1847

The Curtain; or, English Entr'acte, Adapted to the Use of the Royal Italian Opera, Covent Garden. London. Nos 1–[149] 18 Jan 1847 – [29 Dec 1847?] Daily [Nos 1–72]; Every other day [Nos 73–149]   **273**
  ICLoy (microfilm), MB (missing No 99)

The Drama. Glasgow. Nos 1–3. 2 – 16 Dec 1847. Weekly.   **274**
  GU

The Dramatic Mirror and Review of Music and the Fine Arts. [London]: William W. Barth. Nos 1–37. 14 Apr 1847 – 1 Jan 1848. Weekly.   **275**
  BM, ICLoy (microfilm), MB (to Dec 1847), NbU, NIC (Nos 1–36)

The Dramatic News. A journal of theatrical progress and light reading. London. Vol 1. Nos 1–6. 13 Nov – 18 Dec 1847. Weekly.   **276**
  NjP

The Dramatic Review. Glasgow. Nos 1–2. 15–22 Dec 1847. Weekly.   **277**
    GU

Pasquin. A satirical, critical, theatrical, whimsical, and quizzical chronicle. London. Nos 1–9. 14 Aug – 9 Oct 1847. Weekly.   **278**
    BM (missing Nos 1, 9)

The Shakespeare Newspaper. London: Printed and Published by Francis Crew, at the Publishing Office, No 13a Salisbury-square, Fleet-street. Nos 1–2. 1847. [No dates are given for the two issues]   **279**
    BM, ICLoy (microfilm)

Theatrical Beauties and Reigning Stars. London: Mansell, 115, Fleet Street. Nos 1–10. 1 May – 3 July 1847. Weekly. [The title varies slightly]   *280*
    BM (No 1), MH (Nos 1–7, 10), NN (Nos 2–3, 7) NNC (Nos 4–5), Garrick Club (Nos 9–10)

1848

The Dramatic Review. London. Nos 1–8. 15 Mar – 3 May 1848. Weekly.   *281*
    ICLoy (microfilm), MB, NjP

Glasgow Satirist and Dramatic Critic. Glasgow. Nos 1–14. 26 Aug 1848 – 28 Jan 1849. then, *Glasgow Punch, the Satirist and Dramatic Critic.* Nos 15–21. 10 Feb – Apr 1849. Biweekly [except for Nos 17–19, which are weekly]   *282*
    GM (missing No 17), GU, ICLoy (microfilm)

The Opera Glass, a Weekly Amusement Guide. Glasgow. Nos 1–9. 31 Mar – 26 May 1848. Weekly.   *283*
    GU, ICLoy (microfilm)

Puppet Show. London. Vols 1–3. Nos 1–71. 18 Mar 1848 – 14 July 1849. Weekly. [Superseded by, *New Puppet Show*]   *284*
    BM (destroyed), CtY, DLC, MB, NN (1–[3]), NjP (1–69), NPV (Nos 1–66)

The Scene Shifter, or Dramatic Indicator and Panorama of Life As It Is. London. Vol 1. Nos 1–3. 27 Nov – 11 Dec 1848. Weekly.   *285*
    MB

The Stage and Literary and Musical Review. Glasgow. No 1. 9 Sept 1848. Weekly.
    GM, ICLoy (microfilm)   *286*

Tales of the Drama. Being historical accounts of all the popular pieces of the day. London: Printed and Published by E. Lloyd, 12, Salisbury Square. Nos 1–12. [1848] [The date appears in the *British Union Catalogue of Periodicals* IV 282]
    BM   *287*

Theatrical Paul Pry. London: Printed and Published by John Collins, 2, Gresse-street, Rathbone-place, Oxford-street. Vol 1. No 2. 30 Nov 1848. Weekly. [I have been unable to locate any other issues of this periodical. P 10 of No 2 says that "No 3 of the *Theatrical Paul Pry* will be ready for delivery next Thursday morning . . ."]   *287a*
    Garrick Club

1849

Dramatic Omnibus. Edinburgh: R. Reynolds. Nos 1–36. 26 May 1849 – 26 Jan 1850. Weekly. [Nos 1–13 published in Glasgow; Nos 14–36 published in Edinburgh]   *288*
> BM (missing Nos 35–36), CtY, EP (missing No 31), ICLoy (microfilm), MH

The Opera Box. [Her Majesty's Theatre] London: John K. Chapman & Co. [Vols 1–3] [Nos 1–150] [12 Mar] 1849 – 26 Aug 1851. Irregular. [Nos 1–15 are not numbered. The first two issues are not dated. Dating begins with [No 3], 20 Mar 1849]   *289*
> BM (Nos 1–63), ICLoy (microfilm, Nos 1–67), MB, MH (missing Nos 64–150)

The Stage. A weekly magazine of generalities, and a special guide to the sights of London. London: Andrew Vickers, 5, Holywell Street, Strand. Nos 1–14. 23 Mar – 30 June 1849. Weekly. [Also publishes plays in the various issues]   *290*
> BM (destroyed), ICLoy (microfilm), MB, MH, NIC, Garrick Club.

Stage and Scottish Musical and Theatrical Omnibus! Edinburgh. No 15. 11 May 1849. [I have been unable to discover any of the earlier issues]   *291*
> EP, ICLoy (microfilm)

The Stage-Manager; a Journal of Dramatic Literature and Criticism. London: Printed and Published by R. Donaldson, 52, Holywell Street, Strand. Vol 1. 17 Feb – 27 Sept 1849. then, *The Stage-Manager; a Weekly Journal of Music and the Drama.* 4 Oct 1849 – 3 Jan 1850. then, *The Literary Review and Stage Manager.* A journal of literature, music, the drama, and fine arts. Vol 2. 10 Jan – 28 Mar 1850. Weekly.   *292*
> BM (destroyed), DFo, ICLoy (microfilm), ICU, MB (missing 1850), MH, NNC, PU

Supplement to "The Opera Box." London. [Nos 1–61] 15 Mar – 18 Aug 1849. Irregular. [These issues were given out with copies of, *The Opera Box,* for the performances at Her Majesty's Theatre. See, *Opera Box*]   *293*
> BM

The Theatrical Mirror and Playgoer's Companion. London. Nos 1–15. 4 June – [Sept] 1849. Irregular. [The title varies]   *294*
> BM (missing Nos 3–5, and all after No 6), ICLoy (microfilm), MB (missing Nos 9–15)

The Theatrical Programme, and Entr' Acte. London: Printed and Published by E. Baker, at the Office, 5, Whitefriars Street, Fleet Street. Nos [1]–12. 4 June – 20 Aug 1849. then, *The Theatrical Mirror and Playgoer's Companion.* No 13. 27 Aug 1849. Nos 2–6. 3 Sept – 1 Oct 1849. [No 13 is really No 1, under a new title. Numbering begins with No 8. 23 July 1849] Weekly.   *295*
> BM (missing Nos 3–4, 10 Sept, and 17 Sept), MB (missing all after No 8), Garrick Club

Theatrical Review and Author's Miscellany. A monthly journal of the stage. London: S. J. Duffield. Nos 1–5. Sept 1849 – Jan 1850. New Series. Nos 1–6. Feb – July 1850. Monthly. [The subtitle varies]   *296*
> DLC (New Series, Nos 1–6), ICLoy (microfilm), MH (Nos 1–5)

1850

The Brighton Record: Musical, Dramatic, and Literary.   Brighton: E. Wright and
Company, Esplonade Library, 106, King's Road. Vols 1–2. Nos 1–14. 5 Oct 1850 –
4 Jan 1851. Weekly.   **297**
  DFo, ICLoy (microfilm)

The Penny Pictorial Play.   London. Nos 1–32. [1850?] [No dates are indicated for
the various issues]   **298**
  BM, ICLoy (microfilm)

The Playgoer, and Public Amusement Guide.   Glasgow. Nos 1–7. 13 July – 24 Aug
1850. Weekly.   **299**
  EP, ICLoy (microfilm), MH

The Printer's Devil Or the Edinburgh General Review.   A weekly review of the
stage and a guide to the studio. Ed by Paul Vedder. Edinburgh: W. Kent and
Company, 23, 51, and 52 Paternoster Row, E.C. Nos 1–4. 2–23 Feb 1850. then,
Edinburgh General Review. No 5. 2 Mar 1850. then, *The London and Edin-
burgh General Review.* Nos 6–14. 9 Mar – 4 May 1850. Weekly.   **300**
  EP, MH

The Stage Mirror.   A journal devoted to the histrionic and operatic art and literature. London. Nos 1–8. 31 Oct – 21 Dec 1850. Weekly.   **301**
  BM (missing Nos 2–7), BP, MH (missing Nos 2, 4, 5–7)

Tallis's Dramatic Magazine and General Theatrical and Musical Review.   London
and New York: John Tallis & Co. Nos 1–8. Nov 1850 – June 1851. Monthly.
[Followed by *Tallis's Drawing-Room Table Book of Theatrical Portraits,
Memoirs and Anecdotes*]   **302**
  BM, BP, CtY, DFo, DLC, ICLoy (microfilm), ICN, IU, MB, MH, MnS, MnU, NIC, NN,
  NjP, O, OCU

The World.   A dramatic, musical and literary journal. London. Nos 1–14. 9 Mar –
8 June 1850. Weekly. [The subtitle varies]   **303**
  BM (missing Nos 1–8), ICLoy (microfilm), MH, PU

1851

Dramatic Register For 1851.   London: Thomas Hailes Lacy, Wellington Street,
Strand. Vols 1–3. 1851 – 1853. Annual. [A manuscript note, in holograph, signed
by the compiler, in 1853 volume. The initials "T.F.D.C." are written in ink in
1853 volume. The Garrick Club, whose copy it is, attributes the periodical to
Thomas Francis Dillon Croker]   **304**
  BM, ICLoy (microfilm), ICN, MB, MH, NIC, Garrick Club

Dramatic Review: a Weekly Journal of Criticism and Amusement.   Edinburgh:
H. Robinson, 11 Greenside Street; Glasgow: H. Robinson, Lour and Nelson
Street. Vol 1. Nos 1–12. 27 Dec 1851 – 20 Mar 1852. Vol 2. Nos 1–2. 23 Apr – 12
May 1852. Weekly.   **305**
  EP, ICLoy (microfilm)

The Manager's Circular. Or, General Theatrical Directory. London: Printed and Published by Henry Butler, of No. 67, Great Queen-street, Lincoln's-Inn-Fields, in the parish of St. Giles's, Bloomsbury, at the Office of the New Theatrical Agency, No. 21, Bow-street, Covent-garden, London, in the parish of St. Martin's-in-the-Fields. Edited by Henry Butler. No 1 [1] Mar 1851. [On p 1, H. Butler says that the *Circular* will be issued on the 1st of every month] **306**
BM

The Play-goer. London. Nos 1–18. 25 Jan – 24 May 1851. Weekly. [The Yale University copy has written on the flyleaf: "Edited by James Hain Friswell. This was his copy." Inserted on the fly-leaf are two handwritten letters and several clippings. Nos 1–9 were known as, *The Playgoer and Literary Tatler*] **307**
BM, CtY, DLC, ICLoy (microfilm)

Tallis's Drawing Room Table Book of Theatrical Portraits, Memoirs and Anecdotes. London: Published by John Tallis & Company. Parts 1–6. 1851. [Supersedes, *Tallis's Dramatic Magazine*, and superseded by, *Tallis's Shakespere Gallery*] **308**
CtY, DLC, ICN, IU, MB, MBAt, MH, MnU, NN, NjP, PU

Theatre. London: William Winn; Manchester: Abel Heywood; Edinburgh: James G. Bertram & Co. Vols 1–2. 1 Dec 1851 – 2 Oct 1852. Suspended, 15 May – 25 Sept 1852. New Series. Nos 1–2. 25 Sept – 2 Oct 1852. Biweekly. **309**
BM-N (missing New Series), DFo, ICLoy (microfilm, Nos 1–12), MB (missing all after 15 May 1852), Garrick Club (Vol 1)

1852

The Companion to the Theatres and Other Amusements of Edinburgh. Edinburgh: Published by J. G. Bertram and Company, 27 Hanover Street. Nos 1–22. 4–29 Sept 1852. Six days a week. **310**
EP, ICLoy (microfilm, Nos 18, 20), MB (missing No 20)

Tallis's Shakespeare Gallery of Engravings. London: J. Tallis & Company. Parts 1–20. 1852–1853. [Supersedes, *Tallis's Drawing Room Table Book of Theatrical Portraits, Memoirs and Anecdotes*] **311**
DFo, MB, NN (1), NNC

The Universal Guide to the Amusements & Fashions of the Metropolis, for the Use of the Nobility, Gentry, and the Public Visiting London. London. No 6. Mar 1852. [I have not been able to discover any other issues or any additional information regarding this periodical] **311a**
BM-N

The Weekly Review and Dramatic Critic. Edinburgh: H. Robinson. Vols 1–3. [Nos 1–38] 27 Aug 1852 – 13 May 1853. Weekly. **312**
BM, EP, ICLoy (microfilm), KU, MB, MH, MnU

1853

The Crystal Palace Herald. Sydenham. Vol 1. Nos 1–7. Nov 1853 – May 1854. then, *The Crystal Palace Herald and Visitors' Guide.* Nos 8–14. June – Dec 1854.

then, *The Crystal Palace Herald and London Amusements Guide.* Vol 2, No 1 – Vol 3, No 2. Jan 1855 – Feb 1856. then, *The Crystal Palace Herald and Shareholders' Monthly Circular.* Vol 3, Nos 3–7. March – July 1856. Monthly. *312a*
BM-N

Henry Butler's Theatrical Directory and Dramatic Almanack, for the Year 1853. [To be continued annually] Ed by John A. Heraud. London: Printed and Published by Henry Butler. 1853, 1860. Annual [I have been able to locate only these two volumes] *313*
BM, MB (missing 1853)

London. Literature, the drama, music, science, art. With contributions by the first authors & artists of the day. Nos 1–2 conducted by George Augustus Sala. London. Nos 1–9. 24 Dec 1853 – 18 Feb 1854. Weekly. *314*
BM-N

The Shakespeare Repository. [Fennell's Shakespeare Repository] Edited by James Hamilton Fennell. London: Printed for the Proprietor by Thomas Scott, of No. 1, Warwick Court, High Holborn. Nos [1]–4. 1853. [There is no indication of the frequency of publication as the individual issues are not dated] *315*
BM (destroyed), BP, CtY, DLC, ICLoy (microfilm), LU, MB, MH, NN, O, PU, TxHR, WHi

The Weekly Musical Transcript. (A weekly journal of music, the drama, literature and art.) London. Nos 1–6. Sept – 10 Oct 1853. Weekly. then, *Musical Transcript,* Nos 7–69. 15 Oct 1853 – 23 Dec 1854. *316*
BM-N (missing Nos 1–5)

1856

The Glasgow Amateur Public Amusement Record and General Miscellany. Glasgow. Nos 1–15. 1 Oct – 5 Nov 1856. Weekly. *317*
GU, ICLoy (microfilm)

The Soho Courier, West End Advertiser, and London Theatrical and Amusement Guide: An Impartial and Musical Censor. London: Printed by the Proprietor, Cornelius Barrell, of 35, Gerrard-Street, and Published by him. Vol 1. Nos 8–11. 2–23 Jan 1856. Weekly. *318*
BM-N (missing Nos 1–7)

1857

The General Dramatic, Equestrian & Musical Agency and Sick Fund Association. Almanack. By J. Anson. London. 1857–1859. then, *Dramatic, Equestrian and Musical Agency and Sick Fund Association Almanack.* By J. W. Anson. 1860–(1863). then, *Dramatic, Equestrian, and Musical Sick Fund Almanack for 1862* (–64). By J. W. Anson. [The volumes for 1862, 1863, are another edition of the *Dramatic, Equestrian, and Musical Agency and Sick Fund Association Almanac* for the same year] then, *Dramatic and Musical Almanack for 1865.* By J. W. Anson. then, *Dramatic Almanack for 1866* (1867). Annual. *319*
BM

Thespian and Dramatic Record, a Journal Especially Designed to Promote the Interests of the British Stage. [London: Bennett] Nos 1–15. 29 Apr – 5 Aug 1857. Weekly. *320*
ICLoy (microfilm), ICN, MB, MH, NjP

The Weekly Spectator. Glasgow. No 1. 15 Apr 1857.   *321*
   GM

1858

Moliere and Shakespeare. An international review of the stage. Ed by Alfred
   Cheron. London: Bow Street, 35, Covent Garden. No 1. 29 Oct 1858. Weekly.
   [Printed in English and French, in parallel columns. Maurice Godefreid was
   the editor of the French language edition at Paris]   *322*
      BM-N (wanting p 5–8), BP, ICLoy (microfilm)

1860

The Players. A weekly dramatic and literary journal. London: G. Abington. Vols
   1–4. Nos 1–82. 2 Jan 1860 – 20 July 1861. [Vol 1, Nos 1–8, lack numbering]
   Weekly. [Edited by W. Wisgast, 30 Jan – 15 Sept 1860 by J. B. Hopkins, 22
   Sept – Dec 1860]   *323*
      BM, CtY, ICLoy (microfilm), ICU, IaU, MB, MH, NjP, NN (missing Vols 3–4), WEST
      (missing Vols 3–4)

Sporting Telegraph and Daily Record of Music and the Drama. London. Nos
   1–116. 22 Feb 1860 – 13 Mar 1861. Weekly. [Incorporated with, *Sporting Life*]
      BM-N   *324*

1861

The Gaulois and the Universal Caricature. Anglo-French weekly biographical,
   dramatical, musical, fashion, illustrated journal. Conducted by M. de Lavigerie.
   London. Vol 1. No 1. 16 Feb 1861. Weekly.   *325*
      BM-N

1862

The Curtain. Published gratuitously every morning and distributed in the Royal
   Amphitheatre and Theatre Royal as a free programme. Liverpool. 14 Nov
   1862 – 8 July 1864. Daily. [The extent of the run has not been determined] *326*
      LvP (14–29 Nov 1862; 16 Dec 1862; 17 Mar 1863; 4–5 Dec 1863; 8 July 1864)

Dramatic Equestrian and Musical Sick Fund Almanack for 1862. By J. W. Anson.
   [According to the title-page this is the sixth year] London: Printed by H. M.
   Arliss. 1862 – 1864. Annual. then, *Dramatic & Musical Almanack for 1865.* 1865–
   1866. then, *Dramatick Almanack for 1867.* 1867–1868. then, *Dramatic and Musical Almanack for 1869.* then, *Dramatic Almanack for 1870.* 1870–1872. Annual.
      BM   *327*

Illustrated Sporting News. London. Vols 1–4. Nos 1–193. 15 Mar 1862 – 18 Nov
   1865. then, *Illustrated Sporting and Theatrical News.* Nos 194–364; New Series,
   Nos 1–44. 25 Nov 1865 – 19 Mar 1870. Weekly.   *328*
      BM-N (Mar 1862 – 19 Mar 1870)), ICLoy (microfilm, 1862–1868)

The Musician, and Music-Hall Times. A journal for the music-hall, the concert-
   room, and the theatre. London: Printed and published for the Proprietors by
   Walter Graves, at his office, 6 Red Lion Court, Fleet Street, E.C. Nos 1–17.
   28 May – 13 Sept 1862. Weekly. [Contains material on the Provincial music
   halls]   *329*
      BM-N

1863

Mayall's Celebrities of the London Stage, a Series of Photographic Portraits in Character. London: Published by Messrs. A. Marion, Son & Co., 23 Soho Square, W. Nos 1–3. [1863] [The issues are not dated. There is no way to determine the frequency of issue] 329a
O

The Orchestra. A weekly review of music and the drama. London: Crane, Wood and Company, 201 Regent Street. Vols 1–22. Nos 1–561. 3 Oct 1863 – 26 June 1874. Weekly. New Series. Vols 1–14. Aug 1874 – 1887. Monthly. [Later issues are almost exclusively musical in nature] 330
BM (to July 1876), CtY (Vols 1–18), ICLoy (microfilm), MB (to New Series, Vol 10), NN (New Series 1–[4]–[7–8]), O

Prince of Wales Theatre. Play bill and universal evening advertiser. Birmingham. Nos 1–92. 1863 – 10 Nov 1865. Irregular. [No dates are given for the first issues]
BP, ICLoy (microfilm) 331

Royal Dramatic College News. London. No 1. July 1863. 332
BM-N

The Shakespeare Gazette: a Weekly Record of Proceedings Relating to the Tercentenary Celebration. London: H. Thomas. No 1. 3 Dec 1863. Weekly. 333
BM-N, BP, MB

1864

Footlights. [Prince of Wales Theatre] Liverpool. 1864 – 1865. [I have been unable to determine the number of issues, as well as the dates for the first and last issue] 334
ICLoy (microfilm), LvP (9 June, 17 Aug, 14 Oct 1864; 25 Feb, 17 May 1865)

Leading Stars of The London Stage. How, when, and where to see them, with all the theatrical news. London: Printed by Taylor and Greening, at their Printing Office, 4 and 5, Graystoke-place, Fetter-lane, and Published for the Proprietor by the Newsagents' Publishing Company, at their Chief Office, 147, Fleet street, E.C. No 1. 3 Dec 1864. [Registration issue] 335
BM-N

The Little Showman. London. Nos 1–8. [1864] 336
Not located (*British Union Catalogue of Periodicals,* iii p 70)

Musical and Dramatic Review. London. Nos 1–14. 5 Mar – 4 June 1864. Weekly [Nos 1–9 as, *Booseys Musical and Dramatic Review*] 337
BM (missing Nos 2–13), ICLoy (microfilm), MB

The Musical Monthly, and Repertoire of Literature, the Drama & the Arts. Organ of the Muses. London: Published at the Office, 40, Great Marlborough Street, W. Arthur Hall, Smart, & Allen, 25 Paternoster Row, E.C. [Vol 1] Nos 1–7. Jan 1864 – July 1864. then, *The Musical Monthly and Drawing Room Miscellany.* [Vol 1] No 8 – Vol 2, No 21. Aug 1864 – Sept 1865. Monthly. [A note on the cover of the first issue states that the musical contributions are written specially for the magazine. Beginning with No 8, Aug 1864, the name of Vincent Wallace

is inserted as editor of the music. Vol 2 begins with No 13, Jan 1865. The first issue is printed and published by Abraham Gould (p 16). Later it is printed at Regent Press, No. 55, King-street, Golden-square, W., and published by Adams & Francis, at 59, Fleet-street, E.C. Incorporated with the *Mayfair Miscellany*]
  BM, ICLoy (microfilm)   **338**

Tallis's Illustrated Life in London.   London. Nos 1–6. 2–30 Apr 1864. then, *Tallis's Theatrical, Musical, Fine Arts, Literary and General Family Newspaper.* Nos 7–22. 7 May – 27 Aug 1864. then, *The Age, Theatrical, Musical and Sporting.* Nos 23–26. 3–24 Sept 1864. then, *The Sporting Pilot and the Age.* No 27. 10 Oct 1864. then, *The Age.* Nos 28–39. 8 Oct – 24 Dec 1864. Weekly.   **339**
  BM-N, BP (missing all after No 26), MB (missing all after No 26)

1865

The Baton: Musical, Theatrical, and Fashionable Gazette.   London: Printed and Published for the Proprietor by William Henry Elliot, at the Chief Office, 475, Oxford Street. Vol 1. Nos 1–33. 15 June – 22 July 1865. Six days a week.   **340**
  BM-N

The Dramatic Telegram.   A journal of theatrical intelligence and universal dramatic advertiser. London. Nos 1–14. 1 Nov 1865 – 6 May 1866. Biweekly.   **341**
  BM (missing No 13), ICLoy (microfilm), O

Manchester Observer.   [Theatre Royal] Manchester. Nos 1–2903. 17 Apr 1865 – 27 Mar 1875. Six days a week (with some irregularities).   **342**
  MP

The Sporting Times.   Otherwise known as "The Pink 'un." A chronicle of racing, literature, art, and the drama. London. Nos 1–3559. 11 Feb 1865 – 5 Dec 1931. Weekly.   **343**
  BM-N

The Star.   Liverpool. 1865. Daily. [The only issues which I have been able to locate are the two at the Liverpool Public Library]   **344**
  LvP (Nos 85, 733. 9 Sept 1865; 25 Mar 1867)

The World of Magic.   Or Scraps from the note book of a wandering wizard all round the world. London. No 1. 19 Aug 1865. Weekly.   **345**
  BM-N

1867

The Amateur's Guide; or, Stage and Concert Hall Reporter.   Birmingham. Nos 1–2. 29 June – 13 July 1867. Biweekly.   **346**
  BM, ICLoy (microfilm)

London Museum Music Hall, Bull Ring, Birmingham.   Book of words. Birmingham. Vol 3, No 80. 1867. [I have been unable to locate any other issues]   **347**
  BP

The Play.   Liverpool. Nos 164, 176, 294, 561, 602, 638, 1337, 1346. 25 Apr 1867 – 29 Dec 1870. [These are the only issues which I have been able to discover]   **348**
  LvP

Sock and Buskin. The drama, music, entertainments. London. Nos 1–4. 1867.
Weekly.   *349*
  BM (destroyed)

The Weekly Theatrical Reporter and Music Hall Review. London. Nos 1–14.
14 Dec 1867 – 14 Mar 1868. Weekly.   *350*
  BM, MB

1868

Blackpool Visitor. Blackpool. Nos 1–20. 28 May – 9 Oct 1868. Weekly.   *350a*
  BM-N

Blackpool Visitor and Advertiser. Blackpool. Nos 1–4. 3–24 June 1868. Weekly.
  BM-N   *350b*

Dramatic Almanac. By J. W. Anson. London. [Vols 1–4] 1868–1871. Annual. *351*
  MB (missing all before 1871), MiU

The Dramatic News. A journal devoted to the interests of the theatrical and musi-
cal world. London: Printed by the National Steam Printing Company, 11 Crane
Court, E.C. No 1. 16 June 1868. Monthly.   *352*
  BM-N

The Dramatic Review. A weekly journal of literature, art, music and the drama.
Glasgow. Nos 1–7. 1868. Weekly. [I have been unable to discover the dates of
the individual issues]   *353*
  BM (destroyed)

The Era Almanac. Conducted by Edward Ledger. London. Vols 1–2. 1868 – 1869.
Annual. then, *The Era Almanac and Annual.* Vols 3–41. 1870–1919.   *354*
  BM, BP, MB (1868–1913), MH, PU (1868–1916)

The London Mercury. A journal of general information, literature, art, and the
drama. London: Printed and Published for the Proprietors by James Matthews
at the Office, 7, Hyde-Street, New Oxford-street. Vol 1. No 1. 4 Jan 1868. Weekly.
  BM-N   *355*

The Mask: a Humorous and Fantastic Review of the North. Ed by Alfred Thomp-
son and Leopold Lewis. London: 49 Essex Street, Strand, W.C. Vol 1. [Nos 1–11]
Feb – Dec 1868. Monthly.   *356*
  BM, C, CSmH, CU, CtY, DLC, IC, ICN, IU, LGU, MB, MH, NIC, NN, NjP, OU, TxU,
  Garrick Club

Music Halls' Gazette. London. Nos 1–36. 11 Apr – 12 Dec 1868. Weekly.   *357*
  BM-N, ICLoy (microfilm)

*Pictorial Sporting and Theatrical Guide and Record of Music, Literature, and the
Fine Arts.* London: Printed by Joseph Bruton at his Printing Office, 12 Crane-
court, and Published by Alfred William Huckett, at 147, Fleet-street. Vol 21.
Nos 1041–1042. 17–23 Oct 1868. then, *Pictorial, Sporting and Theatrical Guide.*
An authority on sport, music, art, and the drama. Vol 21. Nos 1043–1044. 31
Oct – 7 Nov 1868. Weekly. [At the top of page 1, for 7 Nov 1868, is the word,
"Discontinued." I have not been able to locate the earlier issues]   *358*
  BM-N

The Sphinx. A journal of criticism and humour: art, literature, music, the drama, society, and current events. Manchester: John Heywood, 141 and 143, Deansgate. Vols 1–4. Nos 1–167. 25 July 1868 – 21 Oct 1871. Weekly.   *359*
BM

The Stage; Assembly Room & Music Hall Companion, and General Advertiser. London: Printed and Published for the Proprietor, by Frederick Pickburn, 2, Vineyard-gardens, Bowling Green Lane, Clerkenwell, E.C. No 1. 21 Nov 1868. Weekly.   *360*
BM-N

Theatrical and Musical Review, an Independent Journal of Criticism. London. Nos 1–7. 1 Oct – 12 Nov 1868. Weekly.   *361*
BM (destroyed)

1869

Bill of the Play. [Programmes of St James's Theatre] London. Vol 1. Nos 1–2. 16–23 Oct 1869. Weekly.   *362*
BM-N

The Footlights. A journal of literary, dramatic, and musical interest. London: Printed and Published by Alfred Whitty & Co., Advertising Agents and Publishers, 335, Strand. No 1. 2 Oct 1869. Weekly.   *363*
BM-N

The Gaiety. A weekly record of music, the drama, and amusements. London: Printed and Published for the Proprietor by James Welch, Newspaper Printer, 24, Houghton-Street, Strand. Vol 1. No 1. 3 July 1869. Weekly.   *364*
BM-N

The Gaiety. News-letter and magazine of literature, art, and the drama. [For the Gaiety Theatre] London: Printed and Published by George Berridge & Henry Salmon, of 37 & 42 Eastcheap, E.C. Vol 1. [Nos 1–2] 26 July – 4 Aug 1869. Weekly.   *365*
BM-N

London Entr'acte. London. Nos 1–88. 1869 – 11 Mar 1871. then, *London and Provincial Entr'acte.* Nos 89–137. 18 Mar 1871 – 17 Feb 1872. then, *Entr'acte.* Nos 138–1974. 24 Feb 1872 – 26 Apr 1907. Weekly. [The British Museum copy begins with No 27, 8 Jan 1870]   *366*
BM-N (missing Nos 1–26)

The Play. A journal of literary, dramatic and musical interest. [Programmes of the Theatre Royal, Lyceum] London: Printed and Published by Alfred Whitty & Co., Advertising Agents and Publishers, 335, Strand. [Nos 1–2] Oct – Nov 1869. [The issues are not numbered]   *367*
BM

The Shakespeare Almanack for 1869, Containing a Life of Shakespeare and a History of His Plays. London. 1869, 1874, 1876. [These are the only volumes which I have been able to locate]   *368*
BM

1870

The Day's Doings. An illustrated journal of romantic events, reports, sporting and theatrical news. London. Vols 1–4. Nos 1–82. 30 July 1870 – 17 Feb 1872. then, *Here and There.* Nos 1–44. 24 Feb – 21/28 Dec 1872. Weekly.   *369*
    BM-N, ICLoy (microfilm), ICN (missing Vol 2)

The Dramatic Chronicle and Observer. London. Vol 1. Nos 1–3. 4–18 Jan 1870. Weekly.   *370*
    BM, MB

English Society in Town and Country: a Monthly Illustrated Magazine of Amusement and Recreation. Conducted by J. Hogg. London. [1870, 1871] [I have been unable to determine the number of issues, or the dates of the first and last issues] Monthly.   *371*
    BM (destroyed)

The Ferret. An inquisitive, quizzical, satirical and theatrical censor of the age. London: Printed and published by C. Young, at the Office, 22, Russel-court, Brydges-street, Strand. Nos 1–2. 15–29 Jan 1870. Biweekly. then, *The Ferret.* A weekly literary, satirical, and theatrical journal of the age. Nos 3–5. [New Series, 1–2] 22 Mar – 5 Apr 1870. Weekly.   *372*
    BM-N

The Illustrated Review. A fortnightly journal of literature, science, and art. London. Vols 1–6. Nos 1–105. 14 Oct 1870 – 1874. Biweekly. New Series. Vols 1–2. Nos 106–137. 1 Jan – 5 Aug 1874. Weekly.   *373*
    BM (missing New Series, Vol 2), CtY (missing Vol 5, and New Series), MB (missing all but New Series, Vol 1), O

Music Hall Critic and Programme of Amusements. London. Nos 1–7. 1870. [I have been unable to discover the dates of the first and last issues, or the frequency of publication]   *374*
    BM (destroyed)

1871

The Olio of Literature, Music, the Drama and the Fine Arts. London. Vol 1. Nos 1–26. 19 Aug 1871 – 10 Feb 1872. Weekly.   *375*
    BM, ICLoy (microfilm)

South London Palace and Canterbury Hall Journal. London: Printed by S. Taylor, 4 and 5 Greystoke-place, Fetter-lane, and Published by the Proprietor at the South London Palace and Canterbury Music Hall. Vol 2, No 54. 14 Oct 1871. [I have been unable to locate any other issues]   *376*
    BM-N

The Stage. London: Printed by John Moore, of 4 a, Exeter-street, Strand, and Published by George Richard Genie, at 20, Exeter-street, Strand. Vol 1. No 1. 13 Dec 1871.   *377*
    BM-N

The Vaudeville Magazine. [Ed by E. J. Stinson, and A. C. Skinsley] London: 56 Red Lion Street. Nos 1–5. Sept 1871 – Jan 1872. Monthly.   *378*
    BM, ICLoy (microfilm)

The Wandering Thespian.   Edited by Walter Stephans. London: Published by
Thomas H. Lacy, 89, Strand, W.C. 1871. Annual.   379
   BM, ICLoy (microfilm)

1872

*Mirror; a Weekly Magazine and Review of Literature, the Drama, Science, and
Art.*   London. Vols 1–4. 1872–1874. Weekly. [The subtitle varies]   380
   PPL (Vol 4, 6 June – 19 Sept 1874)

Samuel Eyre's Theatrical Programme.   London. Nos 1–35. 7 Oct 1872 – 2 June
1873. then, *Theatrical Programme.* Nos 36–[174?] 9 June 1873-1876? Weekly.
   BM-N (missing Nos 59–174), NN (1875–1876)   381

1873

The Amphi.   Liverpool. 24 Dec 1873; 9 Mar 1874; 11 Oct 1875; 31 Aug 1878.
[These are the only issues which I have been able to locate]   382
   LvP

The Entr' acte Almanack and Theatrical and Music Hall Annual.   Compiled by
W. H. Combes. London. Vols 1–34. 1873–1906. Annual. [The title varies slightly]
                                                                          383
   BM, C (missing 1873–1882, 1891, 1906), MB (missing 1875, 1877, 1900–1906), MH
   (missing 1875), O (missing 1873–1882, 1884)

1874

The Brighton Echo and Daily Bill of the Play.   Brighton. [No 1. July 1874] [Pro-
grammes of the Theatre Royal]   383a
   BM-N

The Critic.   A weekly review of the drama, music and literature. London: Printed
(for the Proprietor) by James Welch, 6, St. Clement-Inn-Passage, Strand, W.C.
Published at the Office, 23, Leicester-square. Vols 1–2. Nos 1–16. 2 Dec 1874 –
20 Mar 1875. then, *The Critic.* A social and political review. Nos 17–22. (New
Series. Nos 1–6). 27 Mar – 1 May 1875. Weekly. [With No 17, i.e., No 1 of the
New Series, the periodical has a larger format]   384
   BM-N

The Dramatic Record and Theatrical Advertiser.   London: Printed for the Proprietors by Messrs. George Tarrant & Co., 70, Liverpool Road, and Published
by Edward Hastings, 16 Gibson Square, Islington. No 1. 1 Feb 1874. Monthly.
   BM-N   385

Figaro Programme.   [A weekly theatrical journal] London: Printed and Pub-
lished for the Proprietors by Alfred Wilcox, St. Bride Street and Shoe Lane, E.C.
Nos 1–49. 11 July 1874 – 12 June 1875. then, *The London Programme and
Sketch-Book.* Nos 50–52. 19 – 26 June 1875. then, *The Saturday Programme and
Sketch-Book.* 3 July 1875 – 19 Aug 1876. then, [alternate issues are entitled] *The
Wednesday Programme and Sketch Book*, and *The Saturday Programme and
Sketch-Book.* Nos 112–181. 23 Aug 1876 – 21 Apr 1877. then, *The Saturday
Programme and Great City.* 21 Apr 1877. then, *The Wednesday Programme and*

Sketch-Book. 25 Apr – 20 June 1877. [From Nos 114–182, the Wednesday issues are also numbered 2–38, in a consecutive series]   *386*

  BM-N (missing 23 May 1877), BP (missing all after No 51), MH (Nos 1–77, 79–100, 102–181), NN (incomplete)

Illustrated Sporting and Dramatic News.   London. Vols 1–80. Nos 1–3652. 28 Feb 1874 – 1945. then, *Sport and Country.* Weekly. [The title varies somewhat during the long "run" of this periodical]   *387*

  BM-N (1929–1932, 1934–1936, 1938–1939), LVA (missing 1874–1878, and all after 1894), MB (missing Vols 3–16, 36–39, and all after Vols 42), NjR (missing all after 13 Mar 1880), NN (incomplete portions before Vol 47)

The Lorgnette Programme.   London: Printed and published by John Anderson, Metropolitan Buildings, Queen Victoria Street, E.C. Vol 1. Nos 1–5. 23 Sept – 28 Oct 1874. Biweekly. [No 5 has a note saying that "on and after Nov 4th" it will be published under the title of, *The Opera-Glass Programme: Dramatic and Musical Critic*]   *388*

  BM, ICLoy (microfilm)

The New Shakespeare Society's Transactions.   London: Published for the Society by Trübner & Co., 57 & 59, Ludgate Hill, E.C. Vols 1–5. Transactions, 1–14. 1874, 1875 – 1876, 1877 – 1879, 1880 – 1886, 1887 – 1892.   *389*

  CSmH, DFo, ICLoy (microfilm), ICN, IEN, IU, MH, NN, NbU, PU, WaU

The Stage.   London. Vols 1–2, No 1. 1874. [I have been unable to obtain the issues]
  BP   *390*

The Stage.   London. Nos 1–14. 29 Sept – 30 Dec 1874. Weekly   *391*

  BM (missing Nos 8–14), ICLoy (microfilm), NLD

The Visitor's Guide and Journal of Amusements.   London: Printed for the Proprietors, at the Anglo-American Times Press, 127, Strand. No 1. 1 July 1874. Weekly.   *392*

  BM-N

1875

Dramatic Art Circular and Monthly Record of the British Musical and Dramatic Institute.   Ed by Charles Sleigh. London. Vol 1. No 1. 15 Feb 1875. Monthly.
  BM, ICLoy (microfilm)   *393*

Irish Turf Telegraph and Dramatic Gazette.   Dublin. Nos 1–16. 3 July – 16 Oct 1875. Weekly.   *394*

  BM (missing Nos 2–8, 10–15)

Liverpool Programme of Amusements.   Where to go and what to see. Liverpool. Vol 1. No 1. 30 Oct 1875.   *395*

  BM-N

The Programme and Dramatic Review.   London: Printed (for the Proprietors) by S. E. Palmer, 5, Windsor Terrace, Cassland Road, South Hackney, and published at the Office 23, Leicester Square, W.C. Vol 1. Nos 1–2. June – July 1875. Monthly.   *396*

  BM, ICLoy (microfilm)

1876

The Eclipse and Theatrical Programme.   London: Printed for the Proprietor by
   Henry Hughes, at 4, Bouverie-street, Fleet-street, and Published by George
   Hugget at the same address. No 202. 14 Sept 1876. Weekly. [On page 1 the edi-
   tor calls the issue a "New Series." There is no indication of a title for a previous
   series. I have been unable to locate any other issues of the periodical]   *397*
   BM-N

The Fire Fly.   Evening paper & programme. London: W. S. Johnson — "Nassau
   Steam Press," 60, St. Martin's Lane, Charing Cross, W.C. Nos 1–11. 15 Apr – 26
   June 1876. then, [Nos 1–21] 1 Jan – 4 June 1877. [The 1 Jan 1877 issue calls
   itself the first number. It contains the programmes of the Folly and Criterion
   theatres. The publisher changes in 1877]   *398*
   BM-N (15 Apr 1876; 8 Jan 1877), O

The London Album.   [The periodical seems to be edited by the man who edits
   The Eclipse and Theatrical Programme] London: Printed for the Proprietor by
   Henry Hughes, at 4, Bouverie street, Fleet-street, and published by George
   Huggett at the same address. No 1. 4 Oct 1876.   *399*
   BM-N

The London Guide and Photographic Album.   Programmes of concerts, entertain-
   ments, and theatres; and guide to the public buildings and sights of London.
   London: Published by J. Haddon & Co., Bouverie Street, Fleet Street. Vol 1.
   No 1. 13/20 May 1876. Weekly.   *400*
   BM-N

The Minstrel.   [Including the programme of Her Majesty's Opera, Drury Lane]
   London: Printed by W. Brettell, Jun., 336 a, Oxford Street, W. No 1. 16 May
   1876. Two issues a week.   *401*
   BM-N

Rotunda Prompter.   Liverpool. No 236. 18 Nov 1876; No 259. 12 May 1877; No
   266. 30 June 1877; No 267. 7 July 1877. [I have been unable to locate any other
   issues of this periodical]   *402*
   LvP

1877

The Dramatic Observer.   A weekly journal of the drama, music, literature, and
   art. London: Printed and Published for the Proprietor, R. Wilton, 41, Bedford
   Street, Strand. Vol 1. No 1. 5 July 1877. Weekly.   *403*
   BM-N

The Looking Glass.   A reflex of the times; social, satirical, theatrical, musical and
   artistic. Manchester. Vol 1. Nos 1–7. 1 Dec 1877 – 1 June 1878. Monthly.   *404*
   BM, MP

North London Programme.   London: Printed and Published for the Proprietor,
   by William Gee, at 56, High Street, Islington. No 1. 17 Mar 1877. Weekly.   *405*
   BM-N

The Theatre; a Monthly Review and Magazine. London: Wyman & Sons. Vols 1–3. 30 Jan 1877 – 23 June 1878. Weekly. New Series. Vols 1–3. Aug 1878 – Dec 1879. [Second Series] Third Series. Vols 1–6. Jan 1880 – Dec 1882. Fourth Series. Vols 1–30. Jan 1883 – Dec 1897. Monthly. [Subtitle varies slightly. Series 4, Vols 11–13 (Jan 1888 – June 1889), include the monthly supplement, *Dramatic Directory for March 1888 – May 1889.* Ed by Clement Scott, 1878 – 1890. Index]   *406*

> BM, BP, C, ICLoy (microfilm, 1878–1897), ICN, LdP, LvP, MB, NB, NN, O, OCl, PSt, RPB

Touchstone; or, The New Era. Drama, literature, & the arts. London. Vol 1. Nos 1–14. 7 Apr – 7 July 1877. then, *Touchstone; or, The New Era: A Weekly Newspaper, Literary, Artistic, and Social.* Nos 15–21. 14 July – 25 Aug 1877. then, *Touchstone; or, The New Era.* Vols 1–3. Nos 22–79. 1 Sept 1877 – 5 Oct 1878. then, *Touchstone; Artistic, Literary, and Social Review.* Vol 4. Nos 80–113. 12 Oct 1878 – 31 May 1879. Weekly.   *407*

> BM, MB (missing all after No 52)

1878

The Curtain. A weekly programme and review of the drama. London: The Curtain. Nos 1–10. 21 May – 23 July 1878. Weekly.   *408*
> BM, MiU

Dramatic Authors' Society. Provincial Tariff. London. [Nos 1–5] 1878 – 31 Dec 1880. then, *Dramatic Authors' Society Tariff.* Provincial and London. [Nos 6–7] 30 June 1881 – 30 June 1882. Two issues a year (irregular). [Each number is called an "issue"]   *409*
> LU-MM

Dramatic Reform Association. Manchester. No 1. Jan 1878. then, *Circular.* Nos 2–4. Feb – Apr 1878. then, *Journal of Dramatic Reform.* Nos [5]–33. Mar 1878 – May 1883. Irregular.   *410*
> BP (Nos 1–30), MP (missing Nos 31–32), MH (1878–1882), MiU

The Managers' Guide and Artistes' Advertiser. A medium for the managers and members of the theatrical and music hall professions. Manchester. Vol 1. Nos 1–23. 29 June – 3 Dec 1878. Weekly. [Ed by J. H. Cobbe, Vol 1, Nos 1–10. 29 June – 31 Aug 1878; Ed by W. Forest, Nos 11–23. 7 Sept – 3 Dec 1878]   *411*
> BM (missing No 17)

The Mohawk Minstrels' "Nigger" Dramas, Dialogues and Drolleries. By C. Townley. London. [No] 1. [1878] then, *The Mohawk Minstrels . . . Annual.* [Nos] 2–10. 18 . . . ? then, *Francis & Day's . . . Book of Dialogue* &c. [Nos] 11–12. [19--? – 1910]   *412*
> BM (destroyed), O (1878–1881)

1879

The Dramatic & Musical Circular. An epitome of dramatic, operatic & music hall requirements issued weekly, by Brandon & Stevenson. London: Printed and Published for the Proprietors by Arliss Andrews, 31 Museum Street, W.C. Nos 1–27. 27 Mar – 27 Sept 1879. then, *The Dramatic & Musical Circular.* A theatrical and musical critic and advertiser. Nos 28–29. 4 – 11 Oct 1879. then, *London*

Mirror. In which is incorporated *The Dramatic and Musical Circular.* Nos 29–31. 11 – 25 Oct 1879. Weekly. [11 Oct issue is called a "Specimen Number," and repeats the No 29, of the Oct 4 issue. With No 15, Brandon's name is dropped from the title-page, and "Stevenson & Co." is substituted. With No 22 the name "Stevenson & Co." is dropped from the title-page. As *The London Mirror* there is a change of the printing and publishing addresses]   *413*
    BM, ICLoy (microfilm)

Dramatic Notes. An illustrated handbook of the London Theatres. London: Gay and Bird. Vols 1–14. 1879 – 1893. [The title varies slightly] Annual. [Vol 1 (1879), is edited by Charles Eyre Pascoe; Vol 2 (1880) is edited by William H. Rideing; Vol 3 (1881–1882) is edited by T. Walter Wilson; Vols 4–8 (1883 – 1887) are edited by Austin Brereton; Vols 9–14 (1888 – 1893) are edited by Charles Howard. Indexes]   *414*
    BM (missing 1885–1887), BP, CtY (missing Vol 14), ICU (missing Vol 14), MH (missing Vol 14), MiU, MP, NIC, NN (missing Vols 11, 14), O (missing Vols 1, 10), Guildhall Library, London (1879–85, 1885, 1891–92)

The Edinburgh Programme. Edinburgh. Nos 1–33. 7 July 1879 – 14 Feb 1880. then, *The Weekly Programme.* No 1. 21 Feb 1880. Weekly.   *415*
    E (Nos 12, 17, 21)

The Mask. A satirical review of the week in caricature. Ed by Alfred Thompson. London: Seymour. Nos 1–16. 10 May – 27 Aug 1879. Weekly.   *416*
    BM-N, ICLoy (microfilm), ICN, ICU, MH

Saturday Musical Review. A record of music and the drama. With which is incorporated, *The Choir.* [Supersedes, *Choir, and Musical Record*] London. Nos 1–42. 4 Jan – 18 Oct 1879. Weekly.   *417*
    BM, NN (missing Nos 1, 10, 20, 33–42)

Sketch. An illustrated miscellany of art, music, the drama, society and the belles lettres. London. Nos 1–77. 25 Jan 1879 – 25 Dec 1880. Biweekly [Nos 1–25, 25 Jan – 27 Dec 1879] [Edited by Reginald Shirley: Nos 26–47. 3 Jan – 29 May 1880]   *418*
    BM-N, BP (missing No 1), NN (missing Nos 26–77)

1880

Bon Accord; Satire, Music, Art, Drama, Gossip. Aberdeen: [W. J. Clark] Nos 1–85. 3 Jan 1880 – 12 Aug 1881. Weekly.   *419*
    ICN

The Critic. A weekly general review. London. Vol 3, No 8 – Vol 4, No 16. 16 June 1880 – 9 Feb 1881. then, *The Critic.* A weekly dramatic & general review. Vol 5. Nos 1–20. 16 Feb – 29 June 1881. Weekly.   *420*
    BM (missing all before 16 June 1880)

The Green Room. A weekly illustrated record of music and the drama. London: Printed by W. Griggs, at Elm House, Hanover St., Peckham, S.E., and published by E. W. Allen, 11, Ave Maria Lane, E.C. Nos 1–2. 26 June – 3 July 1880. Weekly.   *421*
    BM, MH

The Prompter. London. Nos 1–4. 3 – 24 Jan 1880. Weekly. **422**
    BM-N, ICLoy (microfilm)

The Stage. Sheffield. No 17. 24 Apr 1880. Weekly. [I have been unable to locate any other issues] **423**
    MP (No 17 seems to be the final issue)

The Stage Directory. A London and provincial theatrical advertiser. London. Nos 1–14. 1 Feb 1880 – 1 Mar 1881. Monthly. then, *The Stage.* New Series. Nos 1–4061. 25 Mar 1881 – 12 Feb 1959. Weekly. then, *The Stage and Television Today.* Nos 4062 – . 19 Feb 1959 – . [Includes an occasional supplement] **424**
    BM-N, GM (1943–)

1881

The Actor and Elocutionist. A journal of elocutionary, literary, dramatic, musical, and general artistic interest. Ed by Edwin Drew, and Stuart St. Clair. London: Printed and Published by E. W. Allen, 4, Ave Maria Lane, E.C. Vol 1. No 1. 15 Dec 1881. **425**
    BM, ICLoy (microfilm)

Illustrated Life in London. A journal of general sporting and theatrical news. London: Printed and Published for the Proprietors, by Ernest James, at 32, Tavistock Street, Covent-Garden. Nos 1–4. 7 – 23 May 1881. Weekly. **426**
    BM-N

The Liverpool Entr' Acte. A weekly journal for theatre goers, containing a complete programme of the entertainments at the principal places of amusement in Liverpool. Liverpool. Dec 1881 – [Mar?] 1882. Weekly. **427**
    Not located (Loewenberg p 43)

The Musical and Dramatic World. Liverpool. Nos 1–90. 22 Oct 1881 – 7 July 1883. Weekly. **428**
    BM-N, ICLoy (microfilm)

The Play: A Chronicle of the London Stage. London. Vols 1–3. Nos 1–119. 20 Oct 1881 – 24 Jan 1884. Weekly. **429**
    BM-N, ICLoy (microfilm)

The Theatrical World. London. Vols 1–2. [Nos 1–26] 22 Oct 1881 – 22 Apr 1882. Weekly. **430**
    BM-N, ICLoy (microfilm)

The Umpire. Sport, gossip, and the drama. Ed by Adolphus Rosenberg. London: Printed and Published by Lewis Grose, at 174, Fleet-street. Nos 1–18. 26 June – 23 Oct 1881. Weekly. **431**
    BM-N

1882

The Bill of the Play. An illustrated record of the chief dramas, plays, operas bouffe, etc., produced or revived during the year 1881. With a short story of the plot, a critical analysis of the piece and the actors, and the full cast, and date of production. Ed by J. Higden Thornell. London: "Pictorial World" Office. 1882. Annual.   *432*

MB, MH, NN

The Clarion.   An illustrated theatrical and satirical journal. Liverpool. Nos 1–5. 24 Mar – 22 Apr 1882. Weekly.   *433*

ICLoy (microfilm), MP

Hague's Minstrel and Dramatic Journal.   Ed by Henry A. Duffy. Liverpool. No 1. Sept 1882. Monthly.   *434*

Not located (Loewenberg p 43; Lowe, p 377)

Manchester Pantomime's Annual.   Ed by H. A. Duffy. Manchester: H. Darby-shire. 1882. Annual.   *435*

NN

Old Drury-Lane Christmas Annual. 1882–3.   London: Published for the Proprie-tors, by Alfred Gibbons, at the Offices, 172, Strand, and Printed by R. K. Burt & Co., Wine Office Court, Fleet Street, E.C. Annual. [December 1882 appears on the verso of the last cover leaf]   *436*

BM

1883

The Age and Dramatic Journal.   Glasgow. Nos 1–9. 10 Mar – 12 May 1883. Weekly.
BM-N, O   *437*

The Drama.   London. Vols 1–2. Nos 1–30. 13 Sept 1883 – 3 Apr 1884. Weekly. *438*

BM (missing Nos 23–30), NN (1 [2])

Dramatic and Musical Directory of the United Kingdom.   The manager's guide, theatrical register, and handbook of the Provinces. London. [Vols 1–11] 1883 – 1893. Annual.   *439*

BM (missing 1885, and 1888)

The General Theatrical Programme.   London. Vols 1–2. Nos 1–52. 15 Dec 1883 – 6 Dec 1884. then, *The Theatrical Programme.* Vols 3. Nos 53–113. 13 Dec 1884 – 6 Feb 1886. Weekly.   *440*

BM-N, ICLoy (microfilm), LGU, Guildhall Library, London (Vols 1–3. Nos 1–83)

Lloyds Programme: Drama, Music, Fine Art.   Liverpool. Nos 1–2. 14 – 21 Apr 1883. Weekly.   *441*

Not located (Loewenberg p 43)

The Lorgnette.   [for Theatre Royal] Norwich. [No 1] 8 Dec 1883.   *442*

BM, ICLoy (microfilm)

The Theatrical Times.   London. Nos 1–22. Oct 1883 – 28 June 1884. Bimonthly? [No issues in Nov and Dec 1883. No 2 was issued in Jan 1884. Nos 3–22 were issued weekly]   *443*

BM-N, ICLoy (microfilm)

1884

The Birmingham and Midlands Musical Journal and Dramatic News. Birmingham. Nos 1–18. 29 Sept 1884 – 26 Jan 1885. Weekly. **444**
   BM (missing Nos 9–13, 15–18), BP, ICLoy (microfilm)

Blackpool Visitor and Programme. Blackpool. Nos 1–50. 12 July – 8 Sept 1884. Daily. **444a**
   BM-N

The Box Office Entertainment Guide. London. Vols 1–11. Nos 1–271. 1 Jan 1884 – 1 Apr 1895. Biweekly. **445**
   BM (missing Vol 1, No 2 — Vol 5, Nos 116, 118, to Vol 8, No 168; Vol 9, Nos 175–196, 212–213, 215–219, 223, 231, 243, 245, 248–249, 251–252, 254, 256, 260, 263, 264, 267)

The Fly Paper. A satirical, dramatic, musical, and sporting journal. London: Printed and Published by the Proprietors. Joseph Tabrar, 10 Drury-Court, Strand. No 1. 31 May 1884. Weekly. **446**
   BM-N

Footlights. A journal of theatrical gossip and dramatic news. Manchester. Nos 1–3. 1884. [The issues are not dated] **447**
   ICLoy (microfilm), MP (missing No 1)

The Theatre Annual. Ed by Clement Scott. London: David Bogue, 3, St. Martin's Place, Trafalgar Square, W.C. Vols 1–3. 1884 – 1886. Annual. **448**
   BM, CtY, ICLoy (microfilm), MB (Vols 1–5, 1884–1888), NNC, O (1884–1885)

The Theatrical and Musical Guide. London. Nos 1–15. Nov 1884 – Jan 1886. Monthly. **449**
   BM-N, ICLoy (microfilm)

The Theatrical Manager's Register and Professional Advertiser. London: Managed by Foulger & Co., and Published by them at the Modern Press, 13 & 14 Paternoster Row, E.C. Vol 1. Nos 1–2. 20 – 27 Feb 1884. Weekly. **450**
   BM-N

Under the Clock. A weekly journal for playgoers; album of dramatic celebrities. London: D. Bogue. Nos 1–64. 30 Jan 1884 – 20 Apr 1885. Weekly. [Lowe (p 348), thought only 52 issues were published] **451**
   BM, DFo (incomplete), MB (missing Nos 41–45, 47–48, 50–64), MH

Walter's Theatrical and Sporting Directory and Book for Reference for . . . Ed by E. W. Kempton. London. E. W. Kempton & Co., 48 London Wall, E.C. [Nos 1–4] 1884 – 1888. Annual. [At the British Museum there are also two undated issues, called "Tenth Year," and "Eleventh Year." See also *Optic* (1885)] **452**
   BM

The Wings. A monthly record of general, theatrical, and musical information. Ed by C. Sleigh. London. Vol 1. No 1. 30 May 1884. Monthly. **453**
   BM (destroyed)

1885

The Bat. [A weekly journal of theatrical criticism] Ed by James Davis. London. Vols 1–6. Nos 1–153. 31 Mar 1885 – 28 Feb 1888. Weekly. **454**
   BM-N, MH (Nos 1–92), O (Vols 1–5)

The Birmingham Dramatic News. An illustrated record of the Midland stage. Birmingham. Vol 1. Nos 1–12. 26 Sept – 12 Dec 1885. Weekly.   **455**
  BP, ICLoy (microfilm)

Dramatic Review. A journal of theatrical, musical and general criticism. London. Nos 1–512. 1 Feb 1885 – 26 May 1894. Weekly.   **456**
  BM-N, MH (missing Nos 239–512), O (missing all after 1888)

Interlude: "The Organ of the Variety Profession." London. Nos 1–25. 14 Nov 1885 – 8 May 1886. Weekly.   **457**
  BM-N

The Musical Artists', Lecturers', and Entertainers' Guide, and Entrepreneurs' Directory. For 1884–5. With almanack and diary. Under the patronage of Sir George Alexander Macfarren, and Charles John Plumptre, Esq. London: Frederick Pitman, 20 & 21, Paternoster Row, E.C. [Vols 1–2] 1884/5 – 1886/7. Annual. [The cover title is, *The Musical Artists', Lecturers', and Entertainers' Directory.* For 1884/5. Vol 2 does not have the diary]   **458**
  BM

The Optic. The supplement to *Walter's Theatrical and Sporting Directory.* Ed by E. W. Kempton. London: E. W. Kempton, 53, Lansdowne Road, E. Nos 1–4. 14 Dec 1885 – 1 June 1886. Irregular.   **459**
  BM

Prince of Wales' Journal and Shows' Gazette. Birmingham. 27 Nov 1885. [I have been unable to examine this copy]   **460**
  BP

Sock and Buskin. London. Nos 1–2. 4 – 11 Sept 1885. Weekly.   **461**
  BM-N

1886

The Amateur Actor. Leeds. No 1. Apr 1886.   **462**
  BM, E, ICLoy (microfilm)

The Circulating Library. Review of general literature, science, the fine arts, music, and the drama. London. Nos 1–9. July 1886 – Mar 1887. Monthly.   **463**
  BM (destroyed)

Journal of the Bacon Society. Also containing the first annual report. London: George Redway, York Street, Covent Garden. Vols 1–2. Nos 1–11. 1886 – 1891. then, *Baconiana.* New Series Vols 1– . 1895 –   . [The periodical is included in this bibliography because the Introduction to the first issue states that part of the reason for the magazine is to study Bacon's "connections with the composition of the writings attributed to Shakespeare." p 111]   **463a**
  O

The Liverpool Busy Bee: Illustrated, Comical, Satirical, Social, Sporting, Theatrical, Musical. Liverpool. Nos 1–10. 29 Sept – 1 Dec 1886. Weekly.   **464**
  Not located (Loewenberg p 43; Lowe p 377)

M.H.A.A. Gazette. Issued by . . . the General Committee of the Music Hall Artists' Association. London. Nos 1–11. 30 Aug – 10 Nov 1886. then, *Music Hall Artists' Association Gazette.* Nos 12–42. 17 Nov 1886 – 15 June 1887. Weekly. *465*
    BM-N

Ourselves. An illustrated weekly journal for theatrical & musical amateurs. London: Printed for the Proprietors, by the Boswell Printing Company, 10, Shoe Lane, Fleet Street, E.C., and Published at 3, Whitefriars Street. Vol 1. Nos 1–21. 14 Oct 1886 – 3 Mar 1887. Weekly. *466*
    BM-N

The Playgoers' Pocket-book. Being an illustrated record of the dramatic year 1886 – 87. With descriptions and illustrations of all the new plays of the year; copies of many of the play-bills, and a complete record of dramatic events. By Paul Vedder. London: J. & R. Maxwell [& Blackett] Vols 1-2. 1886 – 1887. Annual. *467*
    CtY (missing Vol 1), DFo, MB, MH, NN

1887

The Artiste. Music hall gossip, theatrical and general news. London: Printed and Published by Read, Brooks, and Co., 25 and 26 Newbury Street, Aldersgate Street, E.C. for the Proprietor James Deacon. Nos 1–18. 1 Jan – 2 May 1887. Weekly. *468*
    BM-N

Entertainment Gazette and Guide to London. A fortnightly journal of entertaining literature and a descriptive and critical guide to London amusements for residents and visitors. London. Vol 1. Nos 1–4. 15 Jan – 26 Feb 1887. then, *Entertainment Gazette Illustrated.* A fortnightly journal of entertainment — art, literature, music, drama and sport. Vol 1. Nos 5–11. [The subtitle varies a number of times] Biweekly. then, *Entertainment Gazette and Echoes of the Week.* Vol 1, No 12 – Vol 2, No 41. 18 June 1887 – 7 Jan 1888. Weekly. [Incorporated into, *Piccadilly*] *469*
    BM-N

The Society Herald. A weekly record of social, political, theatrical, literary and financial events. London. Nos 1–104. 22 Oct 1887 – 8 Oct 1889. Weekly. *470*
    BM-N

The University Shakespeare Journal. Ed by J. C. Wharton. London; Adelaide: W. K. Thomas & Co. Vol 2, No 1. Oct 1887. Quarterly. [This is the only issue which I have been able to locate] *471*
    DFo

The Woodpecker. Otherwise known as the "Oof Bird." Ed by Picus. [A weekly sporting and theatrical review] London. New Series. Nos 9–28. 5 Nov 1887 – 17 Mar 1888. Weekly. [I have been unable to discover the first series] *472*
    BM-N (missing Nos 1–8)

1888

Licensed Victuallers' Mirror. A trade, sporting, and theatrical newspaper. Conducted by B. T. Gale. London: Printed for the Licensed Victuallers Newspaper Company, Limited, by Charles Dickens, and Evans, 24, Great New Street, E.C.,

and Published by Benjamin Thomas Gale, 9, Catherine Street, W.C. Vol 1. Nos 1–880. 10 Feb 1888 – 9 Dec 1904. Weekly. [The subtitle varies. An announcement in No 880 states that the periodical will not be published in the winter season]   **473**
   BM-N

The Licensed Victuallers' Sportsman.   A turf, athletic, cycling and theatrical journal. London: Printed and Published for the Proprietors by Mac Rae, Curtice & Co., Ltd., 12 and 14 Catherine Street, Strand, W.C. Vols 1–2. Nos 1–5. 8 Dec 1888 – 5 Jan 1889. Weekly. [Includes a registration issue, Vol 1. No 1. 1 Oct 1888]   **474**
   BM-N

Liverpool Programme.   Liverpool. 11 May 1888 – 28 June 1889.   **475**
   BM-N, LvP (8 June 1888)

Murray's London Entertainment Guide.   London. Nos [1]–11. 1888 – Aug 1898. then, *The London Entertainment.* No 19. Apr 1890. then, *Reid's London Entertainment Guide.* [No?] – 503. [1892?] – Feb 1931. Monthly.   **476**
   BM (incomplete in early issues)

The Playgoer.   A leaflet for Playgoers. London: Printed and Published for the Proprietors by Harvey & Co., 1 Goldsmith Street, Fleet Street, E.C. Vol 1. Nos 1–2. Nov – Dec 1888. then, *The Playgoer.* Vol 1, No 3 – Vol 3, No 27. Jan 1888 – 31 Oct 1890. Monthly [Vol 1. Nos 1–12. Nov 1888 – Oct 1889] Weekly [Vol 2, No 13 – Vol 3, No 27. 2 Nov 1889 – 31 Oct 1890. The issues are numbered consecutively throughout]   **477**
   BM-N, LU-MM (missing Nos 19–27)

The Playgoer's Magazine, a Monthly Magazine for All Players and Playgoers.   Ed by Paul Vedder. London: Published for the Proprietors by W. Kent & Co., 23, 51, and 52, Paternoster Row, E.C. Vol 1. Nos 1–3. Jan – Mar 1888. Monthly. **478**
   BM, DFo (missing No 3), ICLoy (microfilm), MB, MH, O

Readable Recitations.   Suitable for Entertainments, Smoking Concerts, &c. London. No 1. [Dec 1888] then, *Readable Recitations.* Humourous and sentimental for ladies and gentlemen. No 2. Jan 1889. then, *The Honorary Secretary*, With Which Is Incorporated *Readable Recitations.* Nos 3–8. Feb – July 1889. then, *The Honorary Secretary And Poet's Journal.* Nos 9–14. Aug – Dec 1889. Monthly [except for the last two issues, which are numbered 11 and 12, and 13 and 14] [Beginning with No 10. Sept 1889, each issue consists of an original farce] **479**
   BM

The Salon.   A monthly review of art, fashion, music and the drama. London. Vols 1–6, No 6. July 1888 – Dec 1897. Monthly.   **480**
   BM-N (Vols 1–3, No 36. July 1888 – Dec 1891; Vol 4, No 40 — Vol 5, No 48. Feb 1893 – June 1894; Vol 6. Nos 1–6. Mar 1896 – Dec 1897)

1889

Comedy. A fortnightly review of art. Edited by J. T. Grein. London: Printed and Published by Gee & Co., of 34, Moorgate Street, E.C. Vol 1. Nos 1–12. 20 Mar – 24 Aug 1889. Biweekly. [Registered as a newspaper]   **480a**
   O

Dramatic Opinion.   Conducted by Dr. Charles M. Clarke. [Devoted to Henry Arthur Jones's *The Middleman*] London. No 1. 28 Sept 1889. [A registration issue]   *481*
   BM-N

The Music Hall.   London. Nos 1–30. 16 Feb – 7 Sept 1889. then, *The Music Hall and Theatre.*   Nos 31–42. 20 Sept – 30 Nov 1889. then, *The Music Hall and Theatre Review.* Nos 43–1229. 7 Dec 1889 – 5 Sept 1912. Weekly. [Absorbed, *The Showman*]   *482*
   BM-N (missing Nos 1–44), WEST (Vols [2], 3–4, 19–23, 25–36, 39, 41)

The Prompter and the Footlights.   A music hall and theatrical review. London. No 1. 1 Mar 1889.   *483*
   BM-N

The Rialto.   A financial, social and dramatic review. London. Vols 1–33, No 22. 19 Jan 1889 – 7 Oct 1910.   *484*
   BM-N

Speech. A monthly journal devoted to elocution, oratory and the drama. Conducted by David J. Smithson. London: Published by the Hansard Publishing Union, Limited. Vol 1. Nos 1–8. Oct 1889 – May 1890. Monthly.   *485*
   BM (missing No 2)

The Sporting Review.   London. Nos 1–42. 16 Mar – 28 Dec 1889. Weekly. then, *The Sporting and Theatrical Review.* New Series. Nos 43–133. 4 Jan 1890 – 26 Sept 1891. Weekly.   *486*
   BM (missing Nos 72–90)

Sporting Truth & Dramatic Record.   London. Nos 1–87. 13 Apr 1889 – 6 Dec 1890. Weekly.   *487*
   BM-N

The Weekly Comedy.   A review of the drama, music and literature. London. Nos 1–11. 12 Oct – 21 Dec 1889. Weekly.   *488*
   BM-N

1890

The Author.   The organ of the society of authors [playwrights and composers] London: Published for the Society by Harrison and Sons, Ltd. Vols 1–36, No 4. May 1890 – July 1926. then, *The Author, Playwright and Composer.* Vols 37–59, No 2. Oct 1926 – Winter 1948. then, *The Author.* Vols 60– . Spring 1949 – . [Founded by Sir Walter Besant] Monthly [1890 – 1900]; Monthly [except Aug – Sept 1901 – July 1917]; Irregular [Oct 1917 – Apr 1919]; Quarterly [July 1919 –   .]   *489*
   BM, C, E, NN, O

The Book World.   (A magazine of literary and dramatic news, fiction, and general information.) London. Nos 1–70. Aug 1890 – Apr 1899. Irregular.   *490*
   BM-N

Foot-lights.   London. Nos 1–11. 11 Oct – 20 Dec 1890. Weekly.   *491*
   BM-N

The Liverpool Athletic & Dramatic News. Liverpool. Vols 1–3. 15 Dec 1890 – 26
Jan 1892. then, *The Athletic and Dramatic News.* Vols 4–6, No 139. 2 Feb
1892 – 8 Aug 1893. Weekly.   *492*
  BM-N (1890–1891, being repaired; 1892, lost)

The London Playgoer and Comedy. London: Offices: Pitt, Newcastle Street,
Strand, W.C. Vol 1. Nos 1–4. 1 Mar – June 1890. Monthly.   *493*
  LU-MM

Sporting Summary and Theatrical Tatler. Ed by James Peddie. London: Printed
by the London Printing Co., 8 & 9, Plough Court, Fetter Lane, E.C., and Published for the Proprietors by Trapps, Holmes & Co., 10, Red Lion Court, Fleet
Street, E.C. Nos 1–4. 29 Apr – 20 May 1890. Weekly.   *494*
  BM-N (missing No 3)

Sportive Snatches from Playgrounds and Playhouses. London. 1 –   . [1890?] –   .
[I have not been able to discover any further information regarding this peri-
odical]   *495*
  BM (destroyed)

Theatrical Programme and General Amusements Advertiser. Manchester: Printed
for the Publishers (the Bill Posting and Advertising Agency Limited, 44, Corporation Street) by Henry Smith, Excelsior Printing Works, 23 and 25, Old Hall,
Bolton. Vol 1. No 1. 13 Oct 1890. [Missing Nos 2–4]. then, *Programme of Manchester Amusements.* Vol 1. Nos 5–51. 1 Dec 1890 – 28 Mar 1892. Vol 2. No 22.
28 Mar 1892; No 27. 9 May 1892; No 28. 16 May 1892; No 33. 20 June 1892;
No 37. 24 June 1892. [These are the only issues which I have been able to
locate]   *495a*
  O

1891

Actor, Playgoer, and Dramatic Directory. London. Vol 1. No 1. 1 Oct 1891. *496*
  BM-N

Brighton and Hove Entertainment Chronicle. Brighton. 19 Sept 1891 – 3 Dec
1892. Weekly.   *496a*
  BM-N

Dancing. A journal devoted to the Terpsichorean Art, physical culture and fashionable entertainments. London: Printed and Published for the Proprietors by
The Period Printing and Publishing Syndicate Limited, at 7 and 8, Dyer's Buildings, Holborn, E.C. Vols 1–2. Nos 1–24. 8 June 1891 – May 1893. Monthly. *497*
  BM-N

Dramatic Opinion. London. Nos 1–27. 9 Dec 1891 – Aug 1892. Weekly [to No 25.
25 May 1892]; Monthly [Nos 26–27]   *498*
  BM-N

The Players. An illustrated independent dramatic organ. London. Vols 1–2. Nos
1–47. 16 Dec 1891 – 4 Nov 1892. Weekly.   *499*
  BM-N, MH (missing all before No 37), NN, O

The Playgoer's Review. The organ of the Playgoer's Club. Ed by J. T. Grein. London: Henry and Company, 6, Bouverie Street, E.C. Nos 1–5. Jan – May 1891. Monthly. **500**
> BM, ICLoy (microfilm), O

Programme of Manchester Amusements. Manchester: 44, Corporation Street. Vol 1. No 44. 31 Aug 1891. Weekly. [I have been unable to locate any other issues of this periodical] **501**
> BM

1892

Bill of the Play. London. Nos 1–34. 14 Sept 1892 – Oct 1893. Weekly [to 22 Mar 1893]; Monthly [thereafter] **502**
> BM-N

The Dramatic Peerage . . . Personal notes and professional sketches of the actors and actresses of the London stage. Ed by Erskine Reed, and Herbert Compton. London. 1892. Annual. **503**
> ICU, MB (1891)

The Dramatic Year Book for the Year Ending December 31st, 1891. An annual chronicle of the drama in Great Britain, France, United States of America, and Australasia, and stage directory for the United Kingdom. Ed by Charles S. Cheltnam. London: Trischler and Company, 18, New Bridge Street, Blackfriars. 1892. Annual. **504**
> BM, C, E, MB, O

The Pantomime Annual, Containing the Portraits and Biographies of the Principal Pantomime Beauties. Ed by Henry A. Duffy. London. Vol 1. 1892/93. Annual.
> BM **505**

Professional World. Published in the interests of the musical, dramatic, and artistic professions, and of all artistes who appear before the public. Ed by Alfred Copper and Wilson Newton. London: Printed and Published for the Proprietors by Alexander & Shepheard, 21 and 22, Furnivall Street, Holborn, E.C. Vols 1–3. Nos 1–34. 1 Mar 1892 – Feb 1895. then, *The Audience, A High-Class Dramatic, Musical and Entertainment Journal.* Ed by Alfred Paterson. New Series. Nos 1–6. Mar – Aug 1895. Monthly. [The editor changes to Alfred Paterson with Vol 3, No 23, Jan 1894] **506**
> BM-N, O (Vols 1–3, No 27)

The Sporting and Dramatic Mirror. London. New Series. No 1. 2 May 1892. [Continued from, *The Licensed Victuallers' Mirror*]. then, *The Sporting Mirror.* Nos 2–441. 9 May 1892 – 8 Oct 1900. Weekly. **507**
> BM-N

The Yorkshire Owl Pantomime Annual. Leeds. 5 Oct 1892 – 6 June 1897. Annual.
> BdP **508**

1893

Birmingham Amusements and Souvenir of the Stage. Birmingham. Nos 1–65. 18 July 1893 – 1 Oct 1894. Weekly. **509**
> BP (missing Nos 2, 4, 5–6, 9), ICLoy (microfilm)

Blackpool Programme.   Blackpool. Nos 1–19. 27 May – 30 Sept 1893. then, *Blackpool Programme and Visitor.* Nos 20–24. 19 May – 16 June 1894. then, *Blackpool Visitor and Programme.* Nos 25–263. 23 June 1894 – 26 Oct 1900. Weekly.   *509a*
BM

The Bohemian.   A monthly magazine and review of literature, drama, and art. Ed by S. L. Bensusan. London: Bohemian Publishing Company. Vol 1, Nos 1–6. June – Nov 1893. Monthly.   *510*
CtY, ICN, IaU, IU, MH, NN (missing all after No 1)

Manchester Amusements.   Manchester. Nos 1–347. 6 Feb 1893 – 25 Sept 1899. Weekly.   *511*
BM-N (1893 destroyed; 1894 not available)

The Minim.   A musical magazine for everybody. London. Vols 1–3, No 32. Oct 1893 – May 1896. then, *The Minim.* A Musical Magazine for the Midlands and West of England. [Nos 33–36] June – Sept 1896. [The volume number is dropped, and the issue number is incorrectly given as 21. Nos 34–36 are incorrectly numbered, 22–24. July – Sept 1896. With this issue the magazine was thenceforth printed at Cheltenham]. then, *Minim.* A Musical Magazine for Everybody. Vols 4–5, No 57. Oct 1896 – June 1898. then, *Minim.* A Professional Register and Musical Magazine for Everybody. Vol 5, No 58 – Vol 7, No 84. July 1898 – Sept 1900. then, *The Minim.* A quarterly musical magazine, review and register, for professional and amateur musician. Vols 8–9, No 8. Oct 1900 – July 1902. Monthly [to Sept 1900]; Quarterly [after Sept 1900]   *512*
BM

The Prompter.   An illustrated dramatic and musical record. Ed by J. A. Hammerton. Glasgow. No 1. Mar 1893.   *513*
BM

Theatrical World for 1893 – 1897.   By William Archer. London: Walter Scott, Limited. Vols 1–5. 1893 – 1897. Annual.   *514*
CLU, CU, FiP, IC, IU, IaU, MB, MBAt, MH, MnU, NN, NcU, O (missing 1896), OC, PP, PU

Theatricals.   London. Nos 1–326. Sept 1893 – 9 Apr 1898. Weekly [with some variations]   *515*
BM (missing issues before 6 Oct 1893)

1894

Blackpool Amusements.   Blackpool. [Season 1] Nos 1–13. 2 July – 24 Sept 1894. Season 4 – Season 7, No 18. 7 June 1897 – 1 Oct 1900. [Published during the holiday season only]   *515a*
BM-N

Bournemouth and Boscombe Amusements.   Bournemouth. Nos 1–318. 19 Feb 1894 – 12 Mar 1900. then, *Bournemouth and District Amusements.* Nos 319 – 1881. 19 Mar 1900 – 8 Mar 1930. Weekly.   *515b*
BM-N (wanting 1917)

The Dancing Times. A monthly journal of dancing music, dramatic and kindred arts and subjects. London. Nos 1– . 1894 – 1909. New Series. Vols 1– . 1910 – . Monthly. [I have been unable to discover a full "run" of the first series]   *516*
  BM (far from complete), NN (New Series, Vols 2–)

Dramatic World. London. Vols 1–9. Nos 1–93. Nov 1894 – Aug 1902. then, *Society and Dramatic World.* 1 Sept 1902 – May 1916. Monthly.   *517*
  BM (1894–1909), DLC (Vols 6–9)

Folkestone Amusements. Folkestone. Nos 1–3. 16 – 30 July 1894. Weekly.   *518*
  BM-N

The Graphic Guide to the London Theatres. A succinct and descriptive digest of the plots and characters of all the plays performed at the principal theatres of the metropolis. Ed by H. P. Priestley-Greenwood. London: Printed for the Proprietors, Messrs. Greenwood & Co., 55–56 Chancery Lane, W.C., by Lawrence & Symon, White Hart Street, Strand. Vol 1. Nos 1–7. June – Dec 1894. Monthly.
  BM (destroyed), O   *519*

Hanson's Directory of The Musicians, Music Traders, Dancing Masters, Elocutionists, and Entertainers in Yorkshire for 1894. List of Musical Societies, Bands, Newspapers, Printers, &c., in every town. Armley: West Riding Advertising Agency. [Vol 1] 1894.   *520*
  BM

The Hull, Grimsby & East Yorkshire Programme of Entertainments for Playgoers and Players. Musical, dramatic & equestrian. Hull. 25 Aug 1894 – 28 Sept 1895. then, *Hull and East Yorkshire Illustrated Free Programme.* Oct 1895 – 25 Sept 1897. then, *Hull Entr' Acte.* 2 – 23 Oct 1897. then, *East Yorkshire Comet and Hull Entr' Acte* (New Series). 30 Oct 1897 – 20 Oct 1900. Weekly.   *521*
  BM-N

The Leeds Pantomime Annual. [Leeds] 1894/95. Annual.   *522*
  LdP

Leeds Programme of Amusements. Leeds. Nos 1–113. 22 Jan 1894 – 24 Feb 1896. Weekly.   *523*
  BM-N (missing Nos 10–11, 16, 18, 35, 39, 51–105)

The Mascot. (An illustrated dramatic and sporting weekly) London. Vols 1–7, No 28. 3 Feb 1894 – 28 Mar 1897. Weekly.   *524*
  BM-N

The Musical Exchange Journal and Dramatic Observer. Editor and Proprietor, Mr Percy Notcutt. London: Printed by Hazell, Watson & Viney, Ltd., 52 Long Acre, and Published for the Proprietor, by Simpkin, Marshall, Hamilton, Kent & Co., Ltd., 317, Strand. Vols 1–2. Nos 1–34. 24 Oct 1894 – 9 Oct 1895. Weekly.
  BM-N   *525*

Paisley Society and Dramatic Mirror. Paisley. Nos 1–104. 6 – 20 Feb 1894. then, *Paisley Mirror.* 27 Feb 1894 – 31 Jan 1896. Weekly.   *526*
  BM-N (missing Nos 54, 57–64)

Portsmouth and Southsea Amusements. A weekly programme of forthcoming local events. Southsea: Published for the Proprietors by the Portsmouth Advertising Agency, Bedford House, Bedford Street. Nos 1–31. 18 June 1894 – 14 Jan 1895. Weekly.   **527**
> BM-N (missing Nos 12–13, 18, 25–26)

1895

Boorman's Theatrical Directory of the United Kingdom. Ed by J. H. Boorman. London: Published by J. H. Boorman, 79, Strand, W.C. 1895. Annual.   **528**
> BM

The Dangerfield Entertainment Guide. Containing all the information required by dramatic, touring managers, concert agents, and general entertainment caterers, including upward of 40,000 railway fares. Compiled and edited by Mr. E. Lockwood. London: Printed for the Proprietors, Messrs. Dangerfield & Lockwood, and Published by The Dangerfield Printing company, 22, Bedford Street, Strand. [Vols 1–6] [1895] – 1904. Irregular. [The 1904 edition is the sixth] **529**
> BM

The Dramatic Times. London. Nos 1–13. 2 Feb – 14 Sept 1895. New Series. Nos 1–5. 12 Apr – 5 July 1919. Irregular.   **530**
> BM-N, ICLoy (microfilm)

The Encore Annual. 1894. Ed by Edward Lawrance and Charles Douglas Stuart. London. 1895. Annual.   **531**
> BM (destroyed), MB

Folkestone Programme. Folkestone. Nos 6–703. 22 Apr 1895 – 28 Sept 1908. Weekly.   **532**
> BM-N (all before No 605 were destroyed)

The Glasgow Harlequin. A weekly record of Glasgow pantomimes and pantomimists. Glasgow: Printed and Published for the Proprietors by Wm. Hodges & Co., 26 Bothwell Street. Nos 1–5. 17 Dec 1895 – 14 Jan 1896. Weekly.   **533**
> BM-N, E, ICLoy (microfilm), O

The Glasgow Pantomime Annual and Theatrical Review. Written by "Sir Oracle" of "Quiz" &c. Glasgow. 1895. Annual.   **534**
> BM

Glasgow Theatrical Annual. Glasgow. [Vols 1–7] 1895 – 1901. Annual.   **535**
> GM

The London Bridge Theatre Diary and Amusement List. London. Nos 1–6. May – Nov 1895. Monthly.   **536**
> BM (missing No 1)

London Illustrated Standard. London. Nos 1–210. 26 Oct 1895 – 28 Oct 1899. then, *Sporting and Dramatic Standard.* No 211. 4 Nov 1899. Weekly.   **537**
> BM-N

The Musical World and Dramatic Observer.   London: Printed and Published by
James Biddlecombe, at the Office, 396, Strand. Nos 1–10. 6 Feb 1895 – 11 Feb
1904. Irregular. [Registration issues]   **538**
  BM-N

Roberts Pantomime Annual.   Ed by J. Waddington. Leeds. [Nos 1–3] 1895/96 –
1897/98. Annual.   **539**
  LdP

The Round Table.   London. Vol 1. No 1. 13 Dec 1895.   **540**
  BM

The Shakespearean, a Monthly Magazine Devoted Exclusively to the Shake-
spearean and Poetic Drama and Shakespeareana.   Official organ of the New
York Shakespeare society in Europe, etc. Ed by Alfred H. Wall. Stratford-upon-
Avon: Published at N. 5, Payton Street (Nos 1–17); London: Messrs Dawbarn
and Ward (Nos 18–33). Vols 1–4. Nos 1–33. 15 Nov 1895 – 15 Jan 1898. Monthly.
[The subtitle varies somewhat]   **541**
  BP, CaL, CtY, DFo (missing Vols 3–4), MiU, NN, NNC, PU, O (missing Vol 4)

Sketchy Bits.   A humorous weekly journal of drama, sport & fiction. London. Nos
1–782. 29 Apr 1895 – 9 May 1910. Weekly.   **542**
  BM-N

The Sporting Herald.   A weekly newspaper dealing with sport and the drama.
London. Nos 1–323. 29 May 1895 – 11 Aug 1902. Weekly.   **543**
  BM-N

The Variety Stage.   London: Printed and Published by W. J. Pitt, 30, Newcastle
Street, W.C., Strand. Nos 1–2. Nov – Dec 1895. Monthly. New Series. Vols 1–3.
Nos 1–54. Jan 1896 – 16 Jan 1897. Weekly. [The first two numbers, Nov – Dec
1895, are registration issues]   **544**
  BM-N

1896

A. B. C. Amusement Guide & Record Illustrated.   Being alphabetical particulars
of all the theatres, concerts, music halls, entertainments, with times & prices of
admission. London: Printed for the Proprietors by Lemmon & Son, Limited, 42,
Lower Road, S.E., and published by Gander, Munton & Co., 68, Fleet Street,
E.C. Nos 1–3. 7 – 21 Mar 1896. Weekly.   **545**
  BM-N

The Glasgow Weekly Programme.   Glasgow. Nos 1–70. [1896?] – 1898. Weekly.
then, *The Glasgow Programme.* Nos 71–1311. 1898 – 1922.   **546**
  GM (missing Nos 1–22)

Hastings, St. Leonards & Bexhill Amusements and Visitor's Guide.   A weekly
programme of forthcoming events. Hastings: Printed and Published by Randle
& Son, Queen's Press, 15 & 16, Queen's Road. Nos 1–339. 13 July 1896 – 27 Jan
1903. Weekly. [The subtitle varies somewhat]   **547**
  BM-N

Murray's London Recreation Guide. With map of London, plans of theatres, and illustrations. London: Published by H. Grube, 12 a, Paternoster Row, E.C. Nos 1–4. Nov 1896 – Feb 1897. Monthly.   **548**
   BM

The Playgoers' Guide and Theatrical Notes. Ed by A. Waugh. London: H. Good & Son. No 1. Nov 1896. Monthly.   **549**
   NN

To-Morrow. A monthly review. Conducted by J. T. Grein. London: H. Henry & Co., Ltd., 93 Saint Martin's Lane. [Nos 1–24] Jan 1896 – Dec 1897. Monthly. **550**
   LU-MM

What's On. Manchester. Nos 343–555. 11 May 1896 – 4 June 1900. Weekly. [These are the only issues which I have been able to locate]   **551**
   BM (missing all before No 343)

Yorkshire Harlequin. Leeds. Vols 1–2. [Nos 1–24] 23 Dec 1896 – 9 Mar 1898. Weekly [during the pantomime season]   **552**
   ICLoy (microfilm), LdP

1897

The Amateurs' Handbook and Entertainers' Directory. Compiled by Albert Douglass. London: Potter Bros. [Vol 1] 1897. then, *Douglass' Directory of Amateur Dramatic Clubs, Professional Entertainer.* [Vols 2–18] 1898 – 1914. Annual.
   BM   **553**

Eureka. A monthly theatre and entertainment magazine. London. Vols 1–2. Nos 1–12. 15 Apr 1897 – May 1898. then, *The Favourite Magazine.* Vols 3–9. 1898 – 1903. Monthly.   **554**
   BM

Footlights. Liverpool. No 1. Sept 1897. [I have not been able to discover any other information concerning this periodical]   **555**
   BM (destroyed)

The Glasgow Programme. A weekly record of current events. Glasgow: Printed and Published by the Wilson Advertising Co., 83, Jamaica Street. Nos 1–1311. [1897?] – 15 May 1922. Weekly.   **556**
   BM-N (missing all before No 636. 16 May 1910)

Journal of the Leeds College of Music, Drama and Art. Leeds. Vols 1–10. Jan 1897 – Oct 1906. then, *Leeds Triad.* New Series. Vols 1–5. Jan 1907 – July 1911. Vol 6. May – Dec 1912. Quarterly.   **557**
   LdP

Play-Goer. London. Nos 1–24. 2 Oct 1897 – 24 Aug 1898. Biweekly.   **558**
   BM-N, ICLoy (microfilm), O (missing Nos 1, 23)

The Stage News. Glasgow. Nos 1–8. 1897.   **559**
   GM

The Sunday Mirror and Dramatic and Music Hall Record. London: Printed and Published for the Proprietors by Thomas Vernon, at 6, Wine Office-Court, Fleet-street, E.C. Nos 1–6. 17 Oct – 28 Nov 1897. Weekly.   **560**
   BM-N

The West End.   An illustrated monthly review of politics, society, fashion, art, music, literature & the drama. London. Nos 1–3. Apr – June 1897. then, *The West End Review.* Nos 4–21. Aug 1897 – June 1899. then, *The West End.* Vol 4. Nos 1–28. 22 Feb – 30 Aug 1899. Monthly; Weekly (from Vol 4).   *560a*
  BM-N

1898

The Compass.   A popular up-to-date London guide. London theatres and music halls. Latest items of news. Ed by T. Macready Down. [His name appears only on the first number] London. [No 1] 7 May 1898. then, *The Compass.* The Bijou Journal of London. [Nos 2–6] 14 May – 11 June 1898. Weekly.   *561*
  BM

Critique.   A journal devoted to things theatrical & matters musical. London: Printed and Published by Nelson Arnold, at 111, Fleet Street, E.C. Vols 1–3. Nos 1–40. 1 Oct 1898 – July 1902. Monthly.   *562*
  BM-N

The Playgoer's Magazine.   A journal for theatre-goers, habitués of music halls, and amateur actors. London. Vol 1. Nos 1–2. 1898. [I have not been able to determine the date of each issue]   *563*
  BM (destroyed)

Programme and Playbill.   London. Nos 1–197. 13 Oct 1898 – 7 July 1899. Daily.
  BM-N   *564*

The Proscenium.   An amateur dramatic & musical review. Manchester: Printed and Published for the Proprietors by John Edwards, 27 Lancaster Avenue, Fennel Street. Vol 1. Nos 1–4. Dec 1898 – Mar 1899. Monthly.   *565*
  BM (destroyed), O (missing Nos 2, 4)

Theatrical and Music Hall Life.   London. No 1. 21 May 1898.   *566*
  BM-N

Theatrical and Public Life.   London. Nos 1–8. Dec 1898 – June 1899. Monthly [until March]; weekly [during March] [The next issue is June]. then, *Public Life.* Nos 9–13. June – Oct 1901.   *567*
  BM-N

The Theatrical Public Guide.   London: Printed for the Proprietors by Stenlake & Simpson, 27, Parker Street, Lincoln's-Inn Fields, W.C. Nos 1–7. Jan – July 1898. Monthly. [The printers change]   *568*
  BM-N, ICLoy (microfilm), O

1899

Anglo-French Stage Chronicle.   London. Nos 1–2. 23 June – 14 July 1899. then, *Anglo French Chronicle.* No 3. 29 July 1899. Irregular.   *569*
  BM-N

Beltaine; an Occasional Publication.   [The Organ of the Irish Literary Theatre] Ed by W. B. Yeats. London: At the Sign of the Unicorn. Nos 1–3. May 1899 – Apr 1900. Irregular.   *570*

BM, CtY, D, DLC, E, ICLoy (microfilm), ICN, ICU, MB, MH, MiU, NIC, NN, NjP, O, RPB

The Birmingham Pantomime Annual: a Souvenir of the Pantomimes.   Ed by I. Waddington. Birmingham. 1899. Annual.   **571**
BP, ICLoy (microfilm)

The "Comedy" Gazette.   A Pantomime Annual. Edited by J. Pitt Hardacre. Manchester. Christmas, 1899–1900. Annual.   **571a**
O

Daily Programme and Playbill.   London. Vol 1. Nos 1–100. 30 Nov 1899 – 21 Mar 1900. then, *The Playbill.* Vol 1. Nos 101–440. 22 Mar 1900 – 20 Apr 1901. Daily.
BM-N   **572**

Dramatic Criticism.   London. Vols 1–5. 1899 – 1905. [No volumes were published in 1901 or in 1903. These volumes contain articles by Thomas Grein, previously published in other periodicals]   **573**
LdU (missing Vol 2)

Footlights.   The bulletin of the London and New York dramatic exchange. London. No 1. Oct 1899.   **574**
BM

The Irish Playgoer and Amusement Record.   Dublin. Vols 1–2. Nos 1–30. 9 Nov 1899 – 31 May 1900. Weekly.   **575**
IU, MH

Nottingham Amusements.   Nottingham. Nos 1–12. 13 Mar – 29 May 1899. Weekly.
BM-N   **576**

The Official Music Hall Directory and Variety ABC, Containing a Three Years Diary, Also an Alphabetically Arranged List of Proprietors, Managers, Agents, Artistes, Musical Directors, Apartments and Music Halls.   A ready reference for 1889. Ed by Albert Voyce. London: R. Barrett, 102–104, Pentonville Road. No 1. Mar 1899. Annual.   **577**
BM

The Prompter.   Conducted by William Henderson. Liverpool. Nos 1–7 [1899] – 29 Jan 1900.   **578**
Not located (Loewenberg p 43)

Sights and Shows.   Blackpool. No 1. 11 Jan 1899.   **579**
BM-N (not available, as damaged)

1900

Bristol & Clifton Amusements.   A weekly programme of coming events, theatres, entertainments, excursions, sales, athletic notices, &c. Bristol. Nos 1–157. 10 Dec 1900 – 7 Dec 1903. Weekly.   **580**
BM-N

The Caste.   Being a weekly record of Birmingham plays and players. Birmingham. Nos 1–4. 5 – 26 Mar 1900. Weekly.   **581**
BP, ICLoy (microfilm)

London Theatre Entertainment and Concert Guide. London. Nos 1–16. 7 July 1900 – 23 Feb 1901. then, *The London Theatre, Concert, and Fine Art Guide.* Nos 7–623. 2 Mar 1901 – 19 Oct 1912. Weekly.   *582*
    BM-N

Magic. The magician's monthly magazine. Ed by Ellis Stanyon. London. Vols 1–15, No 9. 1900 – June 1920. Monthly. [Suspended publication from Vol 14, No 5 – Vol 15, No 1. Mar 1914 – Oct 1919]   *583*
    BM (missing Vols 1–2, No 3; Vol 15, Nos 6–9), LU, MH (1–[15]), NN (Oct, Dec 1911 – June 1920), O

Showman. An illustrated journal for showmen and all entertainers. London. Vols 1–4. Nos 1–69. Sept 1900 – 28 Mar 1902. Weekly. then, merged in, *The Music Hall and Theatre Review.*   *584*
    BM, NN

The Stage Society. London. [Vols 1–21] First Annual Report [to] Twenty-First Annual Report. 1899/1900 – 1920/1921. [The Stage Society issues, *Stage Society News*]   *585*
    BM

Will A. Bradley's Pantomime Annual. Ed by "Dromio." Liverpool. Vols 1–4. 1900/01 – 1904. Annual.   *586*
    LvP (missing 1903)

1901

The Clacton Programme of Entertainment and Pleasure. A weekly journal of entertainment, theatres, coming events, excursions, sales, &c., for Clacton-On-Sea, Walton-On-Naze, and Frinton-On-Sea. Clacton. Nos 1–8. 13 July – 31 Aug 1901. Weekly.   *587*
    BM-N

Debrett's Coming Events. A monthly calendar of social fixtures, etc. London: Dean and Son, Limited, 160 a, Fleet Street, E.C. Vols 1–3, No 10. June 1901 – June 1904. Monthly.   *588*
    BM

Eastbourne Amusements. A weekly programme of theatres, entertainments. Eastbourne: Printed and Published by the Plantin Printing Co., 180, Terminus Road. [Nos 1–18] 7/14 Apr – 12/19 Aug [1901] Weekly.   *589*
    BM-N

Folkestone Amusement Guide. Containing official announcements of theatres, pier concerts, entertainments, railway excursions, sea trips, walks and drives, cycling runs, Etc., Etc. Folkestone: Printed and Published at the *Herald* Office. Nos 1–9. 10 July – 4 Sept 1901. Weekly.   *590*
    BM-N

The Hippodrome. An illustrated vaudeville magazine. London. 1901 – . *591*
    BM (missing No 1. Cannot locate)

John Waddington's Annual; the Book for the Playgoer. [Leeds. 1901] Annual. *592*
    LdP

The Kensington. A magazine of art, literature and the drama. Ed by Mrs. Steuart Erskine, and R. J. Richardson. London: Simpkin, Marshall, Hamilton, Kent & Co. Vol 1. Nos 1–7. Mar – Sept 1901. Monthly.   593
    BM, ICN, MnU, NN

Kirkley's Theatrical Apartments Directory. Compiled by F. Russell Kirkley [1st through 11th edition] London: 16, Porchester Gardens, W. 1st – 10th edition. 1901 – 1906. Twice a year. then, *Kirkley's Theatrical, Variety & Apartments Directory.* 11th ed. Parts 1–3. 1907. then, *Kirkley's Theatrical and . . . Variety Apartments and Trades Directory.* 12th ed. 1908. then, *Kirkley's Theatrical and . . . Variety Apartments and Trades Directory, For London, and Provinces* (England, Ireland, Scotland, Wales.) 13th ed. 1909. then, *The Theatrical and Variety Apartments & Business Directory For London and Provinces* (England, Ireland, Scotland, Wales). 14th ed. 1910. Compiled by Charles Vernon, 1908 – 1910. *594*
    BM, O (1908–1910. 12–14th eds)

The Playgoer. Ed by Fred. Dangerfield (S. J. Adair Fitzgerald). London. Vols 1–5. Nos 1–28. Oct 1901 – Apr 1904. Monthly.   595
    BM (missing Vol 4, No 20), BP, IC, MB (missing 1901), MH (missing Vol 5), NIC, O, WEST (missing Vols 1, 4–5)

The Playlet and Monologue Magazine. Conducted by C. D. Hickman. London. Nos 1–5. [1901] [No dates appear in the periodical. The word "monthly" appears on the first number. See, *P.A.D.* (1902)]   596
    BM (missing No 3)

Pleasure and Pastime in the City and Environs. Birmingham. 14 Oct 1901.   597
    BP, ICLoy (microfilm)

Samhain, an Occasional Review. Edited for the Irish Literary Theatre. Ed by W. B. Yeats. [Dublin]: Sealy Bryers & Walker. Nos 1–7. Oct 1901 – Nov 1908. [Suspended, Dec 1905 – Nov 1906] Irregular.   *598*
    CtY, ICLoy (microfilm), ICU, IEN, LU, MH, NN, O (missing 1907)

The Stage Staff Journal. London: Printed by Henry Palmer & Co., 14, Brownlow Street, Holborn, and Published by C. Thorogood, at 29, Wellington Street, Strand, W.C. Vols 1–2, No 17. Dec 1901 – Mar 1904. Monthly.   599
    BM-N

The Tatler. An illustrated journal of society and the stage. London. Vols 1–58. Nos 1–2053. 3 July 1901 – 30 Oct 1940. Weekly. then, *The Tatler and Bystander.* Nos 2054 –   . 6 Nov 1940 –   .   *600*
    BM-N, DLC ([1–58], 79 plus), MH (53–[67]–74 [144]), NN ([1, 27, 30, 62–63]–[65–66])

What's On? A weekly programme of amusements and coming events in Bristol and Clifton. Bristol: Published for the Proprietor by A. Jenkins & Co., Rupert Street. Nos 1–3. 18 Feb – 4 Mar 1901. Weekly.   *601*
    BM-N

1902

The International Entertainer. The Variety Artistes' illustrated magazine. Ed by A. C. Lyster. London. Vol 1. Nos 1–2. Apr – May 1902. Monthly.   *602*
    BM (missing No 1)

London's Daily Guide. A daily journal for pleasure-seekers, playgoers, sightseers, and the public generally. London: Printed by Messrs. Boot and Son, Ltd., E.C., and Published by the Proprietors at 30, Poppin's Court, E.C. Nos 1–6. 17 – 22 Mar 1902. Daily.   **603**
>   BM-N

P. A. D. (Patter and Dialogue for Ventriloquists, Conjurors, Raconteurs, Minstrels, Pierrots, Single-Handed Comedians, Cross-Talkers, and Burlesque Double-Turns. Conducted by Chas. D. Hickman.) London: D. Sydney, 6 Hinley Road, Tooting, S.W. No 1. [1902] Monthly. [Merged in, *The Playlet and Monologue Magazine*]   **604**
>   BM

The Play Pictorial: an Illustrated Monthly Journal. London: The Stage Pictorial Publishing Co., Ltd. Vols 1–75. Nos 1–446. Apr 1902 – Sept 1939. Monthly. [In Vol 5, No 29, are incorporated, *The Play, The Play Souvenir, The Stage Souvenir*]
605
>   BM (missing No 446), CtY (incomplete), MiU (missing Vols 67–69), NCH, NN (1–[28–29]–75), O, WEST (incomplete, Vols 33, 40–41, 46–51, 53–54, 59–61, 64)

The Theatre Journal-Programme. London. No 1. 1902. [Registration number. The title on the wrapper reads, *The Theatre Programme Journal*]   **606**
>   BM

The Weekly Entertainment Guide. London. [Nos 1–3] 9 Feb/15 Feb – 28 Apr/ 4 May 1902. Irregular.   **607**
>   BM

1903

The Clean Slate. A weekly paper for sportsmen and playgoers. Ed by Hannaford Bennett. [His name does not appear in the periodical until the second issue] London: Printed by Odhams, Limited, 19–24, Floral Street, Covent Garden, W.C. And Published by the Proprietors at 12 and 13 Red Lion Court, Fleet Street, E.C. Nos 1–8. 9 Apr – 30 May 1903. Weekly.   **608**
>   BM-N

Dancing. Ed by Fred Browning. London. Vols 1–2, No 4. Sept 1903 – Sept 1904. Monthly.   **609**
>   BM

The Gallery Gazette. London. Vol 2, No 1 – Vol 5, No 4. Jan 1903 – Apr 1905. [plus] No 7. Apr 1909. Irregular. [Reproduced from typewritten copy. This publication is most difficult to untangle. A dispute among the members of the Gallery First-nighters' club was the cause of the appearance of the unofficial journal]   **610**
>   LU-MM

International Theatre. Paris and London. Nos 1–6. Jan – June 1903. Monthly. **611**
>   BM (missing Nos 1–2), O (missing Nos 1–2)

Liverpool and District Programme and Official List of Entertainments and Pleas-ure Sailings. With notes theatrical, musical, dramatical, nautical, artistical,

social and intellectual. [The subtitle varies] Liverpool. Vols 1–5, No 16. 14 Sept 1903 – 12 Mar 1906. Weekly. [1903 is missing 14 and 21 Dec numbers]   **612**
  BM-N

Liverpool Entertainment and Pleasure Programme.   Liverpool. Sept 1903 – 26 Aug 1904. then, *Smith's Liverpool Weekly.* 2 Sept 1904 – 20 Sept 1907. Weekly.
  BM-N (destroyed)   **613**

The London Stage Annual.   Ed by Sidney Dark. London: A. Treherne & Co. [1903] –   . Annual.   **614**
  DLC, E, O (1904–   )

The Oxford and District and Oxfordshire Amusement Guide and Sports & Entertainment Programme.   Oxford: Published by the Oxford and District Billposting and Advertising Co. Nos 1–3. 16 Feb – 2 May 1903. Irregular.   **615**
  BM-N

Paignton's Amusements.   And Visitor's Guide. A weekly programme of coming events. Paignton. Nos 1–416. 18 May 1903 – 10 Sept 1939. [Not published between 1916 and 1919. There are many discrepancies in numbering]   **616**
  BM-N (incomplete)

The Programme.   A weekly journal. London: Printed and Published at the London & County Printing Works. Bazaar Building, Drury Lane, W.C. Nos 1–47. 12 Oct 1903 – 29 Aug 1904. Weekly.   **617**
  BM-N, O

The Stage Society News.   London. Nos 1–26. Nov 1903 – May 1907. [I have not been able to determine the frequency of issue]   **618**
  BM (destroyed)

The Stage Souvenir.   An illustrated monthly journal. With a real photograph as a supplement. [Ed by Fred Dangerfield] London: Simpkin, Marshall, Hamilton, Kent & Co., Ltd. Nos 1–4. 1903. Monthly. [The issues are not dated]   **619**
  BM, LU-MM, O

1904

The First-Nighter.   The organ of the dramatic debaters. Acting Editor, M. J. Landa. London: Printed by the Great Yarmouth Printing Co., Ltd., and Published by Mr. E. L. Bevans, 21, Bedford Place, W.C. Vol 1. Nos 1–2. Jan – Feb 1904. Monthly.   **620**
  BM-N

The Link.   [A theatrical and advertising weekly] London: Messrs. Harper & Co., "The Link," 13 & 14, Great Sutton Street, E.C. [Nos 1–2] 15 – 22 Oct [1904] Weekly.   **621**
  BM-N

London Record.   A weekly illustrated journal of London life, literature, the drama. science, politics and religion. London: Printed and Published by the Proprietors at 26, Bevis Marks, E.C. Vol 1. Nos 1–5. 29 June – 27 July 1904. Weekly.   **622**
  BM-N

The Magician. A monthly journal devoted to magic, spiritualism, hypnotism, and human progress. Liverpool/London. Vols 1–35, No 9. Dec 1904 – Aug 1939. Monthly. **623**

BM-N, LU (missing Vol 25, Nos 9–12), O (very incomplete)

Music Hall Pictorial and Variety Stage. London: 25 Wellington St., Strand. Nos 1–3. Dec 1904 – [Feb 1905] Monthly. [No dates appear after the first issue] **624**

BM-N, O (No 1)

My Programme. London: Printed and Published for the Proprietors by Messrs. King, Sell & Olding, Ltd., 27, Chancery Lane, W.C. Nos 1–28. 7 May – 12 Nov 1904. Weekly. ["Registered as a Newspaper."] **625**

BM-N (missing Sept 3, 10, 17, 24)

The Play. An illustrated monthly. London: Greening & Co. Vol 1. Nos 1–6. 1904. then, *The Play Pictorial.* Nos 1–6. 1905. Monthly. [The issues are not dated] **626**

BM, CaB, CaL, MnU, NjP, NBuG, O (1904)

The Playhouse. London. Nos 1–20. 17 Dec 1904 – 27 Apr 1905. Weekly. **627**

BM-N, ICLoy (microfilm), O

Plays and Players. [The annual of *Smith's Liverpool Weekly*] Liverpool. 1904. Annual. **628**

BM, LvP

Proprietors and Managers Reference Book. London: Printed for the Proprietors, Messrs. Harper, by J. Schunemann, 13 & 14, Great Sutton Street, E.C., and Published at 208, Chapter Rd., Willesden Green, N.W. No 1. 1904–5. **628a**

O

R. P. Watson's Weekly. An illustrated review of sports & stage. London: Printed by W. Wilfred Head & Co., Ltd., "Dr. Johnson Press," Fleet Lane, Old Bailey, E.C., and Published by Charles Davis, at Byron House, 82–85 Fleet Street, E.C. Vol 1. Nos 1–25. 6 Jan – 22 June 1904. Weekly. **629**

BM-N

R. Douglas Cox's Theatrical and C. Douglas Stuart's Variety Directory. London: Whitton & Smith, 22 Tavistock Street, W.C. [1904?] [Annual? The date appears in the British Museum Catalogue] **630**

BM

Stage and Field. A herald of events . . . in Manchester and District. Manchester. Nos 1–55. 28 Nov 1904 – 12 Mar 1906. Biweekly. **631**

ICLoy (microfilm), MP

The Stage Pictorial. London: Printed for Proprietor, and Published by Rudolph Birnbaum, Bloomsbury Mansion, Hart Street, W.C. Vol 1. No 1. Apr 1904. **632**

BM (missing from the shelf), ICLoy (microfilm), O

The Theatre. London: Printed and Published for the Proprietors by J. Fullford, Printer, 261, 263, Pentonville Road, King's Cross, N. Nos 1–3. 1 Nov 1904 – 1 Jan 1905. Monthly. **633**

BM (destroyed), ICLoy (microfilm), O

The Theatrical Employees Journal. London. Nos 1–12. Oct 1904 – Sept 1905.
Monthly.   **634**
    BM-N

To-Day's London Guide. London: Published by the International Hotel Publishing Co., 17 and 18 Telegraph Street, E.C. Nos 1–320. 6 Feb 1904 – 1 Apr 1910.
Weekly.   **635**
    BM

Torquay Amusements. "Where to Go and What to Do." Torquay: Printed and
Published by A. Geo. Reynolds, 20 & 22, George Street. No 1. 14 May 1904. **636**
    BM-N

Wanted. Dates &c. A journal devoted to the requirements of all connected with
the amusement world. Ed by Herbert Darnley. London: Printed for the Proprietors by Hazell, Watson & Viney, Ltd., 4 to 8, Kirby Street, E.C. No 1. 14 June
1904.   **637**
    BM-N

What's On. Cardiff. No 1. 2 May 1904.   **637a**
    BM-N

1905

The Actor Illustrated. A monthly review of the stage. London. Vol 1. Nos 1–13.
Jan 1905 – Jan 1906. Monthly. [1 Oct 1904 is a registration issue]   **638**
    BM, NN (missing Nos 5–13)

The Circle. A monthly periodical of art, music, and the drama. Edited by R. Percy
(to Vol 1, No 10, Dec 1905); Rose D'Evelyn (Vol 1, No 11 –   . Jan 1906 –   ).
London. Vol 1. Nos 1–15. Mar 1905 – May 1906. Monthly.   **639**
    BM (destroyed), O

The Encore Annual. London: Published at 25, Wellington St., Strand, W.C.
Printed by W. I. Richardson, 4, Great Queen Street, Kingsway, W.C. 1905/6.
Annual. [I do not know if this belongs with *The Encore Annual* of 1894 as I
have not been able to locate any volumes for the intervening years]   **639a**
    O

Glasgow Programme and List of Entertainments. Glasgow. Nos 1–19. 30 Jan –
5 June 1905. then, *Glasgow Programme.* Nos 20–1311. June 1905 – 15 May 1922.
then, *Glasgow and District Entertainment Guide.* May 1922 – 26 Sept 1927.
then, *Glasgow Entertainment Guide.* 7 Nov 1927 – 6 Oct 1930. Weekly. **640**
    BM-N (very incomplete, except for 16 May 1910–1922)

Ladies Guild of Francis St. Alban. Report. Nos 1–24. 1905 – 1914. then, *Fly
Leaves of the Ladies Guild of Francis St. Alban.* Edited by Alicia A. Leith. London: Printed and Published by R. Banks & Son, Racquet Court, Fleet Street.
New Series. Nos 2–39. Aug 1914 – 1933. Two issues a year (to 1927); three
issues a year (1928 – 1933). [Devoted to Shakespeare. The printer's address
changes]   **640a**
    BM (missing first series), BP, C (incomplete), O (missing first series, and Nos 1, 5, 6 of
    New Series)

The Millgate Monthly.   Manchester: Cooperative Press, Ltd., 22 Long Millgate. Vols 1–40. Nos 1–458. Oct 1905 – May/June 1945. then, *Playgoer and
Millgate.* Vols 40–46. Nos 459–503. July/Aug 1945 – Jan/Feb 1951. then, *Millgate and Playgoer.* New Series. Vols 1–2. Nos 1–14. Apr 1951 – Spring 1953.
Monthly [and bimonthly]   *641*
>   BM, D, MP, O

The Sporting Globe.   A weekly journal dealing with the turf, finance, theatres,
music halls, athletics, automobilism, etc. London. Vols 1–2. Nos 1–46. 25 Mar
1905 – 3 Feb 1906. then, *The Sporting Globe.* A weekly journal dealing with the
turf, finance, theatres, music halls, athletics, etc. Vol 2. Nos 47–77. 10 Feb – 8
Sept 1906. Weekly. [Includes a "Monday Night Special," Nos 1–82. 24 Apr
1905 – 19 Nov 1906]   *642*
>   BM-N (missing Nos 29, 32, 35, 41, 45, 48)

The Stroller.   A journal devoted to amateur dramatic and musical societies. Lon-
don: Printed and Published by the American Press, at 10, 11, 12, Phoenix Place,
W.C. Nos 1–3 [i.e. No 4] Oct 1905 – Jan 1905 [i.e. 1906] [Two issues are called
No 1. The first No 1, Oct 1905, may be a registration issue]   *643*
>   BM (destroyed), O

Variety Stage and Music Hall Pictorial.   An illustrated magazine. London: Publishing Offices, 25 Wellington Street, Strand, W.C. Vol 1. No 1. Feb 1905.
Weekly. [Registration issue]   *644*
>   BM-N, O

Variety Stage Illustrated.   London. Nos 1–3. 16 – 30 Jan 1905. Weekly. [Registra-
tion issues]   *645*
>   BM-N

The Variety Theatre.   London. Vols 1–3. Nos 1–33. 12 May 1905 – 5 Jan 1906.
Weekly. [Including registration numbers, 27 Jan, 3 Feb 1905]   *646*
>   BM-N

1906

The Amateur Stage.   London: 70, Cambridge Street, S.W. Vol 1. Nos 1–4. 1 Nov
1906 – 1 Feb 1907. Monthly.   *647*
>   BM-N, E, ICLoy (microfilm), O

The Arrow.   Dublin: Published by the Abbey Theatre. Nos 1–5. 20 Oct 1906 – 25
Aug 1909, Summer 1939. [Suspended, 1909 – 1938] Irregular.   *648*
>   CU, CtY, MH, NN

Birmingham Programme of Amusements.   Birmingham. Vols 1–10. Nos 1–133.
15 Jan 1906 – 27 July 1908. then, *Midland Amusements.* Vols 10–29. Nos 134–
416. 3 Aug 1908 – 27 Dec 1913. then, *What's Doing.* Vols 30–32. Nos 417–569.
3 Jan 1914 – 6 Jan 1917. Weekly.   *649*
>   BP

The Book of the Play.   The theatre magazine. London: Globe Press. Nos 1–8. 1906.
Monthly. [Seemingly No 1 was entitled, *The Book of the Play,* and Nos 2–8,
The Theatre Magazine]   *650*
>   BM (No 6), NN (Aug 1906)

Brighton Entertainments and Pleasure Programme. Brighton. Nos 1–39. 9 June 1906 – 2 Mar 1907. then, *Brighton Programme.* Nos 40–960. 9 Mar 1907 – 26 July 1924. then, *Brighton Weekly Programme.* Nos 961–1383. 2 Aug 1924 – 11 Nov 1933. then, *Illustrated Sporting Mail and Brighton Weekly Programme.* Nos 1384–1385. 18 – 25 Nov 1933. then, *Brighton Illustrated Sporting Mail and Weekly Programme.* Nos 1386–1503. 2 Dec 1933 – 29 Feb 1936. then, *The Brighton Weekly Programme.* An authentic guide to topical events, sports, what's on, where to go. Nos 1505–1538. 7 Mar – 24 Oct 1936. Weekly. [No 1504 is omitted in the numbering]   *651*
     BM-N

The Call Boy. [A weekly journal of the theatre] London: Printed by William Cate, Limited, at Hogarth House, Bouverie Street, E. C. and Published by the Proprietors of *The Call Boy*, 12 and 13 Red Lion Court, Fleet Street. Nos 1–46. 9 Mar 1906 – 2 Feb 1907. Weekly. ["Registered at the G. P. O. as a newspaper"]
     BM-N (Sept 22 – Dec 29 issues are imperfect)   *652*

Dancing. An annual and year-book for dancers. London. [Vols 1–2] 1926 – 1927/ 28. Annual.   *653*
     BM (destroyed)

The Dramatic Diary. [Ed by A. C. Drape] London. Nos 1–5. Sept 1906 – Jan 1907. Monthly.   *654*
     BM (destroyed)

The Dramatic Review. London. No 1. Nov 1906. [Registration issue]   *655*
     BM-N

The Green Room Book; or, Who's Who on the Stage. London. Vols 1–4. 1906 – 1909. then, *Who's Who in the Theatre.* 1912 –   . Annual. [Editions have appeared in 1912, 1914, 1916, 1922, 1925, 1930, 1933, 1936, 1939, 1947, 1952, 1957, 1961, 1967. The early editions of, *Who's Who on the Stage,* were edited by John Parker, editor of, *The Green Room Book*, 1908 – 1909]   *656*
     BM, MB, MiU, NN, NwP, PP, PU, TxU

The London Programme of Amusements. London: 140, Leadenhall St., E.C. Vol 1, No 24 – Vol 2, No 36. 14 July – 6 Oct 1906. Weekly. [There seems to be some indication that this periodical may have continued to Mar 1922]   *657*
     BM (missing Vol 1, Nos 1–23; Vol 2, Nos 28–35)

The Magazine Programme. (The Grand Theatre Magazine Programme) Swansea: Grand Theatre. Vol 1, No 42 – Vol 3, No 7. 20 Aug 1906 – 30 Dec 1907. Weekly. New Series. Vols 1–4, No 49. 6 Jan 1908 – 26 Dec 1911. Weekly. [In Vol 3 of the New Series, not published on 12 and 19 December. The inner page title is, *The Grand Theatre Magazine Programme.* With the New Series, Vol 1, No 26, 3 Aug 1908, the title is given on the interior page as, *The Grand Theatre Magazine Programme.* With which is incorporated "Laughter". This heading remains until Vol 4, No 29. 24 July 1911. The name of the printer changes] *657a*
     O

The Magic Circular. A monthly review. Including the Transactions of the Magic Circle. London. Vols 1–54. Nos 1–603. 1 June 1906 – Mar 1960. Monthly.   *658*
     BM (missing Vols 1–49, No 541), NN ([1] 3–6, 14, 23–26)

The Performer.   Official organ of the variety artistes' federation. London. Vols
1–105. Nos 1–2674. 29 Mar 1906 – 26 Sept 1957. Weekly. [Special Christmas
Number, *Performer Annual*, 1907 – 1932]   **659**
    BM-N, WEST (missing Vols 1–74)

Stage and Sport.   London. Nos 1–8. 1 Jan – 23 June 1906. Irregular.   **660**
    BM-N, O (Nos 1–4)

Stage Door.   London. No 1. 1 Feb 1906. then, *Stage Land.* Nos 2–6. 8 Feb – 15
Mar 1906. Weekly. then, *Stageland.* Nos 1–14. 22 Mar – 21 June 1906. Weekly.
    BM-N   **661**

The Variety Theatre Annual.   London. Vol 1. 1906/07. Annual.   **662**
    BM

Variety Time Table and Programme.   London. Nos 1–44. 26 Feb – 31 Dec 1906.
Weekly.   **663**
    BM-N

What's On at the Theatres This Week?   London. No 1. 27 Jan 1906. Weekly.   **664**
    BM-N

Wm. Haslam's Apartment Directory and Theatrical Guide to Manchester.   Ed by
Wm. Haslam. Manchester: Published by Wm. Haslam. First Edition. 1 Mar
1906. Quarterly.   **665**
    BM

1907

Bournemouth Visitors' Programme of Daily Events.   Bournemouth. 8 June 1907 –
16 Oct 1909. then, *Bournemouth Visitors' Daily Events.* 23 Oct 1909 – 25 Mar
1912. then, *Bournemouth Visitors' Daily Events Guide.* 1 Apr – 30 Sept 1912.
then, *Bournemouth & District Visitors' & Residents' Weekly Guide to Daily
Events.* 7 Oct 1912 – 31 Aug 1914. Weekly.   **665a**
    BM-N

Drury Lane Gazette.   A try weekly. Ed by Septem Locum. [According to No 20,
the editor is D. L. Pool] London: Published at the Editorial Offices, Drury Lane
Theatre, No 7, Room P. S. Nos 1–20. 12 Oct 1907 – 7 Mar 1908. Weekly.   **666**
    BM-N

The Favourite.   Sport, satire and the drama. Ed by Charles Villiers-Chapman.
London: Printed for the Proprietor, Charles Villiers-Chapman, and Published
at 18, Buckingham Street, Strand, W.C. Vol 1. Nos 1–12. 12 Oct – 28 Dec 1907.
Weekly.   **667**
    BM-N

Liverpool Theatrical News.   Liverpool. Vol 1. Nos 1–49. 29 July 1907 – 29 June
1908. Weekly.   **668**
    BM-N

Magician Annual.   [Compiled and edited by Will Goldston] London. Nos 1–5.
1907 – 1912. Annual.   **669**
    BM, LU, NN, O (to 1914, from 1908/9)

My Journal. A Monthly Magazine. Dealing with all matters of general interest, literature and the drama. Edited and conducted by Dr. Dobbs. London: Published by Wyman & Sons, Ltd., Fetter Lane, E.C. Vol 1. Nos 1–2. July – Aug 1907. then, *My Journal.* A Monthly Magazine. Nos 3–6. Sept – Dec 1907. Monthly. then, *My Journal.* An Occasional Magazine. Vol 1, No 8 – Vol 2, No 20. June 1909 – June 1910. Irregular. [Vol 2 begins with No 13, Nov 1909]   **669a**
     BM (missing Nos 2, 5, 7)

The Performer Annual. London. 1907 – 1932. Special Christmas Number.   **670**
     BM-N, O (1911–1913; 1920–1921)

The Planet. A journal of social, literary, political, dramatic and topical interest. London. Nos 1–216. 2 Mar 1907 – 11 Apr 1911. Weekly.   **671**
     BM-N

Prompt Box. The official organ of the Liverpool stage club. Liverpool. Nos 1–3. [Oct?] – 2 Nov 1907. Weekly.   **672**
     Not located (Loewenberg p 43)

The Prompter. London. Nos 1–4. 12 Oct – 2 Nov 1907. Weekly. [Registration issues]   **673**
     BM-N

The Robert Arthur Theatres Illustrated Journal Programme. London. Nos 1–21. 1907 – 1908. [I have not been able to determine the dates of the individual numbers]   **674**
     BM (destroyed)

What's On. London. Vols 1–47. Nos 1–598. 9 Feb 1907 – 13 Sept 1919. Weekly [with exceptions: in 1919 only three issues]   **675**
     BM-N

1908

Eastbourne Programme of Entertainments and General Fixtures and Accomodation Register. Eastbourne: Publisher: The South Coast-Programmes Co., Ltd., Eastbourne and Brighton. Nos 1–145. 18 Apr 1908 – 3 Feb 1917. Weekly [irregular]. then, *To-day in Eastbourne.* Nos 146–460. 10 Feb 1917 – 27 Jan 1923. then, *The Eastbourne Mirror.* Vols 1–5, No 215. 7 Feb 1923 – 23 Feb 1927. then, *Eastbourne Courier.* Vol 1 –   . 5 Mar 1927 –   .   **676**
     BM-N

Lancashire Stage-land. Manchester. Nos 1–6. 1 Feb – 7 Mar 1908. then, *Stage-land.* Nos 7–21. 14 Mar – 20 June 1908. Weekly.   **677**
     BM, O

The Stage Year Book, with Which Is Included the Stage Provincial Guide. [Ed by Lionel Carson] London: Carson & Comerford, Ltd. Vols 1–21. 1908 – 1928. 1949 –   . Annual.   **678**
     BM (1908–1919; 1921/25; 1926–1928, 1949–   ), CtY (incomplete), MB (missing 1912, 1918–   ), O

The Theatre. London. No 1. 12 Mar 1908. [Registration issue]   **679**
     BM-N

What's On in Southampton. The Up-to-date official programme of forthcoming events. Southampton: Printed and Published for the Proprietors by W. Mate and Sons, Ltd., 10, Above Bar. Nos 1–1314. 26 Dec 1908 – 7 Apr 1934. Weekly.
BM-N   *680*

1909

Gallery Gazette. London. Ed by P. L. Jackson. No 1. Apr 1909. [This is bound with, *The Gallery Gazette.* New Series. Nos 2–9. Nov 1908 – June 1909. It is larger in size. Reproduced from typewritten copy]   *681*
LU-MM, NN

The Prompter. Edited by Frederick Wood. (Vol 1, No 10 – Vol 2, No 2. Oct 1910 – Feb 1911). London: Printed by Wood and Son, 62 High Street, Perth, and Published by the Proprietors, The Prompter Publishing Co., at 50 Copthall Avenue, E.C. Vol 1. Nos 1–2. Dec 1909 – Jan 1910. then, *The Prompter.* The Organ of the Amateur Stage. Vol 1. Nos 3–9. Feb – Sept 1910. then, *The Prompter.* The official organ of the Dramatic Clubs' Association. Vol 1. Nos 10–12. Oct – Dec 1910. then, *The Prompter.* The organ of the Amateur Stage. Vol 2. Nos 1–2. Jan – Feb 1911. Monthly. [Nos 1–14]   *682*
BM (destroyed), O

The Sheffield Guide and Advertiser. Sheffield: Printed for the Proprietors of the *Sheffield Guide and Advertiser*, 87 Fargate, by J. W. Northend, 8 Norfolk Road. Vol 1. No 1. 12 Nov 1909. then, *What's On.* No 2. 22 Nov 1909.   *683*
BM-N

The Theatre. A monthly magazine for playgoers. Ed by Clifford Young. London. Vol 1. Nos 1–6. 1909. then, *The Playgoer and Society Illustrated.* New Series. Vols 1–9. Nos 1–51. 1 – 9 Oct/Nov 1909 – 14 Jan 1914. Monthly.   *684*
BM, BP (Vols 1–2), MH (Nos 1–6), NN, O

What's On in Southampton. Southampton. Nos 2–1314. 2 Jan 1909 – 7 Apr 1934. Weekly.   *684a*
BM-N

1910

Lotinga's Weekly. An illustrated journal of sports and drama. London. Nos 1–227. 12 Mar 1910 – 18 July 1914. Weekly. [Including registration issues dated, 29 Aug 1914 – 17 Aug 1918]   *685*
BM-N

The Magic Wand. A monthly journal for all entertainers. London. Vols 1–46. Nos 1–256. [Sept 1910] – [1957] Monthly [irregular] [Nos 253–256 are not dated]   *686*
BM (missing Nos 2–5, 7–9, 11, 21, 26, 29–31, 43–46, 51, 52, 54–60, 65–70, 72, 74, 75, 79, 81–88, 94, 98–99, 106, 109–110, 112, 121–132, 134–140, 147–148, 153–154, 157–158, 161–163, 165, 178–179), MH (1–[3–6]–[8–9]), NN (incomplete)

The Magical World. A weekly review of international magic & kindred arts. Ed by Max Sterling. Manchester. Vols 1–2, No 3. 2 Nov 1910 – 17 May 1911. New Series. London. Vols 1–2, No 10. [Nos 1–36] 4 June 1913 – 4 Feb 1914. Weekly.
BM-N (New Series), LU, MH (incomplete), NN   *687*

The Manchester Playgoer. [Manchester Playgoers' Club] Manchester. Vols 1–2. Apr 1910 – May 1912. New Series. Sept 1912 – July 1914. Quarterly [but varying from two to eight months intervals. Edited by O. Raymond Drey, from 1912]
     BM (New Series, 1912–1914), IEN (Missing Vols 1–2), MP   *688*

The Thalia Diary & Directory of Concert Parties and Entertainers. London: Thalia Dramatic & Printing Co. [Vols 1–6] 1910 – 1915. Annual.   *689*
     BM

1911

Art. The magazine of the arts and dramatic club. London: Printed by W. J. Pollock & Co., Ltd., 81 Mortimer Street, W., for the Proprietors, The Arts and Dramatic Club, Clavier Hall, Hanover Square, W. Vol 1. Nos 1–9. 4 Oct – 1 Dec 1911. Weekly. [Beginning with the ninth number the magazine has a larger format]   *690*
     BM, O

The Ball Room. A record of matters appertaining to ball room dancing, music, etiquette and dress. London: Published by the Ball Room Publishing Co., 423, Edgware Road, Paddington, W. Vols 15–19. Nos 187–239. Mar 1911 – Nov 1915. Monthly.   *691*
     BM (very incomplete, with only 19 numbers)

Exeter Day by Day. Exeter. Nos 1–19. June 1911 – Apr 1914. Bi-monthly. *691a*
     BM-N

The Scallop-Shell: the Pilgrim Review. An occasional review: the Organ of the Pilgrim Players. Ed by John Drinkwater. Birmingham. Nos 1–2. Feb and Apr 1911.   *692*
     BM, BP

The Weekly Playgoer. London. Nos 1–26. 22 Mar – 13 Sept 1911. Weekly. *693*
     BM-N (destroyed)

1912

The Independent Theatre Goer. Conducted by J. T. Grein and Herman Klein. London: Publishing and Editorial Offices: Odhams Limited, 93 & 94, Long Acre, W.C. Nos 1–6. 1 Nov 1912 – Apr 1913. Monthly.   *694*
     BM (incomplete), MH (missing Nos 1–2), O

Season's Concert and Entertainment Calendar. Leeds. 1912/13. [Sometime after 1924 the title changed to] *Concert, Lecture, Dramatic Guide.* 1933 – 1938. Annual. [The issues were not intended to form volumes]   *695*
     LdP (1912/13, 1913/14, 1919/20, 1924/25, 1933/34, 1934/35, 1935/36, 1936/37, 1937/38, 1938/39)

"The Stage" Guide. Ed by L. Carson. London: Published by Carson & Comerford, Ltd., Proprietors of The Stage, 19–23 Tavistock Street, W.C. 2. 1912. [Revised edition compiled by A. W. Tolmie, 1946]   *696*
     BM, BP (revised edition)

Theatreland. A journal for playgoers. London: Printed and Published for the Proprietors by L. Upcott Gill and Son, Ltd., at the London and County Printing Works, Drury Lane, W.C. Vol 1. Nos 1–12. 25 Sept 1912 – 12 Mar 1913. Biweekly.
     BM-N, O (Nos 1–3)   *697*

1913

Actresses' Franchise League.   [Annual Report, 1912 – 1913] London. [1913]
Annual.   *698*
    BM

The Blue Review; Literature, Drama, Art, Music. [Ed by John Middleton Mur-
ray] London: M. Secker. Vol 1. Nos 1–3. May – July 1913. Monthly. [Supersedes,
Rhythm, Art, Literature Monthly]   *699*
    BM, CSmH, CU, DLC, ICN, MiU, MnU, NjP, NN, NNC

The Entertainer.   Scotland's amusements weekly, theatrical, vaudeville. Glasgow.
Vols 1–7. Nos 1–285. 4 Oct 1913 – 15 Mar 1919. Weekly.   *700*
    BM

The "Iris" Guide to London's Amusements. London: Printed by E. H. Wheeler,
54–58, Caledonian Road, King's Cross, N., and Published by London's Amusement Co., 55, Pembridge Road, W. Nos 1–55. 4 Oct 1913 – Oct 1915. Weekly,
biweekly, monthly.   *701*
    BM-N

The London Program.   A daily index of forthcoming events and fixtures of general
interest in the metropolis. London: Printed by Unwin Brothers, Ltd., 27 Pilgrim
Street, E.C., and Published by the Proprietors at 120, Bank Chambers, High-
Holborn, W.C. Nos 1–16. 22 Nov 1913 – 13 Mar 1914. then, *The London Program.* A weekly index of all forthcoming events and fixtures of general interest
in the metropolis. Nos 17–21. 20 Mar – 18 Apr 1914. then, *The London Program,
The Weekly Herald,* etc. Nos 22–30. 25 Apr – 20 June 1914. Weekly.   *702*
    BM-N

Man of Today.   A quarterly review of fashion, sport and drama. London. No 1.
Summer edition 1913. Quarterly.   *702a*
    BM-N

Pantomime and Vaudeville Favourites.   Ed by Will Goldston. London. [1913] –
    . [I have not been able to determine the length of the "run," or the date of
the final number]   *703*
    BM (destroyed)

The Playbill.   London. Nos 1–7. Feb – Sept 1913. Monthly [except August]   *704*
    BM-N

Poetry and Drama.   [Ed by Harold Munro] London. Vols 1–2. Nos 1–8. Mar
1913 – Dec 1914. Quarterly. [Superseded by *Chapbook* July 1914]   *705*
    BM, BP, C, CSmH, CtY, ICN, LvP, MB, NCH, NN, O, WEST

Sunday Chronicle.   Pantomime annual. Ed by "Bayard." London and Manchester.
[Nos 1–19] 1912/13 – 1930/31. then, *Sunday Chronicle.* Pantomime and amusement annual. [No 20] 1931/32. Annual.   *706*
    BM

The Theatre. London: Printed and Published for the Proprietors by L. Upcott Gill and Son, Ltd., at the London & County Printing Works, Drury Lane, W.C. Vol 1. No 1. 22 Mar 1913.   **707**
BM, O

The Thespian. London. Nos 1–2. Oct – Nov 1913. Monthly.   **708**
BM-N

The Three Arts Club Journal. London. Vols 1–2, No 10. Jan 1913 – Oct 1914. Monthly.   **709**
BM

Universal Musical and Dramatic Directory. 1913. The English edition of the *Annuaire des artistes.* English section giving all particulars of the music and dramatic trades and professions in Gt. Britain and Ireland. London. 1913. Annual.   **710**
MB

What's On in Portsmouth and Southsea. Portsmouth. Nos 1–14, 16–18. 12 July – 1 Nov 1913. Weekly.   **711**
BM-N

1914

Bacon-Shakespeare. London. Vols 1–3. 21 July 1914 – 12 June 1918. New Series. Vols 1–3, No 4. 15 July 1919 – 12 June 1926.   **712**
AAP, NN (1-New Series, Vol 3, No 4)

The English Folk-Dance Society's Journal. Ed by Perceval Lucas. London. Vol 1. Nos 1–2. May 1914 – Apr 1915. Annual. then, *The Journal of the English Folk Dance Society.* Series 2. Nos 1–4. 1927 – 1931. [No issue was published in 1929]
BM, BP, C, DLC, ICN, ICU, NN, NRU, OCl   **713**

Guide to Selecting Plays. London: Samuel French, Ltd. 1914 – 1965. Annual. then, *The Complete Guide to Selecting Plays.* 1966/67 –   . [Some years have supplementary sections added]   **714**
BM

The London Shakespeare League Journal. Edited by John Booth (to Vol 3, No 10. July 1917); Stewart D. Headlam (Vol 3, No 11 – Vol 8, No 3. Nov 1917 – June 1922); Herbert Farjeon (Vol 8, No 4 – Vol 11, No 2. July 1922 – July/Aug 1925); Lionel Millard (Vol 11, No 3 – Vol 12, No 3. Nov 1925 – Christmas 1925). London: Printed by the East Anglian Daily Times Co., Ltd., 13 Carr Street, Ipswich. Vol 1. Nos 1–8. Oct 1914 – May 1915. then, *Shakespeare League Journal.* Vol 1, No 9 – Vol 8, No 6. June 1915 – Oct 1922. then, *The Shakespeare Journal.* Vol 8, No 7 – Vol 12, No 3. Nov 1922 – Christmas 1926. Monthly (irregular. Some years Aug – Sept form one issue; some years the August issue is omitted).   **715**
BM (destroyed), BP, O (missing Vol 5, No 8)

The Thalia Diary & Directory for Music Halls & Music-Hall Artists. London: Printed and Published by Lorings Ltd. 1914.   **716**
BM

Theatre de Luxe Gazette.   Glasgow. Nos 1–3. Oct 1914 – 27 Dec 1915. Monthly.
BM   *717*

1915

The Bristol Playgoer.   [Bristol Playgoers' Club] Bristol. Nos 21, 22. Apr 1915,
Mar 1924. [I have been unable to obtain any other information regarding the
periodical]   *718*
   BM (destroyed)

British Empire Shakespeare Society.   Official Gazette. London. Vols 1–4, No 13.
Sept 1915 – Aug 1939. [Irregular numbering] Monthly [although no numbers
published in 1919]   *719*
   BM (missing all before Vol 1, No 16), BP

The Magical Record.   Bradford. Vols 1–2, No 3. July 1915 – July 1917. Monthly.
   BM (destroyed), MH (No 1), NN (Nos 1, 3)   *720*

The Playgoer's Calendar for 1915.   London: George G. Harrap and Company,
2 & 3 Portsmouth Street, Kingsway, W.C. [Although this *Calendar* is listed at
the British Museum as a periodical, it is simply a calendar of 1915, and of no
value for theatrical material]   *721*
   BM

The Playgoers' Club Journal.   [Manchester Playgoers' Club] Manchester. Vols
1–13. Nov 1915 – Sept 1934. Monthly [from Oct to Mar, except Oct 1923 – Mar
1924, when it appeared every two months]   *722*
   MP (incomplete)

1917

"A.A." The Official Organ of the Actors' Association. London. Vols 1–2. Nos 1–11.
Jan 1917 – Dec 1918. then, *The Actor for Player and Public.* Vols 1–3. Nos 1–8.
Jan 1919 – July 1922. Monthly.   *723*
   BM (destroyed), NN ([1] 2)

The Actors Association Yearbook.   London: 32, Regent Street. 1917. Annual. *724*
   BM

The Irish Limelight.   The only Irish journal devoted to cinema and theatrical
topics. Dublin. Vols 1–3, No 10. Jan 1917 – Oct 1919. Monthly. [Later issues are
devoted solely to the cinema]   *725*
   BM-N (Jan 1917 – June 1918; Oct 1919)

Shakespeare Association [Papers]   London. Nos 1–21. 1917 – 1937. [A mono-
graph series, published at various intervals, with no indications of date except
for the year]   *726*
   BM, CtY, IaU, NNC, O, PBm, WaU

The Theatre, Music Hall & Cinema Blue Book for 1917.   A list of public amuse-
ment companies with full financial particulars of interest to investors. London:
Keith, Mac Allester & Co., Ltd. Vol 1. 1917. then, *The Theatre, Music Hall and
Cinema Companies' Blue Book.* Vols 2–13. 1918 – 1929/30. Annual.   *727*
   BM

1918

Poetry. A magazine of new lyrics. London. Vols 1–8. Nos 1–74. June 1918 – Sept 1925. Monthly [with a few exceptions] then, *Poetry and the Play.* Vols 8–13. Nos 75–90. Nov 1925 – 1931. Irregular [Monthly (irregular), Oct 1920 – Mar 1925; Quarterly (irregular), July 1925 – Winter 1930. Organ of the Poetry League, July 1926 – Winter 1930. The title varies] **728**
>BP, LvP, NN ([3–5]–[8–10]–13), PP ([6]–13)

1919

Actor for Player and Public. Official organ of the Actors Association. London. Vol 1. Nos 1–12. Jan – Dec 1919. Monthly. [Supersedes the Association's, "A.A." Vol 1, No 7. July 1919, is incorrectly numbered Vol 1, No 6] **729**
>NN (missing No 11)

Arts Gazette; Drama, Music, Art, Literature. Ed by J. T. Grein, and L. Dunton Green. London. No 1. 1 Feb 1919. New Series. Nos 1–41. 18 Mar 1922 – 24 Feb 1923. Weekly. **730**
>BM, O

Drama. A magazine of the theatre and allied arts (British Drama League). London. Nos 1–6. July 1919 – July 1920. Bimonthly. then, *Drama.* The journal of the British Drama League. New Series. Vols 1–17, No 10. Nov 1920 – July/Sept 1939. then, *Drama.* The quarterly theatre review. Summer 1946 – . Quarterly. [From Oct 1939 – Feb 1946 see, *War-Time Drama*] **731**
>BM, BP (incomplete), C, LVA, MH (incomplete), NPV, O

The Honey Pot. The Playgoer's paper. London. Vol 1. Nos 1–2. 1919. [The numbers are not dated] **732**
>BM (destroyed)

The L.A.G.; or London Amusement Guide. With complete index of entertainments, sports, &c. London. [Vol 1. No 1] – Vol 2, No 8. [Numbering begins with Vol 1, No 5. 5 Sept 1919] May 1919 – Aug 1920. then, *London (Official) Amusement Guide.* Vol 2, No 9 – Vol 4, No 4. Sept 1920 – Mar 1922. Monthly. [The subtitle varies] **733**
>BM

London Attractions. A weekly publication devoted to the interests of all in speech, of amusements & recreation. London: Offices: 11, Gt. Turnstile, W.C. 1. Vol 1. Nos 1–3. 12 – 26 Nov 1919. [No 1 is the registration number] **734**
>BM, LGU (missing No 3), Guildhall Library, London (No 1)

The "Old Vic." Magazine. Official organ of the "Old Vic." theatre. London. Vols 1–11, No 10. Oct 1919 – Dec 1930. then, *The Old Vic. and Sadler's Wells Magazine.* Vols 1–3. Nos 1–29. Jan 1931 – Jan 1936. Monthly. **735**
>BM (missing all before Sept/Oct 1932)

Scottish Musical Magazine and Scottish Drama. Edinburgh. Vols 1–12. [Nos 1–137] Sept 1919 – Jan 1931. Monthly. [The title varies slightly] **736**
>BM, DLC, GU, NN, NRU (1–[10]–11)

Stage Mirror. London. Nos 1–3. 8 – 22 Feb 1919. Weekly. [Registration issues]
BM-N   **737**

Theatre-Craft; a Book of the New Spirit in the Theatre. London. Nos 1–5. [1919? –
1921?] Quarterly. [Merged into, *English Review.* The issues are not dated] **738**
C, E, MH, O, WEST (missing No 4)

Wilford Hutchinson's Conjurers Chronicle. Ashton-under-Lynne. Nos 1 – .
1919 –   . [I have been unable to determine the extent of the "run" of this
periodical]   **739**
BM (missing all before Vol 15), LU (1–21, No 3)

1920

Gallery Gazette. Very official organ of the Gallery First Nighters Club. Post-
War Series. London. Vols [1]–3, No 8. Nov 1920 – Dec 1921. Monthly. [Ed by
G. F. Abbott, beginning with Vol 2, No 1. May 1921. Reprinted from typewritten
copy, [Vol 1], Nos 1–6. Nov 1920 – Apr 1921. Printed, from Vol 2, No 1. May
1921. Vol 3 continues the numbering from Vol 2, and has two issues, Nos 7–8.
Altogether there are 14 Numbers]   **740**
BM (destroyed), LU-MM

The Liverpool Programme of Entertainments. Liverpool. Nos 1–17. [?] – 18 Oct
1920. then, *Liverpool and Merseyside Programme of Entertainments.* Nos 18–
40. 25 Oct 1920 – 11 July 1921. Weekly.   **741**
LvP (missing Nos 1–7)

The Palais Dancing News. London. Vol 1. Nos 1–4. Apr – July 1920. Monthly.
then, *The Dancing World.* Vol 1, No 5 – Vol 4, No 10. Sept 1920 – May 1924. **742**
BM (destroyed)

The Proscenium. London. Vol 1. No 1. 1920.   **743**
BM (destroyed)

Screen and Stage. A magazine treating of films, theatres, varieties, music. London: Printed by Vail & Co., Ogle Street, W. 1, and Published by H. Lawrence
Harris, Sole Proprietor, 122 Regent Street, W. 1. Vol 1. Nos 1–2. 1 May – June
1920. Monthly.   **744**
BM-N, O

The Theatrical Apartments and Business Directory. (The Theatrical Artists' Business Directory) Liverpool: Published by Messrs. G. Hardey Graham & Co.
[Nos 1–3] 1920 – 1922. Annual. [A 5th edition, printed in Birmingham, appeared
in 1925]   **745**
BM

1921

Dancing Life. London. Nos 1–3. Nov 1921 – Jan 1922. Monthly. Incorporated
with, *The Dancing World.* [See, *The Palais Dancing News*]   **746**
BM (destroyed)

E.F.D.S. News. London. Vol 1. Nos 1–6. Jan 1921 – Nov 1923. then, *E.F.D.S.
News.* The magazine of the English Folk Dance Society. Vols 1–4. Nos 7–47.

May 1924 – June 1936. [Superseded by, *English Dance and Song*] Two issues a year [Nos 1–15. Jan 1921 – Sept 1927]; three issues a year [Nos 16–37. Feb 1928 – Sept 1934]; six issues a year [Nos 38–43. Jan – Dec 1935]; four issues a year [Nos 44–47. Jan – June 1936. Absorbed, *Bulletin of the English Folk Dance*] **747**
> BM (missing all after No 12?), DLC, ICN, ICU, LdP, MP, NN (1, 3–47), O

English Folk Dance Society News. (English folk dance and song society.) London. Vols 1–4. [Nos 1–47] Jan 1921 – June 1936. Irregular.   **748**
> BM, BP (1–4, No 13), DLC, ICN, ICU, LdP, MP, O

The Gong. Published by the Birmingham repertory theatre. Ed by Alan Bland. Birmingham. Nos 1–11. Dec 1921 – Dec 1922. Monthly.   **749**
> BM, BP, C, MH

The Grand Guignol Annual Review. [Little Theatre] London. 1921. Annual. **750**
> BM (destroyed)

London Weekly Diary of Social Events. London. [No 1] –   . 21/27 Nov 1921 –   . [No issues published from 14 Oct 1941 – 7 May 1945] Weekly. [The British Museum copy skips from 28 Oct 1945, to 9 Oct 1949]   **751**
> BM

The N.A.T.E. Journal. [National Association of Theatrical Employees] Letchworth. Nos 1–11. Jan – Nov 1921. Monthly. then, *The Amusement Workers' News.* London. Vols 1–4. [Nos 1–105] Jan 1922 – Jan 1931. Monthly. [Not published, Nov 1922 – Jan 1923]   **752**
> BM, IU (missing 1921)

"The Performer" Handbook. Ed by John Warr. London: "The Performer" Offices, 18, Charing Cross Road, W.C. 2. [1921]   **753**
> BM, O

What's On in Coventry and District. Coventry. Vol 1. Nos 1–34. 30 Sept 1921 – 22 July 1922. Weekly (irregular).   **754**
> BM-N

1922

Cambridge Guide to "What's On?" Cambridge. Nos 1–209. 19 Oct 1922 – 24 Dec 1926. Weekly.   ***754a***
> BM-N, C (missing Nos 175, 196, 198–199, 206)

The Curtain; a Monthly Review of the Drama. [Ed by Charles Hope, with G. F. Holland, 1926 – 1932] London. Vols 1–11. Nos 1–121. Jan 1922 – Jan 1932. Monthly. [The subtitle varies slightly]   **755**
> BM (missing Vols 9–11), CtY (missing Vols 10–11), DLC (missing Vol 7), MH (missing Vols 7–8, 10–11), NN, O (Vol 4 – Vol 10, No 121)

Danceland. London. Vol 1. No 1. Dec 1922.   **756**
> BM

Glasgow and District Entertainment Guide. Glasgow. Vols 1–6. Nos 1–281. 15 May 1922 – 28 Sept 1927. Weekly.   **757**
> BM-N

Ilford What's On. Ilford. No 1. 19 Aug 1922.   **758**
    BM-N

Ivory Leaves. A Medium of Expression for the New Intensive Study of Shakespeare by Sivori Levey. London: Privately issued at "The Pilgrimage", 12 St. John's Road, Putney, S.W. 15. Vol 1. Nos 1–3. Jan – July 1922. Irregular.   **758a**
    O

London's Entertainments. A monthly review and guide. London: Printed by Fleetway Press, Ltd., 3–9, Dane Street, High Holborn, W.C. 1, for the Publisher, The Holiday Press, Limited, 3, Queen's Square, Southampton Row, W.C. 1. Vol 1. Nos 1–5. Nov 1922 – Mar 1923. Monthly. then, *Round the Town and London's Entertainments Illustrated.* Vol 2. Nos 1–4. 6 – 28 Apr 1923. then, *Round the Town. Illustrated.* Vol 2. Nos 5–13. 5 May – 30 June 1923. then, *Round the Town Illustrated.* The theatre and cinema. Vol 2. Nos 14–22. 7 July – 1 Sept 1923. Weekly.   **759**
    BM-N

The Maskerpiece. An educational magazine profusely illustrated. Showing the link of literature and drama of all ages in the mask and the name. Ed by Sivori Levey. London. Nos 1–2. Nov 1922 – Feb 1923. Three issues a year.   **760**
    BM

The National Amateur Operatic and Dramatic Association. Directory and Constitution. Cheltenham. 1921/22 – 1925/26. Annual. then, *The National Operatic and Dramatic Association Year Book.* 1926/27 – 1930/31. then, *Year Book.* 1931 – 1939/40, 1948 – 1956. London. then, *The National Operatic and Dramatic Association . . . Directory.* 1957 – 1960. then, *Year Book.* 1961 –   . Annual.   **761**
    BM (missing many issues published between 1940 and 1948), O (1955–   .)

The Performing Right Gazette. The official organ of the Performing Right Society. London: Performing Right Society, Ltd., 33, Margaret St., W. 1. Vols 1–6, No 9. July 1922 – July 1939. Quarterly. then, *The Performing Right Society Ltd.* Emergency Bulletin. Nos 1–9. Oct 1939 – Feb 1943. Irregular. then, *The Performing Right Society, Ltd.* An association of composers, authors and music publishers. Emergency Bulletin. Nos 10–13. Apr 1943 – Aug 1944. then, *The Performing Right Society, Ltd.* An association of composers, authors and publishers of music. Bulletin. Nos 14–17. Aug 1945 – Aug 1947. then, *The Performing Right Bulletin.* The official organ of The Performing Right Society Ltd. An association of composers [,] authors and publishers of music. Nos 18–25. Apr 1948 – Sept 1954. then, *Performing Right.* The official organ of The Performing Right Society. An association of composers, authors and publishers of music. Nos 26–44. Sept 1955 – Oct 1966. Twice a year [Nos 33–45. Nov 1960 – Oct 1966. Ed by Eric Crozier. Nos 44–45. Apr – Oct 1966. The last number on the shelf of the British Museum is of 11 Apr 1967, No 44]   **762**
    BM, O

The Spear. No 00001. Huddersfield. 31 June 1922. [A souvenir of the Shakespeare Festival held at the Theatre Royal, Huddersfield]   **763**
    BM-N

T.M.A. Monthly Report. [Theatrical Managers' Association] London. Vols 1–7. Apr 1922 – May 1929. then, *The Theatre Managers Journal.* Vols 8–22. 1929 –

1944. then, *Theatre Industry Journal.* Vols 23–26. 1945 – 1948. then, *The Theatre Industry.* Vols 27–38. 1949 – Mar 1960. Monthly. [Caption title, Nov 1922 – Mar 1927, *Theatrical Managers' Journal*]   **764**
    BM (missing Vols 8–18, and incomplete in others), NN (incomplete, Vols 1–11)

What's On in Birmingham.   Entertainment guide and amusement programmes. Birmingham. Vols 1–2. Nos 1–113. 4 Mar 1922 – 26 May 1924. Weekly.   **765**
    BP

1923

The Amateur Operatic Year Book.   Ed by Tom Bourn. Whitley Bay. Vols [1]–3. 1922/23 – 1924. Annual.   **766**
    BM

Clacton Visitor's Guide.   Clacton. Nos 1–106. 21 May 1923 – 18 Sept 1926. Weekly (irregular).   **766a**
    BM-N

The Critics' Circular.   Official Organ of the Critics' Circle. London. Vol 1. Nos 1–   . Nov 1923 –   . Three issues a year [Vol 1, No 1 – Vol 2, No 7. Nov 1923 – Nov 1925]; twice a year [Vol 2, No 8 – Vol 3, No 12. Mar 1926 – Nov 1927]; Annual [Vol 4 –   . Oct 1928 –   .] [The numbering is from Vol 1, No 1 – Vol 10, No 50. Nov 1923 – Autumn, 1963. Vol 11 begins numbering with No 1, Winter, 1964–65, No 2, Winter 1965–66.]   **767**
    BM

The Dancing Annual. Ed by E. N. Brynildsen. London. 1923. Annual.   **768**
    BM (destroyed)

The Magical Monthly.   A magazine devoted to magic and magicians. Ed by Edward Bagshawe. London: E. Bagshawe & Co. Vols 1–3. Oct 1923 – Sept 1926. Monthly. [The subtitle varies]   **769**
    BM (missing all after Vol 2, No 12. Sept 1925), LU, NN

Oldham Amusements and Shopping Programme.   Oldham: Designed, Printed and Published by the Proprietors — John Albinson, Ltd. Chapel Street, High Street. Nov 1923 – Mar 1926. Monthly.   **770**
    BM-N

Opera.   A magazine for music lovers. London. Vols 1–2. Nos 1–16. Jan 1923 – Apr 1924. then, *Opera and the Ballet.* Nos 1–4. May – Autumn 1924. Monthly.   **771**
    BM

The Programme.   A weekly guide to the stage, platform and pulpit. London: Printed for the Publishers, Verstone & Co., 29, Ludgate Hill, E.C. Vol 1. No 1. 1 Jan 1923. Weekly. [A registration issue]   **772**
    BM-N

Rada News.   Royal Academy of Dramatic Art. London. 1923. [I have been unable to locate any additional information concerning this periodical]   **773**
    BM (destroyed)

The Reandean News-Sheet. London. 1923. [I have been unable to locate any further information concerning this periodical]   **774**
   BM (destroyed)

The Scottish Player. Glasgow: Issued by the Scottish National Theatre Society. Vols 1–4. [July?] 1923 – Apr 1926. Monthly.   **775**
   BM (destroyed)

Stage Props. [Ed by G. Du Maurier] London. 1923. Annual.   **776**
   NN, O

What's On in Margate. Margate. Nos 1–114. 28 Mar 1923 – 27 May 1925. Weekly.
   BM-N   **777**

1924

Blackpool Carnival Pictorial & Programme. Blackpool. Nos 1–10. 11 – 21 June 1924. Daily.   **777a**
   BM-N

The Dancing Record and London Amusements. London. Vol 1. Nos 1–2. Dec 1924 – Jan 1925. Monthly. [Includes also a registration issue dated, Nov 1924]
   BM-N   **778**

Leeds Playgoer. Ed by F. W. Harland-Edgcumbe. Bradford. Nos 1–6. Oct 1924 – Mar 1925. Monthly.   **779**
   LdP

The Link. (The journal of the Association of Teachers of the Revived Greek Dance, The Z Club, the Ginner-Mawer School, etc.) London. Vols 1–5, No 16. Jan 1924 – Oct 1934. New Series. Vols 1–3, No 15. Jan 1935 – July 1940. Irregular. [See, *Parados*]   **780**
   BM

Liverpool "Week-by-Week." Liverpool. Nos 1–26. 1924. [I have been unable to determine the exact dates of the various issues, or the frequency of publication, i.e., whether the periodical is a weekly]   **781**
   BM (destroyed)

The London Programme. London. Vols 1–2, No 14. 16 June – 6 Oct 1924. then, *The London Review.* Vol 2, No 15 – Vol 3, No 6. 13 Oct 1924 – 15 June 1925. Weekly.   **782**
   BM-N

The Magazine Programme. Always enjoyed — never destroyed. London: H. Good & Son. Nos 1–1273. 1924 – 10 July 1939. Weekly (irregular). [Plays performed at the London theatres]   **783**
   BM (missing Nos 1–636)

The Magical News. Ed by Wilfrid G. Jonson. London. Nos 1–2. 15 – 29 Mar 1924. Biweekly.   **784**
   BM

The Municipal Player: a Magazine for Mummers.   Birmingham. Vols 1–3. May
1924 – June 1926. New Series. Vols 1–4. Sept 1927 – Aug 1931. Monthly. [Repro-
duced from typewritten copy]   **785**
     BP

New Plays from Old Stories.   By H. L. Ould. London: Oxford University Press.
Series 1–3 [with three numbers, or plays, in each series] 1924–1935. Irregular.
[This is a series of plays, published in nine parts — one part for each play —
and is not strictly a periodical. I include it as it appears in the *British Union
Catalogue of Periodicals*, and in the British Museum Catalogue of periodicals]
     BM   **785a**

Playgoer.   [Playhouse, William Square, Liverpool] Liverpool. Nos 1–12. Oct
1924 – Mar 1926. Irregular.   **786**
     LvP

                                     1925

Amateur Theatre.   Ed by F. Lloyd. London: Printed by Gibbs & Bamforth, Ltd.,
St. Albans for the National Amateur Operatic and Dramatic Association. Vol 1.
No 1. Nov 1925. [Registration issue]   **787**
     BM-N

Amateur Theatrical World.   Ed by F. Lloyd. London: Printed by Gibbs & Bamforth, Ltd., St. Albans for the National Amateur Operatic and Dramatic Society.
Vol 1. No 1. Nov 1925. [Registration issue]   **788**
     BM-N

Argus.   Political, financial, satirical and theatrical. London: [Haringey] Nos 1–15.
Oct 1925 – Dec 1926. Monthly.   **789**
     BM-N

Birmingham Repertory Theatre News-letter.   By A. Bland. Birmingham. Nos 1–8.
Apr 1925 – June 1926. Irregular.   **790**
     BP

Broadstairs Day By Day.   Broadstairs. Vol 1. Nos 1–24. [9] Apr – 18 Sept 1925.
[Plus a Christmas issue, 18 Dec 1925] Weekly. [Issued weekly in Broadstairs
and St. Peter's]   **791**
     BM-N

The Gilbert and Sullivan Journal.   (Gilbert and Sullivan Society) London: Vols
1–2. [Nos 1–24] Feb 1925 – Dec 1930. Quarterly.   **792**
     BM, NN, O

London Amusements.   What's on at the theatres, variety halls, cinemas, cabarets,
dances, concerts, exhibitions, Etc. London: Printed for The Hereford Times
Ltd., London, Hereford, and Published by the Proprietors *London Amusements*, 10, Lancaster Place, Strand, W.C. Sept 1925. [Registration issue] Vol 1.
Nos 1–10. 14 Nov 1925 – 16 Jan 1926. Weekly.   **793**
     BM-N

The Manager and Stage Business Gazette. A weekly journal devoted exclusively
to the interests of managers resident and touring. Preston. Nos 1–14. 20 May –
19 Aug 1925. Weekly. [Nos 4–8 printed at Manchester]   **794**
    BM-N

The Manchester Playgoer. A monthly review of the stage, screen and sport.
Manchester. Nos 1–5. Mar – July 1925. Monthly.   **795**
    MP

The Midlander. An illustrated review of sport, drama and society in the Midlands. Birmingham. Vols 1–5, No 10. Oct 1925 – Nov 1930. Monthly.   ***795a***
    BM-N, BP

Our Plays and Players. London: Published by S. Presbury & Co., for the Theatre
Advertising Co., Albany Mansion, 87, Charing Cross Road, W.C. 2. Nos [1]–3.
Oct – Dec 1925. Monthly. [This includes a registration issue dated, June 1925.
The first issue, June, is edited by Tom Hood. The other issues are edited by
William Peacock, and are for The Grand Opera House, Harrogate]   **796**
    BM-N

Parade. [The Royal Academy of Dramatic Art] Ed by Rosemary Blackadder.
London: "Parade." The Royal Academy of Dramatic Art, 62–64 Gower St. Vol 1.
No 1. May 1925.   **797**
    BM

The Show. King's Theatre, Southsea. Monthly Programme. Ed by Charles Clarke.
London: Published by S. Presbury & Co., for the Theatre Advertising Co.,
Albany Mansion, 87, Charing Cross Road, W.C. 2 [Nos 1–12] Nov 1925 – Oct
1926. [Including a registration issue dated, 25 June 1925, which was edited by
Alfred Collins]   **798**
    BM-N

The Theatre World and Illustrated Stage Review. (An illustrated monthly review
of London's Theatres.) Edited by Sheridan-Bickers ("Yorick"). London: The
Claremont Publishing Co., Ltd. Vols [1]–4. Nos 1–20. Feb 1925 – Sept 1926.
Monthly. [Absorbed, *Theatre and Film.* The subtitle varies. Sheridan-Bickers is
editor through No 6, July 1925. From that time forward, the editorials are signed
with the initials "S.T.H."]   **799**
    BM-N, C, O

What's On? A weekly guide to Edinburgh entertainments. Edinburgh. Nos 1–59.
25 Oct 1925 – 19 Dec 1926. Weekly.   ***800***
    E (missing Nos 5–6, 8–10, 15, 24, 27, 43–46, 57–58)

What's On in Southsea & Portsmouth District. One week's amusement ahead.
Portsmouth: W. H. Barrell, Ltd., Printers. [Nos 1]–7. 16 Feb – 30 Mar 1925.
Weekly.   ***801***
    BM-N

1926

The Amateur Stage. London: Printed by Gibbs & Bamforth, Ltd., St. Albans for
the National Operatic and Dramatic Association. Vols 1–4. Nos 1–48. Jan 1926 –
Dec 1929. Monthly. [Includes a registration number listed as, Vol 1, No 1, and

dated, Nov 1925. This number, termed a weekly, is edited by F. Lloyd, and is printed for the National Amateur Operatic and Dramatic Association]   *802*
> BM-N, CaOTP, NN

The Ball Room. Theatre and dancing news. Ed by W. Edmund Querry. London. Vol 7. Nos 1–12. Jan – Dec 1926. Monthly. [I have been unable to locate any numbers published before Jan 1926]   *803*
> BM

The Festival Theatre Review. Cambridge. Vols 1–3. Nos 1–63. Nov 1926 – June 1929. then, *The Festival Theatre Programme.* Vols 1–2, No 7. Oct 1929 – 1930. then, *Festival Theatre Review!* Vol 4, No 64 – Vol 6, No 87. 1930 – 1931. then, *Festival Theatre Programme.* Nos 2–8. [No 1 is really Vol 6, No 87, of above] Jan – June 1932. then, *Festival Gate Review.* Vol 6, Nos 87–94. Oct – Dec 1932. then, *Festival Review.* Vol 6, Nos 95–109. 16 Jan – 5 June 1933. then, *Festival Theatre* (new lease) *Programme.* Nos 1–49. Oct 1933 – June 1935. Monthly. [Supplement, *The Festival Theatre Review'd.* 20 May 1927]   *804*
> BM (incomplete), C, CoU, NFQC, O

Theatrical News. Liverpool. Nos 1–8. 23 June – 11 Aug 1926. then, *Theatrical Observer.* Nos 1–10. 18 Aug – 20 Oct 1926. Weekly.   *805*
> BM-N, LvP

1927

The Alexandra Journal. A monthly record of the activities of Leon Salberg's repertory company of Birmingham. Birmingham. Vols 1–4. Nos 1–43. Oct 1927 – July 1932. Irregular.   *806*
> BP

Cylchgrawn Undeb y Ddrama Gymreig. [Welsh Drama League] Swansea. 1927 –   . [I have been unable to locate any further information regarding this periodical]   *807*
> BM (destroyed)

The Dragoman. [What's On in London Today] London: Vols 1–4. Nos 1–37. Jan 1927 – Jan 1930. Monthly.   *808*
> BM

Edward Bagshawe's Magical Journal. London. Vols 1–6, No 6. Aug/Sept 1927 – June/July 1933. Bimonthly (irregular).   *809*
> BM (destroyed)

The Glasgow Entertainment Guide. Glasgow: Published by Universal Advertising Service, 148 Renfield Street. Vols 1–2. Nos 1–151. 7 Nov 1927 – 6 Oct 1930. Weekly.   *810*
> BM-N (missing Vol 1, Nos 2, 5; Vol 2, Nos 117–120, 130–133, 141–143)

Ilford and District Shoppers' Guide & Amusement Programme. Ilford. Nos 1–8. May – Dec 1927. Monthly.   *810a*
> BM-N

The Music Box and British Entertainer. Incorporating "The Entertainment World." A Publication dealing with all that matters in the Realm of Entertain-

ment. [Nos 3–4 are edited by Edward Eve] London: Published for the Proprietor by G. Street & Co., Ltd., at Vernon House, Sicilian Avenue, Southampton Row, W.C. 1, and Printed for them by the Sidney Press, Bedford. Vol 1, Nos 1–4. June – Sept 1927. Monthly.   *811*
BM

The Panton Magazine.   Literature, art, music, drama. London. Vol 1. Nos 1–4. Jan/Mar – Oct/Dec 1927. Quarterly.   *812*
BM, C, NN

Southend Guide to What's On.   Southend. Vol 1. Nos 1–16. 26 Feb – 11 June 1927. Weekly.   *812a*
BM-N

"The Spotlight" Casting Directory for Stage and Screen.   London: Published by W. Keith Moss. Nos 1–90. Aug 1927 – July 1952. Quarterly [Nos 1–61. Aug 1927 – Sept 1942]; three times a year [Nos 62–89. 1942 – 1951. Beginning with No 71, Jan 1946, each number has two parts]. then, *"The Spotlight" Casting Directory for Stage, Screen, Radio and Television.* Nos 91–109. Jan 1953 – Spring 1962. [Beginning with No 102, Autumn, 1958, each number has four parts]. then, *Spotlight.* Nos 110 –   . Autumn 1962 –   . Twice a year [beginning with No 89. Jan 1952]   *813*
BM

14 Apr – 15 Sept 1927. Weekly.   *813a*
What's On.   (Chatham, Gillingham, Rochester and Strood). Chatham. Nos 1–23.
BM-N

What's On.   London. No 1. 8 July 1927.   *814*
BM-N

What's On in Maidstone.   Maidstone. Nos 1–11. 26 Feb – 12 May 1927. then, *Maidstone and District What's On.* Nos 12–282. 19 May 1927 – 14 July 1932. then, *Maidstone Day by Day.* Nos 283–304, 565–690. 21 July – 27 Dec 1932; 6 Jan 1938 – 6 June 1940. then, *Maidstone and District Day by Day.* Nos 691–877. 10 Nov 1947 – Nov 1963. Weekly (irregular)   *814a*
BM-N

Y Llwyfan!   Cylchgrawn Undeb y Ddrama Gymreig; Magazine of the Welsh Drama League. Swansea. Nos 1–8. Dec 1927 – Feb/Mar 1929. Irregular.   *815*
BM (incomplete), D, O

1928

The Amateur Dramatic Year Book and Community Theatre Handbook. 1928–9. Ed by G. W. Bishop. Under the auspices of the British Drama League. London: A. & C. Black. 1928/29. Annual.   *816*
BM, BP, C, E, LGU, LvP, MP, NN, O, SP

The Free Critic: Literature, Art, Music, Drama.   London. Vol 1. Nos 1–12. Mar 1928 – Feb 1929. then, *The Critic.* Vol 2. Nos 1–2. Mar – Apr 1929. Monthly. *817*
BM, C, NN, O

The Dancer. (Official journal of the British Ballet Organization) Ed by Louisa Kay Espinosa. London. Vols 1–10, No 12. Jan [?] 1928 – Dec 1937. Monthly. *818*
BM (missing Vol 1, Nos 1–10; Vols 2–5), NN ([4], 5)

Hardey's Universal Theatrical Directory. Cheltenham: Published by George Hardey, Graham & Co., Limited. First Edition. 1928.   *819*
BM

Hastings Day by Day. Margate. Vol 1. No 1. 16 Apr 1928.   *819a*
BM-N

The Shakespeare Pictorial and Visitors' Weekly Guide. Stratford-Upon-Avon: E. P. Ray. Nos 1–4. 23 May – 13 June 1928. then, *The Shakespeare Pictorial.* A monthly illustrated chronicle. Nos 5–139. July 1929 – Sept 1939. then, *The Shakespeare Pictorial Occasional Papers.* New Series. Vols 1–10. Nos 1–53. [July 1940] – Sept 1946. then, *The Shakespeare Pictorial.* An intimate monthly chronicle of events in Shakespeareland. Nos 54–60. Feb/Mar – Sept 1946. Monthly. [Subsequently incorporated in, *Stratford-upon-Avon Scene*]   *820*
BM (incomplete), BP, DLC, ICU, NN

The Shakespeare Review; a Monthly Magazine Devoted to Literature and the Drama. Ed by A. K. Chesterton. Stratford-on-Avon: The Shakespeare Review. Nos 1–6. May – Oct 1928. Monthly.   *821*
BM (missing Nos 3, 5), BP, C, Cst, CaQMM, O

The St. Pancras People's Theatre Magazine. London. Vol 1–   . 1928 –   [?] [I have not been able to obtain any further information regarding this periodical]
BM (destroyed)   *822*

Theatre and Film Illustrated. London. Vols 1–4. [Nos 1–24] Feb 1928 – Mar 1930. Monthly. [Merged in, *Theatre World*]   *823*
BM-N

The Theatre Manager's Handbook. Compiled and edited by James M. Glover. London: Published by the editor at 19, Sackville Street, Piccadilly, W. 1. 1st ed. 1928.   *824*
LU-MM

The Theatrical Manager. With which is incorporated, *The Acting Manager and Musical Director.* The official organ of the association of touring and producing managers. London. Vols 1–2. Nos 1–18. Dec 1928 – Jan 1931. Monthly (irregular)   *825*
NN

What's On in Tottenham. Tottenham. Nos 1–75. Aug 1928 – Feb 1935. Monthly.
BM-N   *826*

1929

Current Events: an Authentic Guide to All That Is Going on in Birmingham. Birmingham. Vol 1. Nos 1–7. Jan – July 1929. Monthly.   *827*
BM, BP

Everyman.   Books, drama, music, travel. London. Nos 1–243. 31 Jan 1929 – 23 Sept 1933. Weekly. then, *Everyman.* The world news weekly. New Series. Nos 1–54. 29 Sept 1933 – 5 Oct 1934. New Series (Series 3). Nos 1–32. 12 Oct 1934 – 17 May 1935.   *828*
> BM-N, NN (1-New Series; Series 3. Nos 20–23)

The Festival Theatre Programme.   Anmer Hall's Company. Cambridge. Vol 1. Nos 1–24. [12 Oct] 1929 – 14 June 1930. Weekly (irregular).   *829*
> BM (missing Nos 1–2, 4–6, 13–18, 20–23)

Malvern Festival.   Worthing: Printed by M. T. Stevens, Ltd., Malvern, and Published by Advisers, Ltd., Worthing. 1929 – 1939. Annual.   *830*
> BiR

Pictures, Pleasures, Pastimes.   An indispensable guide to London's amusements. London. [Nos 1]–20. Oct 1929 – June 1931. Monthly. [The subtitle varies] *831*
> BM

Plays and Players.   Director: B. W. Findon. London: Printed for the Proprietors, Findon Ltd., by Williams, Lea & Co., Ltd., Clifton House, Worship Street, E.C. 2, and Published by Findons Ltd., 9 Adam Street, Strand, W.C. 2. Vols 1–3, No 24. 19 Oct 1929 – 19 Sept 1933. Monthly.   *832*
> BM, O

The Prince of Wales Courier.   Published by the Prince of Wales Theatre. Birmingham. Nos 1–31. July 1929 – Mar 1934. Irregular.   *833*
> BP

The Royal Tatler: Gossip about Coming Attractions at the Theatre Royal, Birmingham.   Birmingham. Nos 1–44. Mar 1929 – Dec 1936. Irregular. Nos 1–15. Nov 1936 – Aug/Sept 1939. then, Apr/May 1947 – Dec 1948 [?] [There is an overlap in numbering: Dec 1936 is called No 44, and also 3rd issue. Presumably Nov 1936 [No 43] is 1st issue, and Nov – Dec 1936 [No 43] is 2nd issue, although neither bear this numbering]   *834*
> BP

Salisbury Observer and What's On.   Salisbury. Nos 1–2. Nov – Dec 1929. Monthly.
> BM-N   *834a*

Shakespeare Club.   Annual Report. For the Session 1928–29, together with a summary of papers read before the club, and the Shakespeare sermon. Stratford-Upon-Avon. [Nos 1–7] 1928/29 – 1934/35. Annual.   *835*
> BM

The Theatrical Artistes Road Book and Medical List.   London: Theatrical Organising Co. [Vols 1–5] 1929 – 1939. Irregular.   *836*
> BM

1930

The Arcadia, Doncaster, Monthly Post.   [Issued by the Arcadia Theatre, Doncaster] Doncaster. Vols 1–2. Nos 1–12. June 1930 – May 1931. Monthly.   *837*
> BM-N

Avon News. Stratford-upon-Avon. Issued as a supplement to, *Shakespeare Pictorial.* Nos 1–56. 26 Mar 1930 – 21 Apr 1931. Weekly.   ***838***
  NN

The Call Board. The quarterly organ of the actor's church union. London. Nos 1–32. Feb 1930 – Nov 1937. Quarterly.   ***839***
  BM

The Clarion; Politics, Books, Drama, the Open Road. London. Vols 1– . 1930 – . Monthly.   ***840***
  NN

The Erith, Belvedere and District Free Press and Entertainment Guide. London [Bexley] Vols 1–17. Nos 1–364. 15 Nov 1930 – 30 Oct 1937. Weekly. then, *The Bexley and Erith Bulletin.* Vols 7–9. Nos 365–385. Dec 1937 – Aug 1939. Monthly.
  BM-N   ***841***

The Malvern Theatres Monthly Post. Malvern. Nos 1– . 1930 – . Monthly. [I have not been able to determine the numbers or the dates of the issues published]   ***842***
  BM (destroyed)

The Operatic Association Gazette. The official organ of the association of operatic dancing of Great Britain. London. Vols 1– . 1930 – . Quarterly.   ***843***
  BM (begins May 1941)

The Rep. The journal of the Repertory Theatre Co., Ltd. Newcastle upon Tyne. Vol 1. Nos 1–9. Jan – May 1930. Vol 2. Nos 1–12. Aug 1930 – Jan 1931. Biweekly.
  NwP   ***844***

The Scottish Stage. The journal of the drama in Scotland. [Scottish community drama association] Glasgow: Printed by Aird & Coghill, Ltd., 24 Douglas Street, for the Publishers "The Scottish Stage," 227 Bath Street. Vols 1–4, No 1 [Nos 1–37] Sept 1930 – May 1934. Monthly. [Merged in, *The Amateur Theatre.* The sub-title varies. The printer changes]   ***845***
  BM (destroyed), EP, NN, O

The Week-End Review of Politics, Books, the Theatre, Art and Music. London. Vols 1–8. Nos 1–200. 15 Mar 1930 – 6 Jan 1934. Weekly. [Incorporated with, *The New Statesman*]   ***846***
  BM-N, CU, CaOOP, ICN, MBAt, MH, NB, NN

What's On and Where. London: Printed by King & Jarrett, Ltd., Holland Street, Blackfriars, S.E. 1, and Published by *What's On and Where,* at Their Office, 1, Mitre Court, Fleet Street, E.C. 4. Vols 1–2. Nos 1–21. Apr 1930 – Feb 1932. Monthly. [The subtitle varies]   ***847***
  BM-N

1931

British Equity . . . Annual Report. British Actors' Equity Association. London. 1931/32 – 1932/33. then, *What Equity Is Doing.* 1935/36 – . Annual.   ***848***
  BM (missing No 1. 1931/32)

Era Screen and Stage Pictorial.   London. Vols 1–2. [Nos 1–16] 29 Apr – 12 Aug
1931. Weekly.   *849*
> EP (missing [Nos 14–16]), NN

The Red Stage.   Organ of the workers' theatre movement. London: Published by
the Workers' Theatre Movement, 59 Cromer St., W.C. 1, printed by Ajax Press,
T.U., 1 Gatton Rd., S.W. 17. Vol 1. Nos 1–5. Nov 1931 – Apr/May 1932. then,
New Red Stage. Nos 6–7. June/July – Sept 1932. Irregular. [The printer changes]
> BM (destroyed), O   *850*

Repertory.   A journal of drama and ideas. Oxford: Printed for the Publishers, the
Oxford Repertory Company, by the Oxford Times, Ltd., New Inn, Hall-street.
[Vols 1]–4, No 5. 18 Apr 1931 – 29 May 1933. Weekly. [With Vol 4, No 1, 1 May
1933, the title appears as, *Repertory.* Official Organ of the Playhouse Guild. As
the Bodleian copy skips from 13 Mar 1933 to 1 May, I cannot be sure of the
exact date the new sub-title was adopted. Thea Holme's name appears as editor
from Vol 2, No 1 – Vol 3, No 8. 5 Oct 1931 – 6 Mar 1933. Stamford Holme was
editor from Vol 4, No 1, to the end. 1 – 29 May 1933. Seemingly the magazine
was not published from Dec 1931 – early Jan 1933]   *850a*
> O (Vol 1, Nos 1–9. 18 Apr – 15 June 1931; Vol 2. Nos 1–9. 12 Oct – 30 Nov 1931; Vol 3.
> Nos 1–8. 23 Jan – 13 Mar 1933; Vol 4, Nos 1–5 [Bodleian missing No 3] 1–29 May 1933)

The "Spotlight" Yearbook.   Ed by W. Keith Moss. London: Published by the
Proprietors of *"The Spotlight" Casting Directory*, Ancaster House, 43, Cranbourn Street, W.C. 2. Vols 1–3. 1931 – 1933. Annual.   *851*
> BM, O (missing Vol 1)

Variety, Music, Stage and Film News.   London. Vols 1–5. Nos 1–106. 2 Sept 1931 –
6 Sept 1933. then, *Variety Cabaret Film News.* Vols 6–8. Nos 107–251. 13 Sept
1933 – 18 June 1936. Weekly.   *852*
> BM-N

What's On in Sheffield and District.   Sheffield. Vol 1. Nos 1–12. Jan – Dec 1931.
Monthly.   *852a*
> BM-N

1932

Amateur Stage.   London. Vols 1–3. Nos 1–13. Dec 1932 – Dec 1933. Monthly.
[Supplement to, and continued in, *Theatre World*]   *853*
> IaU, NN

Amusement World.   [A weekly journal for amusement centers, seaside and pleas-
ure proprietors] London: Printed and Published by the Proprietors, Oldhams
Press, Ltd., Long Acre, W.C. 2. Vol 1. No 1. 22 Jan 1932. then, *Amusement World.*
Professional amusement caterers, showmen, and public entertainers. Vol 1.
Nos 2–7. 29 Jan – 4 Mar 1932. Weekly.   *854*
> BM-N

The Courier.   The magazine of the King's Theatre and Lyceum Theatre. Edinburgh. Vols 1–6, No 1. 1932 – 1939.   *855*
> EP, O (Vol 1, Nos 1–6)

The Courier. The Opera House, Manchester. Edited by Gordon Courtney (Nos 1–2); Francis R. H. Bolton. Manchester: Printed by Whittaker & Robinson Ltd. Vol 1. Nos 1–6. May – Dec 1932. Monthly (irregular) [Advertised as "Manchester's First Theatre House Organ"]   *856*
    BM (destroyed), C, MP (Nos 1–4), O

The Dancer and Cabaret. London. Vol 1. Nos 1–6. July – Dec 1932. Monthly. [Continued as, *Dancing and Film News*]   *857*
    BM (destroyed)

The Garrick Spectator. Southport. No 1. Dec 1932.   *858*
    SptP

The Greater London Players' Magazine. London. 1932. [I have not been able to determine the number or the dates of the various issues]   *859*
    BM (destroyed)

Journal of the English Folk Dance and Song Society. Ed by Frank Howes. London. Vols 1–2. [Nos 1–4] Dec 1932 – International Festival Number, 1935. Annual.   *860*
    BM

The London and Suburban Programme and Amusement Guide. London. No 1. 20 Feb 1932. Weekly.   *861*
    BM

Motley. [The Dublin Gate Theatre Magazine] Ed by Mary Manning. Dublin. Vols 1–3, No 4. Mar 1932 – May 1934. Monthly.   *862*
    BM (destroyed)

Musicians Directory. Incorporating The Dance Musicians Directory. Compiled by David D. Arram, & L. Ash-Lyons. London: Published by The Musicians' Directory. Palace House, 128–132, Shaftesbury Avenue, W. 1. First Issue. Oct 1932. [The foreword says that the magazine is to be issued "twice yearly in March and September . . ." p 5]   *863*
    BM

The Occasional Magazine. Dealing with theatrical matters in general and the Birmingham repertory theatre in particular. Birmingham. Vols 1–2. Nos 1–7. Sept 1932 – Jan 1934. Irregular.   *864*
    BP

Southport Dramatic Club Magazine. Southport. No 1. Sept 1932.   *865*
    SptP

Stage Stars of To-day. Portrayed by Theatre World. London: Printed in Great Britain by Thomas De La Rue & Co., Ltd., 110 Bunhill Row, E.C. 1. First Series. [1932] [This periodical is also listed at the British Museum under, *Theatre World*]   *866*
    BM

Who's Who in Dancing. 1932. Being a list of alphabetically arranged biographies of the leading men and women in the world of dancing. Ed by Arnold Haskell

and P. J. S. Richardson. London: Published by The Dancing Times, Ltd. 1932.
[In the preface the editors look forward to another edition in 1934. The British
Museum lists the work as a periodical]   *867*
    BM

1933

The Amateur Theatrical Review. Incorporating, *Southport Dramatic Club Maga-*
zine. Southport. No 1. Mar 1933.   *868*
    SptP

Davenport's The Demon Telegraph. London: Published by L. Davenport & Co.
Vols 1–6. Nos 1–56. Aug 1933 – Jan 1941. Irregular. then, *The 'Demon' Tele-*
graph. [The Ace Magical Magazine] Nos 57–150. Feb. Mar. Apr 1941 – Dec
1951. [Volume numbers are not used after Volume 6]   *869*
    BM, LU (1943–1948, incomplete)

Let's Go. A weekly review and programme of London's Amusements. London:
Printed by Charles Phipps, Printer, 6 Vicarage Parade, West Green, N. 15, for
the Proprietors and Publishers, Stage & Screen Publicity. Vol 1. No 1. Jan 1933
[registration issue] Vol 1. Nos 1–2. 27 Jan – 3 Feb 1933. Weekly.   *870*
    BM-N

People's National Theatre Magazine. Ed by Nancy Price. London. Vols 1–18,
No 4. Oct 1933 – Winter 1945. Monthly. then, *Pedlars Pack.* Spring 1955 –   .
Quarterly.   *871*
    BM, NN

Poetry Quarterly and Dramatic Review. London. Vol 1. Nos 1–6. Spring 1933 –
Spring 1934. Quarterly.   *872*
    BM, D, E, KyU, NN

The Theatre Illustrated Quarterly. A quarterly illustrated guide and souvenir of
the theatre. London. Published by Keith Prowse and Co., Ltd., 42/43 Poland
St., W. 1, and Printed by Henry Good & Son, Ltd., 33–39 Moor Lane, E.C. 2.
Vols 1–3, No 4. [Nos 1–12] Spring 1933 – Winter 1935. Quarterly.   *873*
    BM

1934

The Amateur Theatre and Playwright's Journal. Edited by John Bourne [Vol 3,
No 54 – Vol 5, No 102. Aug 1936 – 30 Sept 1938] London: Published and
Printed by the Garamond Press, Ltd., Maltravers House, Arundel Street, Strand,
W.C. 2. Vols 1–5. Nos 1–102. 31 Jan 1934 – 30 Sept 1938. Biweekly (Sept – Apr);
Monthly (May – Aug); Irregular. [Each issue contains an original play or
plays. Absorbed, *The Scottish Stage*]   *874*
    BM, BP (missing Vol 3, No 55), NN, WEST (Vols 2–5)

East London Sports and Entertainment Mirror. London. New Series. Nos 1–34.
17 Nov 1934 – 20 July 1935. Weekly.   *875*
    BM-N

Garraway's Directory of Concert and Variety Artistes.   London. 1934. [I have not been able to discover any additional information regarding this periodical] *876*
BM (missing from shelf)

Goldston's Magical Quarterly.   [Supersedes the, *Magazine of Magic.* Official Organ of the Magician's Club, London] Ed by Will Goldston. London. Vols 1–6, No 4. June 1934 – Sept 1940. Quarterly. *877*
BM, NN

The Journal of the Institute of Magicians.   Ed by W. J. Giddins, Dec 1945 – May 1949; W. H. Gent, Aug 1949 – Mar/Apr 1956. London: Edited and Published by The Institute of Magicians. Nos 1–15. 1934 – June 1940. [No more published until 1945] Nos 1–58. Dec 1945 – Mar 1956. [The numbering begins anew with the issue of Dec 1945] Quarterly. [Both printed issues and issues reproduced from typewritten copy] *878*
BM

London School of Dramatic Art Magazine.   Ed by G. Shaw-Mackenzie [Vol 1, Nos 1–14]; Ed by M. Love [Vol 2, Nos 1–4] London. Vols 1–2. [Nos 1–18] Jan/ Mar 1934 – Spring 1939. Irregular. *879*
BM

The Modern Dance.   London. Vols 1–4, No 3. 1934 – Dec 1937. then, *The Modern Dance and the Dancer.* Vols 4, No 4 – Vol 31, No 8. Jan 1938 – June 1965. Monthly. [The journal had a succession of editors] *880*
BM (missing all before Vol 2, No 3. Dec 1935)

Rep.   [The Magazine of the Westminster & Croydon Theatre] Croydon. Vol 1–   .
1934 –   . *881*
CROY

The Scottish Amateur Theatre and Playwright's Journal.   London. Vols 1–5. Nos 1–102. 1934 – 30 Sept 1938. Bimonthly. *882*
EP

Sheffield Repertory Company.   Repertory News. Sheffield. Nos 1–90. 15 Sept 1934 – Aug 1938. then, *Playhouse News.* Nos 91–121. 1 Sept 1938 – 6 Apr 1940. Biweekly [in general. Published before each production] *883*
SP

The Spotlight Gazette of Artists at Liberty or Open to Offers.   A supplementary service to Spotlight Casting Directory, etc. London: Ancaster House, 43, Cranbourn Street, W.C. 2. Nos 126, 141, 153. 4 Oct 1934; 19 June 1935; 15 Jan 1936. [Reproduced from typewritten copy. These are the only numbers of the periodical which I have been able to locate] *884*
BM

1935

The Authors', Playwrights, & Composers' Handbook for 1935.   Compiled and Edited by D. Kilham Roberts. London: John Lane. [Vols 1–6] 1935 – 1940. Annual. *885*
BM

Dance Tone. London. Vol 1. Nos 1–2. Mar – Apr 1935. Monthly.   *886*
> BM (destroyed)

East Surrey and District Entertainment Guide. London [Croydon] Nos 1–20.
2 Nov 1935 – 22 Aug 1936. then, *Croydon Entertainment Guide.* Nos 21–35.
19 Sept 1936 – Aug 1937. Irregular.   *887*
> BM-N

The Hippodrome Tatler. Coventry. Vols 1–3. Nos 1–22. July 1935 – Sept 1939.
then, *Theatre News.* Vol 4. Nos 23–28. Nov 1939 – Apr 1940. Monthly.   *888*
> CvP (missing Aug 1938, Dec 1939, or Jan 1940, and Mar or Apr 1940)

London Sports and Entertainments Mirror. London: Printed by The Wimbley
News, Ltd., 12, Neeld Parade, Wembley, and Published by the Proprietors,
London Sports and Entertainments Mirror, 131, Fleet Street, E.C. 1. Nos 1–29.
27 July 1935 – 7 Feb 1936. Weekly.   *889*
> BM-N

London Week. [A guide to London entertainments] London. Vols 1–2, No 52.
15/24 Mar 1935 – 18/24 Sept 1936. Weekly. then, *What's On.* Vol 3, Nos 53–79.
25 Sept/1 Oct 1936 – 26 Mar/1 Apr 1937. then, *What's On in London.* Vol 3,
No 80– . 8 Apr 1937 –   .   *890*
> BM

The London Weekly Programme and Guide to Theatres, Cinemas, Dances, Caba-
ret Shows, Exhibitions, Sport Events and All Amusements and Attractions.
London: Strange the Printer, Ltd., 59, New Oxford Street, W.C.1. Nos 1–35.
1 Feb – 27 Sept/5 Oct 1935. Weekly.   *891*
> BM, O

The Manchester Repertory Theatre Magazine. Manchester. Vols 1–2. 1935/36 –
1937/38. Annual.   *892*
> MP

The Mime Review. A quarterly magazine for those interested in the study and
practice of the art of mime. West Dulwich. Vols 1–3. [Nos 1–16] July 1935 –
Apr 1939. Quarterly. [Merged with, *School Drama.* May/Sept 1939]   *893*
> BM (destroyed), NN

N.O.D.A. Bulletin. The official organ of The National Operatic & Dramatic Association. London. Vol 1. No 1–   . Sept 1935 –   . Irregular. [From Vols 1–4,
No 9. Sept 1935 – May 1939, nine issues a year. Monthly, Sept – May. Then
sporadic issues during the war, and post-war years. Seven issues from Jan 1940 –
Oct 1946. There is no numbered Volume 5. Three issues a year from 1946 to
the present]   *894*
> BM, O (missing all before 1955)

The Oxford Repertory Company Limited. Oxford. Annual Report and Statement
of Accounts. [Nos 1–2] 1934 – 1935, 1936 – 1937. Annual. [Apparently no number was issued for 1935 – 1936]   *895*
> BM

Piping and Dancing. A monthly journal for pipers, dancers & drummers. Ardros-
san. Vols 1–6, No 6. Aug 1935 – Feb 1941. Monthly.   *896*
> BM

"The Spotlight" Pocket Telephone Directory of Subscribers. Also of the London theatres, film companies, and film studios. London. [Vol 1. Nos 1–2] Summer – Autumn 1935. then, *"The Spotlight" Pocket Telephone Directory of Advertisers.* Also of the London theatres, film companies, and film studios. [Vol 1, No 3 – Vol 2, No 4] Winter 1935 – Winter 1936. Quarterly.   **897**
   BM

Theatre Royal: Brighton Repertory Theatre Magazine. Brighton. Nos 1–5. Feb – May, July 1935. Monthly.   **898**
   BiP

Voici Londres. London. [Nos 1–3] May – D'Eté 1935.   **899**
   BM

What's On in London. London. Vols 1–   . 1935 –   . Weekly. [Volume numbering ceased with Vol 21, Mar 1950]   **900**
   CROY, EALG

1936

Beckenham and Penge Entertainment Guide. London [Bromley] Nos 25–28. 14 Nov 1936 – 2 Jan 1937. Irregular. [I have been unable to locate the earlier numbers of the periodical]   **901**
   BM-N

English Dance and Song. The magazine of the English Folk Dance and Song Society. London. Vol 1. Nos 1–   . Sept 1936 –   . Monthly (and bimonthly). [Supersedes, *English Folk Dance Society News*]   **902**
   DLC, ICN, ICU, IU, MB, MH, MnU, MoU, NN, NNC, NbU, NcD, NjP, OCL, OU, ViU

Garrick Magazine. A periodical for the members of the Altrincham Garrick Society. London. Vol 1. Nos 1–7. Oct 1936 – Nov 1937. Bimonthly (irregular).
   BM (destroyed)   **903**

The Highbury Players' Bulletin. Sutton Coldfield. Nos 1–17. Mar 1936 – July 1937. then, *The Highbury Bulletin.* Aug 1937 –   . Monthly. [Reproduced from typewritten copy]   **904**
   BP

London. Shops, theatres, films, sports. [An entertainment guide] London: Printed by Skinner & Co., Limited, 7, Butler Street, E.C. 2; Published by Crabtree Press, Fleet House, 58, Fleet Street, E.C. 4. Nos 1–5. Christmas Eve 1936/New Year 1937 – 23 Jan 1937. Weekly.   **905**
   BM-N

Purley and Couldson Entertainment Guide. Croydon. Nos 21–28. 19 Sept 1936 – 2 Jan 1937. Biweekly. [I have been unable to discover the earlier numbers of the periodical]   **906**
   BM-N (missing Nos 1–20)

The Southampton Repertory Magazine. Southampton. Nos 1–5. Aug – Dec 1936. Monthly.   **907**
   SoP

Unemployed Drama News.   Introductory issue. Ed by Kathleen Edwards. London: Published by Kathleen Edwards for Unemployed Drama Groups. [1936] Monthly. [A letter in the issue is dated, 1st July 1936]   **908**
   BM

Wallington Entertainment Guide.   Wallington. Nos 25–28. 14 Nov 1936 – 2 Jan 1937. Bi-weekly.   **908a**
   BM-N (missing all before No 25)

What's On in the City.   Manchester, Salford & Districts. A monthly programme for the citizens of and visitors to Manchester & Salford. Manchester. [Vols 1]–7. [Nos 1–80] Apr/May 1936 – Nov 1942. Monthly.   **909**
   BM-N

1937

The Call Sheet.   A casting directory of small-part players. London: Published by The Call Sheet, 66, Shaftesbury Ave. Vol 1. Nos 1–[3] July 1937 – [1938] [Included is an autumn supplement for 1937] Quarterly (irregular).   **910**
   BM

Danceland.   London. Vol 1, No 1 – Vol 3, No 28. Oct 1937 – June 1941. Monthly. then, *Dance News.* Nos 29–68. 19 July 1941 – 18 Apr 1942. then, *Danceland.* Nos 69–139. Sept 1943 – Feb 1952. [There seems to be some evidence which points to the continuation of the periodical to Vol 29, No 42, Apr 1954. *Danceland* was first edited by C. L. Helmann, and Byron Davies, and then by C. St. J. Murphy]   **911**
   BM (very incomplete), NN ([1949] plus)

Friendship.   Kettering: Printed by Messrs. T. Beatty Hart, Ltd. Vols 1–2. Nos 1–15. Aug 1937 – Oct 1938. Monthly. [With Vol 1, No 4, Nov 1937, the size of the page is enlarged. The magazine is printed through Vol 1, No 7, Feb 1938, and mimeographed from Vol 1, No 8, Mar 1938, to the end. The name of Mollie Moncrieff Hart appears as editor with Vol 1, No 5, Dec 1937. She remains the editor to Oct 1938]   **911a**
   BM

The "Little" Magazine.   A monthly publication dedicated to the interests of the Southport dramatic club and the little theatre. Southport. Nos 1–10. 1937 – 1939. Monthly (irregular)   **912**
   SptP (missing Nos 1, 4)

Pastime.   The London entertainment weekly. London: Printed and Published by Periodical Press, Ltd., 48, Fetter Lane, E.C. 4. No 1. 26 Apr 1937. Weekly. **913**
   BM-N

The Theatre.   London. Nos 1–4. 26 May – 16 July 1937. Biweekly.   **914**
   BM-N

Weekly Sporting Review.   London. Nos 1–145, 350–629. 20 Mar 1937 – 1 June 1940; 23 Feb 1946 – 14 July 1951. then, *Show Business and the Weekly Sporting Review.* Nos 630–741. 21 July 1951 – 4 Sept 1953. then, *Weekly Sporting Review*

and Show Business. Nos 742–1094. 11 Sept 1953 – 10 June 1960. [Also Christmas and New Year editions, 1948/49 – 1952/53] Annual.   **915**
BM-N

1938

The Oldham Repertory Club. The Oldham repertory magazine. The official organ of the Oldham repertory club. Oldham. Nos 1–3. Apr – June 1938. Monthly. **916**
BM (destroyed), MP

Perforwritings. P.R.S. [Performing Right Society] Staff Magazine. London. Vols 1–2, No 3. Oct 1938 – Oct 1948. Irregular. [Reproduced from typewritten copy]
BM   **917**

School Drama. London. Vols 1–3. [Nos 1–10] Feb 1938 – May/Sept 1940. Quarterly. [See *Mime Review*]   **918**
BM (destroyed), BP

Theatrecraft. Ed by John Bourne. London: Printed in Great Britain for Theatrecraft, Ltd., by Samuel Temple & Co., Ltd., 2711 King Street, W. 6. [Stratford-upon-Avon for later numbers] Nos 1–32. Dec 1938 – [1942] [The last dated number is Oct/Nov 1941, No 31] Monthly [Nos 1–28. Dec 1928 – Mar 1941]; Quarterly [Nos 29–32. June 1941 – 1942. The issues contain a one act play. No 32 really incorporates the Newsletter]   **919**
BM (missing Nos 11–28), E

Theatre Forum. A Bi-Monthly Magazine. Oxford: Published by Frederick Farley and Eric Hobbs, at 187 Divinity Road. Vol 1. Nos 1–4. June/July – Dec 1938/Jan 1939. Bi-monthly.   **919a**
O

1939

A.C.U. Paper. [The quarterly news sheet of the actor's church union] London. Nos 1–83. Nov 1939 – Sept 1955. Quarterly.   **920**
BM (missing Nos 41, 63–64)

Ballet. London: Edited and Published by Richard Buckle at 107 Charlotte Street. [Vol 1] Nos 1–2. July/Aug – Sept/Oct 1939. [No more published until 1946] [Vol 1], No 3 – Vol 12, No 10. Jan 1946 – Oct 1952. Monthly. [Index for Vols 1–6, 1939 – 1948, in 1948. In Oct 1948, the title became, *Ballet and Opera.* In January 1950 the title became once again, *Ballet*]   **921**
BM (Vols 1–10), E, FU, LU, NN

The British Ballet Organization Bulletin. London: Published by the British Ballet Organization. Woolborough House, 39 Lonsdale Road, S.W. 13. 1939 –   .
Quarterly [with some irregularities]   **922**
BM (missing Vols 1–3, No 8)

British Puppet and Model Theatre Guild. Wartime Bulletin. London. Nos 1–17. 1939 – 1945. Irregular. then, *The Puppet Master.* The journal of the British Puppet and Model Theatre Guild. Ed by Arthur E. Peterson. Vol 1, No –   .
Jan 1946 –   . Quarterly.   **923**
BM (missing Nos 1–15), CaQMM (missing Nos 15–16), NN (missing Nos 1–11)

Dance Review. A News-Magazine. London. Vols 1–2, No 9 [13 issues] Mar 1939 –
June 1940. Monthly.   **924**
    BM (destroyed)

*New Theatre; a Magazine Devoted to the Interests of the Modern Theatre and
Associated Arts.* London. Vol 1. Nos 1–2. Aug – Sept 1939. Monthly. [Sus-
pended publication, Sept 1939 – Dec 1945] Vols 2–5. [Nos 1–44] Jan 1946 – July
1949.   **925**
    BM, E, MH, NN

The Repertory World. The magazine for the repertorygoer. York. 1939. [I have
not been able to discover any additional material concerning this periodical]
    BM (destroyed)   **925a**

Theatre. London. Nos 1–2. 24 Feb – 24 Mar 1939. Monthly.   **926**
    BM-N

War-time Drama; an Occasional Bulletin from the British Drama League. London. Nos 1–39. [No 32 is repeated in the numbering] Oct 1939 – Feb 1946.
Irregular. [Issued during the temporary suspension (due to the war) of *Drama,*
a monthly record of the theatre in town and country at home and abroad. The
subtitle varies slightly. Nos 35–36. May – July 1945, the title is, *VE-Time Drama.*
No 37. Oct 1945, the title is, *VJ-Time Drama.* Nos 38–39. Nov 1945 – Feb 1946,
the title is, *Interim Drama*]   **927**
    BM (incomplete), NN

1940

C.E.M.A. Bulletin. London. Nos 1–62. May 1940 – June 1945. [The title varies
slightly]. then, *The Arts Council of Great Britain Monthly Bulletin.* Nos 64–71.
Aug 1945 – Mar 1946. then, *The Arts Council Bulletin.* Nos 72–140. Apr 1946 –
Dec 1951. Monthly.   **928**
    BM (missing Nos 24–26, 28, 30, 31, 43, 45, 57, 58, 67, 90, 96), NN (missing Nos 1–30),
    NjP, NNFr

London Off Duty. London. [Vol 1. No 1]–Vol 7, No 2. Spring 1940 – Spring 1947.
then, *London Leisure.* Vol 7, No 3 – Vol 10, No 6. 5 May 1947 – Dec/Jan 1951.
Irregular. [Larger format, beginning with Vol 8, No 3. May 1948]   **929**
    BM, O

Merseyside Unity Theatre. Membership Bulletin. Liverpool. 1940 – 1948. New
Series. 1948 –   . Monthly [occasionally bimonthly. Reproduced from typewritten copy]   **930**
    LvP (missing all before 1948)

Parados. The gateway to dance and drama. The journal of the Greek Dance Asso-
ciation, The Institute of Mime, The Old Ginner-Mawer Club, The Ginner-
Mawer School, and of all interested in the dance and drama. London. Vol 1.
Nos 1–25. Oct 1940 – Sept 1949. Irregular. [Originally *The Link*]   **931**
    BM

Top-Spin. A periodical devoted to the interests of North London Dancers. [Pub-
lished by the Royal Dance Hall, Tottenham] London [Haringey] Nos 1–3.
1 Apr – 1 June 1940. Monthly.   **932**
    BM-N

1941

British Puppet and Model Theatre Guild Junior News. Worcester. Nos 1–2. 1941 – 1942.   **933**
   CaQMM

Commentary. The Magazine of the Picture Hire Club. A Causerie for Artists, Actors, Picture Lovers, Playgoers and Writers. Edited by Sean Dorman. Dublin: Trueman's Gallery, 24 Molesworth Street. Vol 1. No 1. Nov 1941. then, *Commentary.* Art. Drama. Literature. The Magazine of the Picture Hire Club. Vol 1. No 2. Dec 1941. then, *Commentary.* Art. Drama. Literature. Vol 1. Nos 3–6. Jan – June 1942. then, *Commentary.* Ballet, Drama, Painting. Vol 1. Nos 7–8. June – July 1942. then, *Commentary.* Literature. Music. Theatre. Vol 1. No 9. Aug 1942. then, *Commentary.* Literature. Music. Painting. Vol 1. No 10 – Vol 5, No 3. Sept 1942 – Mar 1946. [Sub-title continues to change]. then, *Irish Commentary.* Vol 5, No 4 – Vol 6, No 2. Apr 1946 – Feb 1947. then, *Irish Cinema,* Vol 6, Nos 3–4. Mar – Apr 1947 [Publisher and place of publication varies] Monthly.   **933a**
   BM, GaU

Gazette. The Royal Academy of Dancing. London. Nos 43–   . May 1941 –   . [I have not been able to locate any earlier numbers] Quarterly (irregular). **934**
   BM (missing all before No 43)

The Magical Gazette. Official organ of the London Society of Magicians. London. Vols 1–2, No 3. Nov 1941 – Jan 1943. Monthly. [Reproduced from typewritten copy] New Series. Vols 1–17, No 8. Dec 1946 – Sept/Oct 1963. Monthly (irregular).   **935**
   BM (missing New Series, Vol 1, Nos 1–11)

Theatrecraft News-Letter. Supplement[s] to *Theatrecraft.* Nos 29–30. June – Aug 1941. Ed by John Bourne. London: Printed in Great Britain for Theatrecraft, Ltd., by Samuel Temple & Co., Ltd., 2711 King Street, W. 6. Quarterly. [Editorial Office: Stratford-upon-Avon]   **936**
   BM

1943

Flash Backs from "London off Duty." London. [Nos 1–2] July 1943 – June 1945. Annual (irregular).   **937**
   BM

The Prompter. The bulletin of the Citizens' Theatre Society. Glasgow. Nos 1–89. Nov 1943 – Jan 1957. Monthly [somewhat irregular in early issues, and very irregular in later numbers. The title was adopted with No 7, the earlier issues being nameless]   **938**
   GM

Tabs. Published in the interests of the theatre by The Strand Electric and Engineering Co., Ltd. London: The Strand Electric & Engineering Co., Ltd., 29 King Street, Covent Garden, W. 2. Vol 1, No 1–   . 1943 –   . Irregular.   **939**
   BM (missing all before Vol 18, No 3), WiM (4–   .), NN ([1–3] 17 plus), WmP (4 plus)

What's On in Birmingham. (Birmingham Hospitality Committee) Birmingham. Nos 1–135. 21 Nov 1943 – 23 June 1946. then, *What's On in Birmingham: Programme of Events in the City.* Birmingham: Published by the City of Birmingham Information Department. 30 June 1946 –   . Weekly.   ***940***
  BP

1944

The Cornish Pixie. A tract on white magic for magicians only. Ed by Vivian St. John. Wolverhampton. Vols 1–[2] Nos 1–45. 19 Jan 1944 – Sept 1946. Monthly. [Reproduced from typewritten copy]   ***941***
  BM

Puppet Year Book. Educational Puppetry Association. London: Educational Puppetry Association, 41, Mowbray Road, Brondesbury, N.W. 6. Nos 1–2. 1944/45 – 1946. [No 1 is edited by Ellen M. Marks; No 2 is edited by Ellen M. Codlin] Annual. [The title on both covers is, *EPA Year Book*]   ***942***
  BM

1945

Ballet. The Russian ballet league periodical. Tunbridge Wells: Published by Roxburgh Press. Vol 1, No 1 – Vol 2, No 9. Sept 1945 – Sept 1947. then, *Ballet World.* Ed by Mme. Nicolaeva-Legat. Vol 1. Nos 1–4. Sept 1948 – Summer 1949. Quarterly.   ***943***
  BM, BP

Footlights. Coventry. Vols 1–7. Nos 1–68. Mar 1945 – June/July 1951. Monthly. [Formerly, *Coventry Amateur Stage: a Magazine of Amateur Drama and Opera*]
  CvP   ***944***

The London Artiste. The medium between the artiste and the booker. London. Vols 1–9, No 3. 1945 [?] – Feb 1954. then, *The London Artiste and General Advertiser.* Vol 9, Nos 4–5. Mar – Apr 1954. Monthly. [Vol 9, No 5. Apr 1954, the editor announced that the magazine was for sale]   ***945***
  BM (missing all before Vol 6, No 3)

The Prompter. Southampton: Published by the Southampton Theatre Guild. No 1–   . Oct 1945 –   . Monthly. [The early numbers are reproduced from typewritten copy. Printed since July 1946]   ***946***
  SoP

Script. The journal of the association of Ulster dramatic societies. Belfast. Nos 1–4. Feb – June 1945. New Series. Sept 1945 – May 1948. Monthly.   ***947***
  Not located (Loewenberg p 62)

Theatre. Bradford: Issued from the Bradford civic playhouse. Nos 1–11. July 1945 – Winter 1948. Three issues a year. [No 2, Winter 1945/46, lacks numbering]   ***948***
  BM, BP, LdP, NN (incomplete), O (Nos 1–8), WmP, WEST

Theatre Notebook: a Quarterly of Notes and Research. London: Published for subscribers only by I. K. Fletcher. Vol 1–   . 1945 –   . Quarterly. [Includes the, *Bulletin* of the Society for Theatre Research]   ***949***
  BM, BP, BU, C, CtY, DFo, IEN, NN, NNC, O

1946

Abracadabra. The only magical weekly in the world. Ed by Goodliffe. Birmingham. Vol 1. Nos 1–20. 2 Feb – 15 June 1946. then, *Goodliffe's Abracadabra.* Vol 1. No 21–   . 22 June 1946 –   . Weekly.   *950*
    BM, DLC, NN ([12–18] plus)

The Amateur Stage. Edited by George Taylor. London: Published by Vawser & Wiles, Ltd., Guardian House, Forest Road, E. 17. Vols 1–3, No 12. Sept 1946 – Dec 1948. then, *The Amateur Stage.* The National Independent Monthly Magazine for the Amateur Player, Producer and Playwright. Vol 4, Nos 1–8. Jan – Aug 1949. then, *The Amateur Stage.* The Only National Independent Magazine for the Amateur Theatre. Vol 4, No 9 – Vol 5, No 3. Sept 1949 – Mar 1950. then, *The Amateur Stage.* Vol 5, No 4 – Vol 10, No 12. Apr 1950 – Dec 1955. Monthly [With Vol 5, No 7, July 1950, published by Stacey Publications, 356–8 Kilburn High Road, N.W. 6. With the same issue Roy Stacey became managing editor. An editorial board guided the policies from Vol 4, No 10 – Vol 5, No 6. Oct 1949 – June 1950. The publishing address changes several times]   *951*
    BM, E, NN, O

Ballet Carnaval. London: Pendulum Publications Limited. 10, Old Square, Lincoln's Inn, W.C. 2. Nos 1–6. June 1946 – June/July [1947] Bimonthly. [Ed by A. L. Nash, Nos 1–4. June 1946 – Jan/Feb 1947]   *952*
    BM

Ballet Today. London. Vols 1–17. Mar/Apr 1946 – Nov/Dec 1967. [Ed by P. W. Manchester. Vol 1, No 1 – Vol 5, No 4. Mar/Apr 1946 – Apr 1952; Ed by Peter Craig-Raymond, Oct 1953 – Feb 1955; Ed by Estelle Herf, Apr 1955 –   .] Bimonthly [with some variations]   *953*
    BM, InU, ICN, NN, NwP, O (incomplete before Vol 2)

Behind the Scenes. A monthly review for all tastes. Stage, screen, radio, sport, literature, music. London. Nos 1–11. Dec 1946 – Dec 1947. Monthly. [Issues for August and September are combined into No 8]   *954*
    BM

British Theatre. London. 1946. Annual.   *955*
    BP, FiP, GU, LGU, LU, NwP

Call Boy. Bristol guild of players monthly magazine. Bristol. Vol 1–   . 1946 –   . Monthly.   *956*
    BrP

Christian Drama. (Religious drama society of Great Britain.) London: Published for the Religious Drama Society by the Society for Promoting Christian Knowledge. Vols 1–5, No 1. Nov 1946 – Spring, 1963. Three issues a year. *957*
    BM, O (incomplete), WmP

Con Brio. A Scots magazine for the modern music lover. Glasgow. Vol 1. No 1. [1946]. then, *Con Brio.* The modern magazine for music lovers. Vol 1. Nos 2–3. [1947 – 1948]. then, *Scottish Music & Drama.* Incorporating 'Con Brio.' Nos [4]–6. 1949 – 1951. Annual [beginning with No 6, 1951. The issues for 1949 and 1950 bear no series numeration, and the issue for 1949 bears no date]   *958*
    BM (missing No 1), E (missing No 1), O (missing Nos 1–3)

Dance News Weekly. (Incorporating, *London Dance News, Northern Dance News, and Scottish Dance News.*) Ed by Rowland T. Davis. London. Nos 1–194. 7 Dec 1946 – 2 Sept 1950. then, *Dance News.* 9 Sept 1950 –   . Weekly. **959**
BM-N, NN (1949 plus)

Film and Stage Digest. Glasgow. Nos 1–2. [1946] [No dates are given for the two numbers]   **960**
BM

The Gen. Ed by Harry Stanley. East Barnet. Vol 1. No 1– . [1946?] –   . [No dates appear in Vol 1, Nos 1–12. Vol 2, No 1, is dated Dec 1946] Monthly. [From No 9 on, London: Published by Jack Hughes and Harry Stanley] **961**
BM

The Green Room Mirror. Portsmouth. Nos 1–4. Spring 1946 – Summer 1947. **962**
Not located (Loewenberg p 53)

Lancashire Dance News. Ed by Rowland T. Davis. London: Vol 1. Nos 1–6. 27 Apr – 1 June 1946. Weekly. then, *Northern Dance News.* Nos 7–9. 8 – 22 June 1946. then, *Northern Dance News Weekly.* Nos 10–32. 29 June – 30 Nov 1946.
BM-N   **963**

The Lantern. London. Vol 1. Nos 1–8. Aug 1946 – Mar 1947. then, *The Lantern.* Stage, screen, radio, the arts. Nos 9–[13] June/July – Nov 1947. Monthly. [The last four issues are not numbered]   **964**
BM

Leisure Topix. The real pocket size entertainment monthly. Ed by Victor L. Pettett. London. Nos 1–3. Dec 1946 – [Mar 1947?] Monthly. [No 2 is dated, Jan/Feb 1947; No 3 is not dated]   **965**
BM

London Dance News. Ed by Rowland T. Davis. London: Printed by Welbecson Press, Ltd., 39/43 Battersea High St., S.W. 11. Vol 1. Nos 1–9. 27 Apr – 22 June 1946. then, *London Dance News Weekly.* Nos 10–32. 29 June – 30 Nov 1946. Weekly. [Incorporated with, *Dance News Weekly*]   **966**
BM-N

London Music Diary. Published by Everybody's Books. London: Denmark Street, W.C. 2. [Nos 1–3] 6/12 – 20/26 May 1946. Weekly.   **967**
BM

London Musical Events. Concert, ballet, opera. Ed by Michael Hadley. London. [No 1]– . Dec 1946 –   . Monthly. [The subtitle varies]   **968**
BM, DLC ([2] plus), ICN ([3] plus), NN (4 plus), O (Vol 7, No 1 — Vol 10, No 5. 1952–1955), WEST

The Masque, a Theatre Notebook. Ed by Lionel Carter. London: Curtain Press. Nos 1–9. Dec 1946 – 1949. Irregular.   **969**
BM, BP, DLC, ICN, IEN, IaU, IU, LU, LVA, LvP, NIC, NN, NNC, O, PU, WEST

The Model Stage. The quarterly magazine of Pollock's Toy Theatre Club. London: Benjamin Pollock. Nos 1–3. 1946 [?] – 1950. Quarterly (irregular). [The issues are undated]   **970**
BM, BP (1–3)

Peter Warlock's Pentagram. An independent monthly bulletin for all who want
good magic. Bramcote. Vols 1–14, No 3. Oct 1946 – Dec 1959. Monthly. [Later
the periodical is published at Enfield]   *971*
  BM

Pot-pourri. Magazine for entertainment. Ed by M. A. Hadley. Brighton. [Vols
1]–2, No 1. Aug 1946 – Spring 1947. Irregular. [Three issues of the periodical]
  BM   *972*

Proscenium. [Erith theatre guild] London. Vols 1–4. [Nos 1–15] Autumn 1946 –
Autumn/Winter 1950. Quarterly (irregular). [Vol 1, No 4, is edited by Marjorie
Ramsey]   *973*
  BM, ERIT

Queue. An entertainment digest for the city of Belfast and district. Belfast. Vols
1–4, No 6. 4 Feb – 18 Nov 1946. Weekly. [The subtitle varies]   *974*
  BM

The Royal Academy of Dramatic Art Magazine. Journal of the Students of the
R.A.D.A. Ed by Stefan Lane. London. Nos 1–2. May 1946 – Mar 1947. Irregular.
[This is a new series. All earlier issues seem to have been destroyed. The title
inside the cover is, *The RADA Magazine.* Journal of the students of the Royal
Academy of Dramatic Art]   *975*
  BM

Scots Theatre [Glasgow Unity Theatre] Glasgow: Published by Glasgow Unity
Theatre at 358 Sauchiehall Street, C. 2. Nos 1–6. Sept 1946 – May 1947. Monthly.
[Nos 2–4 are edited by W. M. Coulter and Donald Cameron. Nos 5–6 are edited
by Donald Cameron]   *976*
  BM, EP, O

Scottish Dance News. Ed by Rowland T. Davis. London: Printed by Hardy Press,
Ltd., Bournemouth, for the Publishers, Danceland Publications, Ltd., 34, Exeter
Street, London, W.C. 2. Vol 1. Nos 1–8. 27 Apr – 15 June 1946. Weekly. then,
Scottish Dance News Weekly. Vol 1. Nos 9–32. 22 June – 30 Nov 1946. [Incor-
porated with, *Dance News Weekly*]   *977*
  BM-N

Scottish Music and Drama. An annual review published during the Edinburgh
festival. [Glasgow: W. Mac Lellan] Vol 1–   . 1946 –   . Annual.   *978*
  DLC

Shaw Society Bulletin. London. Nos 1–50. Sept 1946 – Sept 1953. then, *The
Shavian.* New Series. Nos 1–   . [Also called No 51–   ] Dec 1953 –   .
Irregular.   *979*
  CtY, IEN, NN, O (*The Shavian*)

Show World. London. Nos 1–517. 11 Sept 1946 – 12 Jan 1957. Weekly. then, *Show
World and Film & T.V. Advertiser.* Nos 518–525. 19 Jan – 9 Mar 1957. then,
Show World, Film, Radio, Record & T.V. Advertiser. Nos 526–535. 16 Mar – 10
Aug 1957.   *980*
  BM-N

Stratford-upon-Avon Scene.   Ed by Lester Taylor. Stratford-upon-Avon: Printed by Edward Fox & Son, Ltd., for the Proprietors, Charles Lester Taylor, Percy Roland Grail and George Kenneth Boyden, and Published at 20, Chapel Street. Vols 1–3. Nos 1–[30] Sept 1946 – Oct 1950. Monthly (Irregular) [Absorbed, *Shakespeare Pictorial.* The numbering ends with No 29]   **981**
    BM, BP, DLC, MH, MiU, NN, NNC, NjP, PBL, RPB, TU

Theatre Mirror.   Issued by the New Yiddish Theatre, Folk House (Beth Am). [In English and Yiddish] London. Vols 1–2. Nos 1–16. Mar 1946 – June/July 1947. Monthly. [Nos 15–16 form a combined issue]   **982**
    BM-N, NN

Theatre Newsletter   [Ed by Ossia Trilling, 1946 – 1950; Ray Walker, 1951–1953] London: Published by Theatre News Service, 20, Buckingham Street, W.C. 2, and Printed by T. G. Norris & Son, N.W. 8. Vols 1–6. Nos 1–139. 15 July 1946 – 19 Jan 1952. then, *Theatre.* Vol 6, No 140 – Vol 7, No 166. 2 Feb 1952 – 14 Feb 1953. Biweekly (slightly irregular) [The printing information changes]   **983**
    BM, BP, InU, NIC, NN, NNC, O, WEST

Theatre Today.   Ed by M. Slater. London: Fore Publications, Ltd. Nos 1–7. Mar 1946 – Jan 1949. then, *Film and Theatre Today.* No 8. Aug 1949. Irregular.   **984**
    BP, C, CtY, MnU, MH, NN (missing No 7), NwP, O, WEST

This Week in London.   Everybody's pocket guide. London: Published by Everybody's Books. [Vols 1–2. Nos 1–40] 19 Jan – 19 Oct 1946. then, *This Week in London.* London's leading pocket guide. Vol 2, Nos 41–[128] 17 Oct 1946 – 29 May 1948. [The numbering runs from Vol 2, No 41 – Vol 3, No 54. 17 Oct 1946 – 17 Jan 1947]. then, *This Week in London.* The leading entertainment guide. [Nos 125–148] 5 June – 6 Nov 1948. Weekly. [Ed by A. Fraser White, 17 Oct 1946 – 17 Jan 1947; by Gordon S. Sheppard, 24 Jan 1947 – 29 Oct 1948]   **985**
    BM

Variety Fare.   London: Published by Ellison-Barlow Productions, Ltd. Vols 1–3, No 2. May 1946 – Aug 1947. then, *Night Life.* Vol 3, No 3 – Vol 4, No 2. Sept 1947 – Apr 1948. Monthly (irregular). [Twenty issues of the periodical]   **986**
    BM

Vic-Wells Association.   [Bulletin] London: D. Whitton, 14 Alderbrook Rd, S.W. 12 [1946] [Supersedes the, *Old Vic and Sadler's Wells Magazine*]   **987**
    BP

What's On?   The Manchester Entertainment Guide. Manchester: 98 Grosvenor Square. [Nos 1–12] 14 Dec 1946/11 Jan 1947 – 13 Dec 1948/9 Jan 1949. Bimonthly.   **988**
    BM

1947

The Artistes Bulletin.   Ed by Cary Ellison. London: Issued by EL-BA Direction. Theatrical & Film Agency. Nos 1–2. Dec 1947, Feb 1948. Monthly [?]   **989**
    BM

The Ballet Annual.   A record and year book of the ballet. London: Adam and Charles Black, 4, 5 & 6 Soho Square, W. 1. Vols 1–18. 1947 – 1964. Annual. [Vols

1–14, are edited by Arnold L. Haskell; Vols 15–18, are edited by Arnold L. Haskell, and Mary Clarke]   **990**
BM, BP, C, CoU, IEN, IU, KyU, LU, LdP, MP, NIC, NNC, NjP, NwP, O, OC, OCl, PmP

Ballet Review.   Edinburgh: The Albyn Press, 42 Frederick St. No 1. 1947.   **991**
BM, C, DLC, MP, NN

Ballroom Dancing Annual.   London: Published by Dancing Times Ltd. [Vols 1–9] 1947 – 1955. Annual.   **992**
BM

Bristol Diary of Events.   [Bristol Development Department] Bristol [Nos 1–49] July 1947 – July 1951. Monthly. [July 1951 issue says that the magazine will discontinue publication "after the present issue." p 12]   **993**
BM

Cast.   [Ellison-Barlow productions. Ed by Cary Ellison] London. No 1. 1947. Monthly.   **994**
BM

Cinema and Theatre Annual Review and Directory of Ireland.   Dublin: The Parkside Press, Ltd. 1947. Annual.   **995**
BM, BP, C, E

Equity Letter.   A bi-monthly report to the members of the British Actors' Equity Association. London. [Nos 1–23] Mar 1947 – July 1951. then, *Equity Letter.* A quarterly report to the members of the British Actors' Equity Association. [Nos 24–58] Oct 1951 – Feb 1966. then, *Equity Letter.* A report to the members of the British Actors' Equity Association. [Nos 59–   ] Jan 1967 –   . Irregular.
BM   **996**

Exits and Entrances.   Organ of the Durham County drama association. Durham. Nos 1–6. Jan 1947 – Jan 1950. Irregular.   **997**
DuC

Festival News.   Published for the International Festival of Music and Drama. Edinburgh: Published by the Scottish Features, Ltd., 19 Forth Street [Nos 1–4] [1947] – 1950. Annual [?]   **998**
BM

Goodliffe's Magic Monthly.   A magazine for the amateur magician. Ed by Goodliffe. Birmingham: Published by Goodliffe the Magician. Vol 1. Nos 1–8. Jan – Oct 1947. Monthly (irregular). [Skips publication in May and June]   **999**
BM

The Green Register, 1946–47.   A comprehensive index and register of theatrical artists of stage, screen, radio, music, covering the United Kingdom of Great Britain and Northern Ireland, and Eire, etc. Ed by I. Wm. De Pinna. London: Putnam & Du Bree [1947] Annual. [This is called a "Confidential Issue To The Theatrical Profession"]   **1000**
BM

The Londoner Annual.   The What's On Year Book for 1946–7. Ed by F. Maurice Speed. London: Published by Gramol Publications, Ltd. 1947. Annual.   **1001**
BM

The Magic Wand Year Book, 1946 – 1947.   London. 1947. Annual.   *1002*
  BM (destroyed)

The Metropolitan Times.   Your news-magazine which covers the whole of London
  and suburbs. Special London edition. London: Published by Wm. Slatter & Co.,
  223 Blackfriars Road, S.E. 1. Nos 1–2. Apr/May – June/July 1947. Bimonthly.
  BM   *1003*

New Plays Quarterly.   Edited by John Bourne. London: Printed and Published
  by Rylee, Ltd. Nos 1–64 [1947] – Winter 1964. Quarterly [There is also a Supplement to *New Plays Quarterly*, Nos 1–54]   *1004*
  BM, BP, BrP, EdP, GM, LvP, O, WEST

Now-a-days.   Book reviews, theatre, music, poetry, art. Brighton. Vol 1. Nos 1–5.
  Spring 1947 – Spring 1948. Quarterly.   *1005*
  BM (missing since 1956), BiP, DLC, MH, NN

Phoenix.   [People's theatre art group] Newcastle upon Tyne. 1947. Quarterly. *1006*
  Not located (Loewenberg p 48)

Puppet Post.   The quarterly journal of the Educational Puppetry Association.
  London. Vol 1. No 1–   . Spring 1947 –   . Quarterly [1947 – Winter 1951/
  52; Two issues a year [1952 –   ] [Ed by F. Hook, Spring 1947; by M. R.
  Poulter, Winter 1947 – Autumn 1951; by D. Hawkes, Winter 1951/52 – Spring
  1954; A. R. Philpott, Spring 1955 – Spring 1958. This is the last date an editor's
  name appears. Also, from Spring 1958, reproduced from typewritten copy] *1007*
  BM, NN (missing all before 1950), WM ([1951/52]–59)

S.C.D.A. Advisory Service.   Compiled by E. J. P. Mace. Edinburgh: Published by
  the Scottish Community Drama Association. No 1. 1 Feb 1947. [This publication
  is a pamphlet rather than a periodical, although the *British Union Catalogue of
  Periodicals* lists it as a periodical. For this reason I include the work]   *1007a*
  BM

The Shakespeare Fellowship News-Letter.   Edited by W. Kent, 1947–1953; by
  Miss G. M. Bowen, and Miss R. M. D. Waivewright, Spring 1957 – Autumn 1958
  [London] R. H. Johns Ltd., Newport, Monmouthshire, Printer. Sept 1947 –
  Autumn 1958. Two issues a year [The Sept 1954 issue mentions that the periodi-
  cal had been edited by W. Kent since 1947, but I have not been able to locate
  any issues previous to Sept 1954. The issues are not numbered. Superseded by
  Shakespeare Authorship Review, No 1, Spring 1959]   *1007b*
  BM (1954 on), LU (Sept 1951 on), O (Sept 1954 on)

Shakespeare Quarterly.   London. No 1. Summer 1947.   *1008*
  DFo

Spotlight.   The journal of the Swindon and district theatre guild. Swindon. No
  1–   . 1947 –   . Monthly.   *1009*
  SwC

Stage and Screen Miscellany.   Edited by Peter Noble. London: Published by
  Pendulum Publications Ltd., 100 Old Square, Lincoln's Inn, W.C. 2 [Vol 1.
  No 1] Spring 1947. then, *Stage and Screen* [No 2] Summer 1947. Quarterly. *1010*
  O

Stage Door. [Brighton and Hove operatic society] Brighton. 1947 – 1954. Monthly
[1947 – Oct 1952]; Bimonthly [Nov/Dec 1952 – Aug/Sept 1953]   *1011*
   BiP (missing all before Vol 2, No 10)

The Stage, Screen and Variety News. Southsea. Vol 1. No 1. June 1947. Monthly.
   BM   *1012*

Theatre in Education. A bulletin of the drama in university, college, school or
youth group. London. Vols 1–5. Nos 1–28. 15 Feb 1947 – Oct/Nov 1951. Irregular.   *1013*
   BM, LU, NN, O

The Tyneside Phoenix. Journal of the people's theatre arts group. Newcastle upon
Tyne. Nos 1–18. Spring 1947 – Autumn 1952. Three issues a year. [Nos 2–10 are
edited by Henry D. Davy]   *1014*
   BM, NwP

What's On? The Stockport entertainment guide. Manchester. [Nos 1–5] Oct/Nov
1947 – Apr/May 1948. Bimonthly.   *1015*
   BM

The Wizard. The modern magic monthly. London. Vols 1–8. Nos 1–95. Apr 1947 –
July 1956. Monthly. [Ed by George Armstrong. Vols 1–6, No 72. Apr 1947 – Jan
1954; Ed by Jack Lamonte. Vols 7, No 73 – Vol 8, No 95. Feb 1954 – July 1956]
   BM   *1016*

1948

B.D.T.G. Bulletin. [Birmingham district theatre guild] Birmingham. Nos 1–8.
July 1948 – Jan 1950. then, *Theatre Guild Review.* Sept 1950 –   . [Birming-
ham and district theatre guild, a branch of the British drama league] *Monthly*
(irregular). [Reproduced from typewritten copy]   *1017*
   BP

"Broadsheet." London. Nos 1–2. [1948] – 5 Mar 1948. then, *Greek Drama (Amateur
Players).* Broadsheet. Nos 3–4. Apr – May 1948. Monthly. [Reproduced from
typewritten copy]   *1018*
   BM

The Children's Theatre. [Magazine of the Educational Drama Association] Ed
by A. E. Thomas. Birmingham. No 1. Jan 1948. then, *Creative Drama.* Sept
1950 –   . Semiannual.   *1019*
   BP, DeU, GU, MiDW, NN

Civic Entertainment; Theatre, Music, Visual Arts. London. Vols 1–2. [Nos 1–10]
Nov/Dec 1948 – Mar/Apr 1950. Bimonthly. [No 10, of Vol 2, lacks volume
designation]   *1020*
   BM, CLU, KeP, LU, NN

Dobson's Theatre Year Book. Ed by John Andrews, and Ossia Trilling. London.
Vol 1. 1948/49. Annual.   *1021*
   BM, BP, C, DLC, FiP, MP, NP, O

English Folk Dance & Song Society Bulletin. London. Nos 1–13. Apr 1948 – May
1950. Irregular.   *1022*
   BM, BP, DLC (missing Nos 4–5), O

Footlights. Issued by the Gloucester Theatre Guild. Gloucester. Nos 1–2. Mar –
Apr 1948. Monthly.   **1023**
    Not located (Loewenberg p 36)

The Laban Art of Movement Guild. News Sheet. Ed by Benedict Ellis. Sheffield.
[No 1]–36. [1948] – May 1966. Irregular. [The British Museum copy has '[1947]'
written on the title page of the first number. In an editorial, however, in No 3,
Jan 1949, the editor says that the first issue was in July 1948]   **1024**
    BM, CoU (No [1–20] plus), NcGW (No [1–20] plus)

Leisure Year. Annual of London Leisure. London. [1948] Annual.   **1025**
    BM

Little Theatre News. Portsmouth. No 1. 1948.   **1026**
    Not located (Loewenberg p 53)

The Living Theatre. Darlington: Published by the Darlington Repertory Theatre,
the Royal Astoria Theatre, Darlington. Nos 1–12. Mar 1948 – Mar 1949. Monthly.
    DaP   **1027**

Mercury. A review of the arts in Wessex. "The Journal of the Winter gardens
society." Ed by Jon Evans. Bournemouth. Nos 1–9. Oct 1948 – Oct 1950. Quarterly. [The subtitle varies slightly]   **1028**
    MH (missing No 1), NN, WmP

Movement. An international magazine. Ed by George Deckmann. London: Published by The Laban Art of Movement Guild. Vol 1. Nos 1–2. Summer – Winter
1948. Quarterly.   **1029**
    BM, NcGW

The Piping, Drumming and Highland Dancing Journal. Ed by Hugh Ross. Edinburgh: Published by the Proprietors of *The Piping, Drumming and Highland
Dancing Journal.* Vols 1–3, No 2. May 1948 – June 1950. Monthly.   **1030**
    BM, EP

Plays of the Year. Chosen by J. C. Trewin. London: Paul Elek [Vols 1]–   .
1948/49 –   . Annual [Numbering begins with Vol 5]   **1030a**
    BM, BP, O

Scottish Drama Year Book. Ed by Jack House. Edinburgh: The Albyn Press, 42
Frederick Street. 1948. Annual. then, *Scottish Drama*: the *Scottish Drama Year
Book. 1950.* [The 1950 edition is edited by Jack House and G. O. Cribbes] **1031**
    BM, BP, NN, O

Shakespeare Quarterly. Issued under the auspices of the Austrian Shakespeare
Society. London: 3, Braham Gardens, S.W. 5. No 1. Summer 1948. Quarterly
[On p 120 the editor gives a list of the articles which will appear in No 2, and
says that the third number, in six months' time, will be entirely American] **1031a**
    BP, BU, GU, LU, O

Shakespeare Survey. An annual survey of Shakespearian study and production.
Ed by Allardyce Nicoll. Cambridge: At the University Press; New York: The
Macmillan Company. 1948 –   . Annual.   **1032**
    AU, BM, BP, BU, C, CSmH, CtY, GM, ICN, ICU, IEN, LU, MH, MiU, MP, NIC, NN,
    NNC, NU, O, OCl, PU, SU

Supplement to New Plays Quarterly. London. [Nos 1]–54. [1948] – 1962. Quarterly (irregular).   ***1033***
BM

Theatre Digest. To interest. To stimulate. To entertain. [Nos 1–3 are edited by Anthony Merryn, and G. K. Jeannette; Nos 4–8 are edited by G. K. Jeannette] London. Nos 1–8. [1948 – 1950. The issues are not dated] Quarterly (Bimonthly). [Nos 2–6 are published quarterly; No 8 is published bimonthly]   ***1034***
BM, CLU

What's On in Ilford. Ilford. Nos 1–15. Feb – Sept 1948. Biweekly.   ***1035***
BM-N

The Working Light. Organ of the Northumbrian and Durham division of the British Drama League. Newcastle. No 1. Feb 1948.   ***1036***
Not located

The Year's Work in the Theatre. Ed by J. C. Trewin. London: Published for the British Council by Longmans, Green & Co. Vols 1–3. 1948/49 – 1950/51. Annual.
BP, CaOTU, EP, IEN, LU, MH, MiD, MP, NIC, O   ***1037***

1949

British Puppet Theatre. London: Published by Puppet Theatre Limited, 5 New Bridge St., E.C. 4. Vols 1–3, No 5. Dec 1949 – Jan 1953. Monthly.   ***1038***
BP, MH, MoS, NN

Call-boy. Magazine of Bristol & West entertainments. Bristol. No 1. June 1949.
BM   ***1039***

Creative Drama. [Educational drama association] London: Stacey Publications, 9 Houndsden Rd., N. 21. Vol 1–   . 1949 –   . Quarterly.   ***1040***
BM, NN

Cue. Film. Sport. Entertainment. London: Published by Central News Agency Ltd. Vol 1. Nos 1–4. Oct 1949 – Jan 1950. Biweekly.   ***1041***
BM (missing Vol 1, No 1. Oct 1949)

Curtain Call. The South Wales stage recorder. Swansea. Vol 1. No 1. [Apr 1949]
SwP   ***1042***

"The Magical Digest" (*and Viewsletter*). A monthly magazine giving publicity and information of interest to all devotees of the magic art. Ed by Oscar Oswald. London. Vols 1–9, No 6. Sept 1949 – 1959. [After Vol 9, No 1, Mar/Apr 1959, the remaining five numbers are not dated] Monthly (irregular). [The subtitle varies slightly]   ***1043***
BM, LU

The Meteor. A star magazine focussing its light on magic and magicians. [Editorials are signed, "Elliott," who is also the publisher] Rotherham. Vol 1. Nos 1–4. Mar – June 1949. Monthly.   ***1044***
BM

Southport Playbill. The magazine of the Southport repertory company. Southport. Nos 1–2. 1949. Irregular.   ***1045***
SptP

Souvenirs de Ballet. A book for lovers of ballet to be published annually. Ed by Duncan Melvin. London. No 1. 1949. Annual.   **1046**
   BM

Spotlight. Stage and screen casting directory. American and European Edition. London: Published by "The Spotlight," Ltd. Ed by E. M. Mann. No 1. 1949. Annual.   **1047**
   BM, O

Spotlight-Contacts. Stage and screen. London: "The Spotlight." [No 1]–   . Jan 1949 –   . [Three issues a year, to No 30, Oct 1958; two issues a year since No 31, Apr 1959]   **1048**
   BM, NN (missing Nos 1–22)

Theatre World Annual. A pictorial review of West End productions with a record of plays and players. London. 1949/1950 –   . Annual.   **1049**
   BM, CLU, CoU, DLC, NjP, NN, O, PSt

West Middlesex Entertainment Review. Ed by H. W. Thompson. Southall: Printed at Hayes, Middlesex. [Nos 1–2?] Mar – Apr 1949. Monthly.   **1050**
   BM

What's On and Where. Dundee. Nos 1–13. 1949.   **1051**
   DnP

What's On in Ealing. Social Events. Ealing. [Nos 1–25] Oct [1949] – Autumn and Christmas Number, 1951. Monthly.   **1052**
   BM

What's On in the West Country. Weston-super-Mare. Vol 1. Nos 1–4. 27 Mar/9 Apr – 8/21 May 1949. then, *Events in the West.* Vols 1–9. Nos 5–120. 22 May/14 June 1949 – Jan 1958. then, *Events in Bristol.* Vol 9. Nos 121 – Vol 18, No 225. Feb 1958 – Oct 1966. then, *Events in Bristol & Cardiff.* Vol 18. No 226–   . Nov 1966 –   . Monthly. [For Taunton, Wells, Glastonbury, Weston-super-Mare, Bristol, Cardiff]   **1053**
   BM

1950

Dance and Dancers. Ed by Peter Williams. London: Mersey House, 132–4 Fleet St., E.C. 4 [then, published by Hanson Books] Vols 1–13, No 12. Jan 1950 – Dec 1962. Monthly.   **1054**
   BM

Dance Journal. The Imperial Society of Teachers of Dancing Incorporated. With which is embodied The Cecchetti Society and the Federated Association of Teachers of Dancing of Australia and New Zealand. Ed by Cyril Beaumont. London: Published by Order of the Council, Headquarters, 70, Gloucester Place, W. 1. 1950. Quarterly. [It is most difficult to untangle information concerning Numbers 1–43]   **1055**
   BM (Nos 44–   . 1950–   .)

In Town. Chesterfield's monthly entertainment and shopping review. Ed by Wyndham C. Baylis. [His name appears until Feb 1953. After that date no editor is listed] Chesterfield. Vols 1–4, No 10. Sept 1950 – July 1954. Monthly.
BM   *1056*

Intimate Theatre Group News-letter. The Intimate Theatre Group, Highbury Theatre Centre. Sutton Coldfield. No 1. Mar 1950. [Reproduced from typewritten copy]   *1057*
BP

Opera. London. Feb 1950 –   . Monthly. [Supersedes, in part, *Ballet and Opera*]
BM (incomplete), CtY, DLC, ICN, ICU, MiD, NN, O   *1058*

Proscenium. Ipswich: Published quarterly by the Ipswich Theatre Club. Vols Vols 1–3, No 4. Dec 1950 – 1954. Quarterly (irregular). [No issues in 1952, except the issue, Winter 1952 – 1953. One issue in 1954. In all, eleven numbers]
BM, NN (missing Vol 2, No 4)   *1059*

Quarterly News-Sheet. Issued by The Greek Dance Association, The Ginner-Mawer School and The Old Ginner-Mawer Club. London. [Nos 1–8] Mar 1950 – Dec 1951. then, *The News-Sheet.* Issued by The Ginner-Mawer School & The Ginner-Mawer Old Girls' Club. [Nos 9–18] Aug 1952 – Sept 1958. Quarterly (irregular). [The subtitle varies. The last number is issued by The Ginner-Mawer Club]   *1060*
· BM

Repertory. A weekly magazine devoted to the interests of repertory. Ed by Angus Mac Innes. Northgate-Halifax. [Published at the Grand Theatre Buildings] Vol 1. Nos 1–10. 2 Jan – 6 Mar 1950. Weekly.   *1061*
BM, O

Scottish Drama. Edinburgh. Vol 1. 1950. Annual. [Incorporated, *Scottish Drama Year Book*]   *1062*
MH, O

Shakespeare Memorial Theatre. A photographic record. London. 1948/50 – 1959.
AU (1948/50), BM (1951/53), MBU (1948/50–1959)   *1063*

Shavian Tract. [Shaw Society] London. 1950 –   . Irregular.   *1064*
CLU, CU, CtY, ICU, IEN, IaU, IU, KyU, MH, NIC, NN, NNC, WU

Society for Theatre Research. London. Vol 1–   . 1950/51 –   . Annual. *1065*
BP, CLU, CtY, KyU, LU, LvP, MoU, OCU

Spotlight: a Bulletin on the Activities of the Hall Green Little Theatre. Birmingham. Nos 1–5. 1950 – 1954. Irregular. [The issues are not dated. Reproduced from typewritten copy]   *1066*
BP

Stage and Variety Artistes Guide and Handbook. London. Vol 1. 1950. Annual.
DLC   *1067*

Theatre Holiday Bulletin. [Theatre Holiday Plan] London. Nos 1–2. Jan – Feb
1950. Monthly. [Reproduced from typewritten copy]   **1068**
     BM

1951

British Puppet and Model Theatre Guild Newsletter. Ed by John Dudley. London. [Nos 1–3] 4 – 20 Mar 1951 – Feb 1953. Irregular. [Reproduced from typewritten copy] New Series. No 1–   . Apr 1956 –   . Monthly (irregular).
[The last number located, as of June 1967, is for No 127, Nov 1966]   **1069**
     BM (missing Nos 7, 11; New Series, No 1)

Dance Music Annual. London: John Dilworth, Ltd., 63, Perham Road. 1951.
Annual.   **1070**
     BM

Foyer; a Quarterly of Music, Opera and Ballet. [London] Nos 1–2. Autumn 1951 –
Winter 1951/52. Quarterly.   **1071**
     BM, BP, DLC, ICN, LU, LVA, MiD, MP, WmP, WEST

Music and Theatre Digest. [Formed by the union of, *Musical Digest,* and *Theatre
Digest*] Ed by G. Martin. London: Published and Distributed by Lyford Publication Limited, 240 High Holborn, W.C. 2. Nos 1–4. June 1951 – 1952. Six issues
a year. [Only the first issue is dated. The address changes]   **1072**
     BM, CLU, DLC, O, OCl

What's On. The journal of club entertainment in Nottinghamshire and Lincoln-
shire. Ed by "The Showman." Lincoln. Vol 1. Nos 1–5. Jan – May 1951. Monthly.
     BM   **1073**

1952

District Club News and Local Entertainment Guide. Grays, Essex: Published by
J. Bevis. Vol 1. Nos 1–2. Jan – Feb 1952. Monthly. [No 1 is a "Specimen Copy"]
     BM   **1074**

In Town. Derby's monthly entertainment and shopping review. Ed by Wyndham
C. Baylis. Derby. [Nos 1–3] Mar – May 1952. Monthly.   **1075**
     BM

Magazine 4. A review of the visual arts, literature, music and drama. Ed by Garry
Denbury. Glastonbury. Vol 1. No 1. Oct 1952.   **1076**
     BM

The Magic Magazine. For all magicians. Ed by Max Andrews. London: Published by Max Andrews. Vols 1–5, No 6. Apr 1952 – Sept 1956. Monthly. **1077**
     BM

Opera, Ballet, and Music-Hall in the World. London. No 1–   . Oct 1952 –   .
Quarterly.   **1078**
     GU

Speech and Drama. [Society of Teachers of Speech and Drama] London. No
1–   . 1952 –   .   **1079**
     LIE, LU, OU ([1–3, 7]–   )

The Young Ballet Dancer.   Ed by N. Nicolaeva-Legat. London: Published monthly by the Proprietors, "The Young Ballet Dancer Publishing Company." Cliffords Inn, Fleet Street, E.C. 4. Vol 1. Nos 1–5. Jan – May 1952. Monthly.   *1080*
BM

1953

Cymdeithas Ddawns Werin Cymru.   Welsh Folk Dance Society Cylch-Lythyr — News-letter. Wrexam. Nos 1–6. 1953 – 1958. then, *"y Cylchlythyr" "The News-letter."* The Welsh Folk Dance Magazine. No 7. 1959/60. Annual. [No 1 is edited by Ifan O. Williams; Nos 2–5 are edited by Gwen Taylor; No 6 is edited by Lois Blake; No 7 is edited by Gwyn Williams. This number is published in Bangor]   *1081*
BM

Dance Notes.   News & Views of Midland Dancers and Midland Dancers Guide. Dudley: The Modern Press, 84a, Hall Street. No 1. Nov 1953.   *1082*
BM

French's Play Parade.   Supplement to the Guide to Selecting Plays. London: Samuel French, Ltd. No 1–   . Feb 1953 –   . Irregular.   *1083*
BEDD

Highlights from the Folkestone-Hythe Operatic and Dramatic Society.   [Ed by R. Dawe, in 1953; by Kenneth Miles, 1954 – 1956; by John A. Oates, 1957 – 1959; by R. Dawe, 1960 – 1961; by Mrs. Rae Giles, 1962 – 1966] Folkestone. [Vol 1] No 1–   . Oct 1953 –   . Irregular. [Reproduced from typewritten copy to 1955, then printed]   *1084*
BM

Hughes News.   London: Published by John Hughes. [Vols 1]–3, No 3. Dec 1953 – [Summer 1956?] Quarterly. [Eleven numbers in all]   *1085*
BM

The Isis Theatre Supplement.   Edited by Christopher Bell. Oxford: Printed for University Newspapers Ltd., by Holywell Press, Ltd., and published at 9 Alfred Street. Vol 1. No 1. Michaelmas 1953 [Oxford University]   *1085a*
O

The London Entertainer and Concert Artiste.   Ed by George Le Roy. London. Vols 3, No 1 – Vol 5, No 8. Jan 1953 – Aug 1955. Monthly. [A note in the *British Union Catalogue of Periodicals, Supplement,* p 521, says that numbers 1–2 were not published]   *1086*
BM

Plays and Players.   London: Hanson Books, Ltd., 21 Lower Belgrave St., Buckingham Palace Rd., S.W. 1. Vol 1–   . 1953 –   . Monthly. [This periodical has gradually incorporated, *Theatre World, Encore, Play Pictorial, and Shows Illustrated*]   *1087*
BM, C, CSt, E, LvP, LU, MiD, NN, O, WM

SCR. Society for Cultural Relations with the U.S.S.R.   Theatre Section Bulletin. London. Vols 1–2, No 1. July 1953 – Jan 1955. then, *Soviet Theatre Bulletin.*

Vol 2, No 3 – Vol 3, No 1. Oct 1955 – Apr 1956. Irregular. [Superseded by, *The Arts in the USSR*. SCR Bulletin, Jan 1957. Eight numbers. The July 1953 issue, No 1, does not have a volume number]   **1088**
BM, NN (1[2])

The Shakespeare Stage.   The quarterly bulletin of the Shakespeare Stage Society. Ed by C. B. Purdom. London: Claridge, Lewis & Jordan, Ltd., 68–70 Wardour Street, W. 1. Nos 1–6. 7 June 1953 – Sept/Dec 1954. Quarterly. [The final issue is numbered 6–7. Sept/Dec 1954]   **1089**
BM, BP, CLU, CoU, MH, MoU, NN, PU

Sport & Show News.   London: Published by Jocal Productions, Ltd., 20, Rupert Street, Piccadilly. Nos 1–14. 24 Oct 1953 – 13 Mar 1954. Weekly.   **1090**
BM-N

Theatre World Monographs.   London: Berrie and Rockliff. Nos 1–12. 1953 – 1958. Irregular.   **1091**
CU, DLC, MH, OU

Welsh Folk Dance Society News-letter.   (Welsh Folk Dance Society.) Denbigh. No 1. 1953.   **1092**
BM, O

What's On.   Coming events in Norwich. Cambridge. [Nos 1–2] Nov – Dec 1953. Monthly. then, *What's On.* Coming Events in Norwich, Gt. Yarmouth and Lowestoft. [Nos 3–5] Jan – Mar 1956. then, *What's On.* Norwich, Great Yarmouth, Lowestoft. [Nos 6–79] Apr 1956 – May 1960.   **1093**
BM (missing June 1956, June 1957, Oct 1957, Feb 1959)

What's On in Cambridge.   Cambridge. [Nos 1–5] May – Oct 1953. Monthly. then, *What's On in Cambridge, Ely, Newmarket & Royston.* [Nos 6–7] Nov – Dec 1953. [Includes a supplement, *What's On in Ely, Newmarket, Royston & Soham.* Nov 1953]. then, *What's On.* Cambridge, Ely, Newmarket, Royston, Saffron Walden. [Nos 8–10] Jan – Mar 1954. then, *What's On.* Cambridge, Ely, New-market, Royston, Saffron Walden, St. Ives. [Nos 11–84] Apr 1954 – May 1960.
BM   **1094**

1954

Encore; the Review of World Theatre.   London: 52 Hyde Park Gate, S.W. 7. Vols 1–12, No 5. 1954 – Sept/Oct 1965. Quarterly [bimonthly from Vol 3. Incorporated into, *Plays and Players*]   **1095**
BM (3–   ), CoU (3), KyU (3–   ), NN (3–   )

The Folk Dancer.   Exclusively devoted to the development of folk dancing of all nations for the enjoyment of leisure and the promotion of a better international understanding. Ed by Hugh A. Thurston. London. Vols 1–3, No 6. Mar/Apr 1954 – Jan/Feb 1957. Bimonthly. then, *The Folklorist.* The international maga-zine. Incorporating "*The Folk Dancer*" and "*The Folk Musician and Singer.*" Ed by Henry R. Baldrey. Vols 4–7, No 6. Mar/Apr 1957 – Spring 1963. then, *Folk Musician and Singer.* Vol 8, Nos 1–6. Summer 1963 – Autumn 1964. Ed by Henry R. Baldrey.   **1096**
BM

The Imperial Society of Teachers of Dancing Incorporated. (Embodying: The Cecchetti Society, The Federal Association of Teachers of Dancing of Australia and New Zealand, and the Greek Dance Association) Report of Council and Accounts for the Year. London. [Nos 1–8] 1954 – 1961. Annual. [The 1953 (1954) report mentions that the 10th Ordinary and General Meeting of the Society will take place July 25, 1954]   *1097*
BM

In London Now. Theatres, cinemas, society, restaurants, fashions, art, sport. London. [Nos 1–46] 26 Feb 1954 – 2/15 Feb 1956. then, *The Londoner.* [Nos 47–96] 12 Apr 1956 – 24 Nov 1960. Biweekly.   *1098*
BM (missing 1958 – July 1960)

Masque. [Royal Academy of Dramatic Art] Ed by Robert Corder. London. [No 1] Sept 1954. [Called a "First Edition"]   *1099*
BM

Masque. The journal of the Masque Theatre Club. London: 3 Neate House, Lupus St., S.W. 1. Nos 1–2. Winter 1954 – 1955. Quarterly (irregular). [Reproduced from typewritten copy]   *1100*
BM

Music, Music and Dancing, Cinematograph, Stage Plays, Boxing and Wrestling Licenses and Sunday Cinematograph and Musical Entertainment Licenses and Permissions Granted by the Council and in Force. [London County Council] London. 1954 –   . Annual.   *1101*
LGU

Opera Annual. Ed by Harold Rosenthal. London. Nos 1–8. 1954/55 – 1962. Annual.   *1102*
BM, ICN, IaU, MB, MiU, NIC, NN, O, PU, WU

Seats: a Bi-Monthly Journal Devoted to Entertainment Bookable through Civic Radio Services Limited. Concert and theatre department. Birmingham. Nos 1–25. Feb – Mar 1954 – June/July 1958. Bimonthly.   *1103*
BP

Shakespeare at the Old Vic. London. Vol 1–   . 1954/55 –   .   *1104*
IEN

The Showgirl. Leicester: Published by Hart of St. Johns. Vols 1–2. Nos 1–22. Summer 1954 – [1957?] Quarterly [Nos 1–8. Nos 10–22 are undated]; Monthly [Nos 14–22 say that the periodical is a monthly]   *1105*
BM

Theatre. Ed by Ivor Brown. London: M. Reinhardt. Vols 1–2. 1954/55 – 1955/56. Annual.   *1106*
AU, BM, BP, CU, DLC, IEN, NIC, NN, NNU, O

1955

Act; the Drama Magazine. [Patrons: The National Union of Students: Leeds University Union. Theatre Group] Ed by Richard Courtney. Leeds. Vols 1–2. [Nos 1–7] Winter 1955 – Winter 1956/57. Quarterly.   *1107*
BM, NN, NNC

Cymdeithas Ddawns Werin Cymru. Welsh Folk Dance Society. Annual Report. Dinbych. 1954/55 – 1961/62. Annual. [At the British Museum the work begins with the 6th Annual report, 1954/55; the seventh report, 1955/56 is called the Sixth. The error is continued in succeeding years. Seven numbers at the British Museum] *1108*
BM

The New Elizabethan. The journal of the Southend Shakespeare. Southend. No 1. [July 1955] *1109*
BM

The 1955 Directory of Concert and Cabaret Artistes. A comprehensive directory of artistes engaged in concerts, cabarets, after-dinner entertainment, summer shows, etc., etc. London: Pullman Press, Ltd., 97–99 Praed Street, W. 2. 1955. Annual [Subsequently incorporated in, *Pullman Casting Directory*] *1110*
BM (p 15–18 are mutilated)

Play Reviews. National Union of Townswomen's Guilds. London. First — Twentieth Supplement. Dec 1955 – Dec 1965. Twice a year [June and December] [Reproduced from typewritten copy] *1111*
BM (missing the 3rd supplement)

Puppetry Year Book. Official Publication of the British Puppet and Model Theatre Guild. Ed by Eric Bramall. Wallington. 1955. Annual. *1112*
BM, N, O

The Shakespeare Memorial Theatre. Report of the Council. Stratford-upon-Avon. 79th–   . 1955 – 1960. then, *The Royal Shakespeare Theatre. Report of the Council.* 1961 – 1962. then, *Royal Shakespeare Company. Report of the Council of the Royal Shakespeare Theatre.* 1962/3 –   . Annual [For private circulation only] *1112a*
O

Show. A candid magazine of international film, theatre, cabaret, television. London: Axtel Publications, Ltd. Nos 1–29. 1955 – 1958 [The issues are not dated] *1113*
BM (missing Nos 4, 9, 11)

Showgirl Glamour Review. Ed by Ralph Coveney. London: 20 Welbeck Street, W. 1. Vol 1. No 1. [1955] [The issue is not dated] *1114*
BM

Theatre Organ Review. [Theatre Organ Club] London: Published by Theatre Organ Club, 121 Clifford Road, Ruislip Gardens. Vols 9, No 33 – Vol 20, No 78/79. Mar 1955 – June/Sept 1966. [Vols 13–20 are edited by Frank A. Hare. I have not been able to locate any volumes before Mar 1955] *1115*
BM (missing all before Vol 9, No 33)

What's On. Ipswich, Felixstowe, Colchester, Clacton. Cambridge. [Nos 1–10] July 1955 – June 1956. Monthly. *1116*
BM

What's On. Luton, Dunstable, Harpenden, Hitchin and Districts. Cambridge. [Nos 1–58] Aug 1955 – May 1960. Monthly. *1117*
BM

1956

The Ballroom Dancing Times. London: The Dancing Times, Ltd., 12 Henrietta
Street, Covent Garden, W.C. 2. Vol 1. No 1 –   . Oct 1956 –   . Monthly. *1118*
BM

Carnival Parade. Britain's magazine of pleasure. Ed by Herbert Stoneley. London.
Vol 1. Nos 1–2. May/June – July/Aug 1956. Bimonthly.   *1119*
BM

The Directory of London Theatrical Agents. London: Pullman Press, Ltd., 97–99
Praed Street, W. 2. First Edition. 1956. Annual [?]   *1120*
BM

Fore-Stage. The magazine of the Quaestors. Ed by Basil Hull. Ealing. Vol 1. Nos
1–3. Nov 1956 – May 1957. Irregular. [The Quaestors, who founded The Little
Theatre Guild, began in 1929]   *1121*
BM

International Theatre Annual. Ed by Harold Hobson. London: John Calder, 17
Sackville Street, W. 1. Vols 1–5. 1956 – 1961. Annual.   *1122*
    BM, DLC, ICU, IU, MB, MiU, NIC, OU, PU

New Plays Annual for Women. Ed by John Bourne. London: Published by Hugh
Quekett, Ltd., 35, Dover Street. Nos 1–9. [1956] – [1965] Annual. [The issues
are not dated]   *1123*
    BM, DLC, E, NN, O

Offstage. Harpenden, Herts: Printed and Published by K. Green. [For Harpenden's "dramatic life"] No 1. 24 Apr 1956. [Reproduced from typewritten copy]
BM   *1124*

*Pullman Casting Directory, Incorporating "Directory of Concert and Cabaret
Artistes."* Variety. Television. Concert. Radio. Revue. Cabaret. London: Pullman Press, Limited. 1956.   *1125*
    BM (p 37–38 are mutilated)

Showmen's Year Book. The official organ of the Showmen's Guild of Great Britain.
Ed by F. C. Roope. London: Showmen's Guild of Great Britain, 230 Abbey
House, Victoria Street, S.W. 1. [Vols 1–4] 1956 – 1959. Annual.   *1126*
BM

This Is London. What to do and where to go. London: Published Weekly by
Chalrey, Ltd. Nos 1–   . [8 Oct 1956] –   . Weekly.   *1127*
BM

1957

Books and Art, Films, Theatre, TV, Music, Painting. London. Nos 1–6. Oct 1957 –
Mar 1958. Monthly. [Incorporated in, *Books of the Month*]   *1128*
    CU, KyU, MH, NIC, NN

The Concert Goer's Annual. Ed by Evan Senior. London. No 1. 1957. Annual.
BM   *1129*

Harlequin. News-letter of the Federation of Russian Classical Ballet. Ed by John Gregory. London: Printed by Carey and Claridge, 253–255 Fulham Road, Chelsea, S.W. 3. [Nos 1]–2. Autumn 1957 – Autumn 1958. **1130**
    BM

London's Festival Ballet Annual. 1956–57. Ed by A. George Hall. London: The Grays Inn Press Publications, 42, Grays Inn Road, W.C. 2. 1957. Annual. **1131**
    BM, O

Lytton's Theatre Seating Plans and Concert Hall 1957 – 1958. Plans of the theatres and main concert halls, with historical notes and topical commentary. Ed by Douglas Gardner. London: Published by Vinton & Company, Limited. 1957 – 1962/3. [The publisher changes] **1132**
    BM (1957), O (1960/61–1962/63)

Marlovia. Magazine of the Marlowe Society. Edited by Clifford W. Russell. Hinckley, Leicester: Printed for the Publisher by Lawrence Warmer, Printer, 25 Middlefield Lane. Vol 1. No 1. Summer 1957. [This is not the same as the *Marlowe Chronicle*, which was reproduced from typewritten copy, and not printed. The other was published in "Mid-March 1957". The editorial in *Marlovia* makes no mention of the earlier work] **1132a**
    O

Marlovian Chronicle. Ed by C. W. Russell. Chislehurst: Published by the Marlowe Society. No 1. Mid-March 1957. To be issued, "From Time To Time." [Reproduced from typewritten copy] **1133**
    BM

The National Operatic and Dramatic Association Directory. Compiled by authority of the council of the association. London. [Vols 1–4] 1957 – 1960. Annual.
    BM **1134**

The National Operatic and Dramatic Association. Member's Handbook. Compiled by authority of the council of the association. London. 1957. **1135**
    BM

Photo-Cast. London: Published by Cast Publications, Ltd., 322 High Holborn, W.C. 1. Vol 1. Sept 1957. [Directory of Variety Artists] **1136**
    BM

Threshold. Ed by Mary O'Malley. Belfast: Published by the Lyric Players. Vols 1–5, No 1. Feb 1957 – Spring/Summer 1961. Quarterly. No 18 [Undated. Ed by Roy McFadden] **1137**
    BM (missing Vol 2, No 1; Vol 3, No 3; Vol 4, Nos 3–4), CU, DCU, DLC, ICU, IEN, IaU, LU, MH, NIC, NN, NNC, PSt, PU, PV, ViU

1958

Ballroom Dancing Year Book. London: Published by the Dance Teachers Association (Great Britain). [Vol 1]– . 1958 – . Annual. **1138**
    BM

Diary of Entertainment and Events. Nottingham. [No 1] June 1958. [Issues are reproduced from typewritten copy until Jan 1966, when they are printed] [Nos

2–14] Mar 1959 – Mar 1960. Monthly. [Publication is resumed in March 1959] then, *Nottingham Diary of Entertainment and Events.* [Nos 15–32] Apr 1960 – Aug 1961. then, *City of Nottingham Civic News and Diary of Events.* [Nos 33–107] Sept 1961 – Nov 1966. then, *City of Nottingham Civic News and What's On.* [Nos 108]– . Dec 1966 – .   *1139*
   BM

The Questors Theatre. [Newsletter] London. [1958] [On page 4 is a statement that the next issue is to appear in February. There are no dates]   *1140*
   BM

Royal Opera House Annual Report [Covent Garden] London. [Nos 1–3] 1957/ 58 – 1959/60. then, *Royal Opera House, Covent Garden.* Annual Report. [Nos 4–5] 1960/61 – 1961/62. Annual.   *1141*
   BM

The Swan. An occasional publication of the Swan Players. Ed by G. Elmer. London: 8, Harewood Road, S.W. 19. No 8. July 1958. Irregular. [Reproduced from typewritten copy. I have not been able to locate any of the earlier numbers]
   BM   *1142*

Theatre Guild News. Journal of the theatre guild of Coventry. Coventry. No 1– . 1958 – . Quarterly [approximately] [Reproduced from typewritten copy]   *1143*
   CvP

Vues from Revues. [Irving Theatre] London: Published by D. P. Chaudhuri, The Irving Theatre, W.C. 2. Summer 1958.   *1144*
   BM

1959

Drama. Cylchgrawn y ddrama. Gymraeg. Denbigh. Vol 1– . 1959 – .   *1145*
   BnU

Ethnic. A quarterly survey of English folk music, dance & drama. London: 8 Eldon Park, S.E. 25. Vol 1. Nos 1–4. Jan – Autumn 1959. Quarterly. [Reproduced from typewritten copy]   *1146*
   BM

[*Folkstone-Hythe Operatic and Dramatic Society*]   Bulletin. Folkstone. Apr 1959. [Reproduced from typewritten copy]   *1147*
   BM

John Bourne's Newsletter. London: Published by Evans Brothers, Ltd., Publishers of *Plays and New Plays Quarterly.* Montague House, Russell Sq., W.C. 1. Dec 1959. [Reproduced from typewritten copy]   *1148*
   BM

The Mermaid Theatre Review 1959. London. 1959.   *1149*
   LU-MM

New Theatre Magazine. The quarterly magazine of repertory and university drama. Bristol: Published by the Green Room Society of the Drama Depart-

ment, University of Bristol. [Vol 1], No 1–   . Oct 1959 –   . Quarterly [with variations] [First edited by Christopher Ellison, and Harry Thompson. Nos 1–4. Oct 1959 – July 1960. Through 1966 a succession of some ten editors followed]
>   BM, CLSU, E, GM, MH, NN, NcU, NhU, OClW, O   **1150**

On Stage.   Bulletin of the Romford and Hornchurch Theatre Association. Ed by Ian Wilkes. [Romford] Nos 1–[7] Mar 1959 – Dec 1960. [Nos 3–7 are not numbered] Monthly (irregular). [Reproduced from typewritten copy]   **1151**
>   BM

Repertoire: the Official Newspaper of Sadler's Wells.   London. Vol 1. No 1. Sept 1959. Every six weeks.   **1152**
>   Not located

Seven Arts Digest.   London. Vol 1. Nos 1–7. Sept 1959 – Feb 1960. Monthly. [Nos 6 and 7 are both dated, Feb 1960. Reproduced from typewritten copy]   **1153**
>   BM

Shakespearean Authorship Review.   (The Shakespearean Authorship Society) London. Vol 1–   . Spring 1959 –   . Semiannual. [Supersedes, *Shakespeare Fellowship-Newsletter*]   **1154**
>   BP, CLU, DLC, LU, MH, MdBP, NIC, O

1961

British Actors' Equity Hotel and Apartment Guide.   Ed by W. Livingstone. London: Published annually on behalf of The Actors' Equity Association by Kemp's Commercial Guides Ltd. 1961. then, *Actors' Equity Hotel and Apartment Guide.* 1962 – 1963. Annual.   **1155**
>   BM

Show Pictorial.   The world of entertainment in words and pictures. Ed by Isidore Green. London: 22 Greek Street, W. 1. Nos 1–44. 20 May 1961 – 19 May 1962. Weekly. [It appears that the number for 30 Dec was not printed]   **1156**
>   BM-N

Theatre Royal.   Lowestoft. Nos 1–10. [1961] [The first numbers of the British Museum copy has "Feb. '61." written on the verso of the title page. The numbers are not dated]   **1157**
>   BM

Who's Who in Show Business.   London: Published by Show Business Publications, Ltd. 1960/61. [Called the "first edition," on p 3]   **1158**
>   BM

1962

About the House.   [A magazine devoted to ballet and opera] Ed by Kensington Davison. London: Published by The Friends of Covent Garden Limited, Royal Opera House. Vol 1. No 1–   . Nov 1962 –   . Quarterly [Four issues a year, except for three in 1964]   **1159**
>   BM (missing Vol 1, No 10. June 1965), E, LU-BTM (No 1)

International Stage & Film Review. Television. Film. Theatre. An independent
monthly world survey of current interest to buyers of film, television and theatre
productions. London: Published by Lion Mail, Ltd., 68 Mill Lane. [No 1] Feb
1962. Monthly.   *1160*
  BM

The Monitor. The bulletin of the Monmouthshire Drama League. Ed by Miss
  K. V. Barry. Newport: Issued by the Monmouthshire Drama League, Com-
  munity House. 8, Pentonville. Nos 8–9. Spring – Autumn 1962. Quarterly [?]
  [Reproduced from typewritten copy. I have not been able to locate any of the
  earlier numbers]   *1161*
  LU-MM

Prompt. (University College, London Dramatic Society). London. No 1–   .
  Summer 1962 –   . Three issues a year (irregular).   *1162*
  BrP, DLC, LdP, NIC, NN, O

Scene. Ed by Francis Hitching. London: Nicholas Luard Associate, 56 Fleet
  Street, E.C. 4. Vol 1–   . Sept 1962 –   . Weekly.   *1163*
  Not located

Seven Arts. [Incorporating, *Art and Artists, Books and Bookmen, Dance and
  Dancers, Films and Filming, Music and Musicians, Plays and Players, Records
  and Recordings,* and *Look and Listen.* London. [Nos 1–7] Oct 1962 – Apr 1963.
  Monthly. [This is simply a collection of seven different periodicals bound to-
  gether under one cover, with the title, *Seven Arts*]   *1164*
  BM (missing [No 5])

1963

Gambit. An international quarterly. Ed by Robert Rietty, Cav. London. Nos 1–3.
  1963. Quarterly. [The numbers are not dated. Contains original plays]   *1165*
  BM, E, O

Shaw-Script. Worcester. Nos 1–8. Autumn 1963 – 1965. Quarterly (irregular)
  BP, O   *1166*

Stagecast Directory. (Theatre, Films, Radio, Television) Ed by Derek Young.
  Dublin: Published by Stagecast, 23 Essex Quay. [Nos 1–3] 1962/63 – 1964/65.
  then, *Stagecast Directory.* Irish stage and screen. [No 4]–   . 1965/66. –   .
  Annual.   *1167*
  BM

Student Theatre. Leeds University Union. Leeds. No 1–   . Dec 1963 –   .
  LdP   *1168*

Who's Who in Show Biz. [London. 1963]   *1169*
  BM

1964

Scottish Community Drama Association Bulletin. Official organ of the Scottish
  Community Drama Association. Edinburgh. No 1–   . Summer 1964 –   .
  E, O (1966/67)   *1170*

Scottish Opera News.   Glasgow. No 1–   . 1964 –   .   *1171*
    E

1965

Jury.   A magazine of film and theatre criticism. London: Nos 1–8. 1965 – 1966.
    HLU, O   *1172*

London by Night.   A weekly guide to London's entertainment. London: Published by the Alpha Publishing Company, 12, Archer Street, W. 1. Nos 1–3. 28 May – 18 June 1965. Weekly.   *1173*
    BM

Proscenium: the Magazine of the Birmingham Repertory Theatre.   Birmingham. No 1–   . 9 Feb 1965 –   .   *1174*
    BM, BP

1966

EPA Spotlight.   Newsletter of the Educational Puppetry Association. London: 23 A Southampton Place, W.C. 1. 1966. 8 issues a year. [Listed in, *Newspaper Press Directory*, 1966]   *1175*
    Not located

Encore.   The Magazine of the Alexandra Theatre. Birmingham. No 1–   . 1966 –   .   *1176*
    BP

1967

Act One, Scene 2.   (Official Magazine of the Oxford Playhouse Company.) Edited by Michael Healy and Glynn Robbins. Oxford: Oxford Playhouse. Printed by Hunts Limited, Broad Street. Nos 1–3. Sept/Oct 1967 – May/June [1968] Every two months (irregular) [No 3 is called a "Special Issue: *The Tempest.*" The size of the periodical changes with No 3]   *1177*
    O

Appendix I

Number of Periodicals Published Outside of London

Aberdeen	1	East Barnet	1	Nottingham	2
Androssan	1	Eastbourne	1	Oldham	2
Armley	1	Edinburgh	43	Oxford	6
Ashton-Under-Lynne	1	Exeter	1	Paignton	1
Bath	1	Folkestone	5	Paisley	1
Belfast	3	Glasgow	44	Plymouth	3
Birmingham	39	Glastonbury	1	Portsmouth	3
Blackpool	7	Gloucester	1	Preston	1
Boscombe	1	Grays	1	Romford	1
Bournemouth	3	Hampstead	1	Rotherham	1
Bradford	3	Harpenden	1	Salisbury	1
Bramcote	1	Hastings	1	Sheffield	7
Brighton	11	Hinckley	1	Southall	1
Bristol	8	Huddersfield	1	Southampton	4
Broadstairs	1	Hull	2	Southend	2
Cambridge	8	Ilford	3	Southport	5
Cardiff	1	Ipswich	1	Southsea	3
Chatham	1	Kettering	1	Stratford-Upon-Avon	8
Cheltenham	2	Leeds	11	Sutton Coldfield	1
Chesterfield	1	Leicester	1	Swansea	4
Chislehurst	1	Letchworth	1	Swindon	1
Clacton	1	Lincoln	2	Sydenham	1
Coventry	3	Liverpool	42	Torquay	1
Croydon	2	Lowestoft	1	Tottenham	1
Darlington	1	Maidstone	1	Tunbridge Wells	1
Denbigh	2	Malvern	2	Wallington	2
Derby	1	Manchester	34	Warwickshire	1
Dinbych	1	Margate	2	West Dulwich	1
Doncaster	1	Newcastle	4	Weston-super-Mare	1
Dublin	28	Newcastle Upon Tyne	5	Whitley Bay	1
Dudley	1	Newport	2	Wolverhampton	1
Dundee	2	North Shields	2	Worcester	2
Durham	1	Northgate	1	Wrexam	1
Ealing	1	Norwich	3	York	2

Appendix II

Number of New Periodicals Published Each Year

Year	No.	Year	No.	Year	No.	Year	No.	Year	No.
1720	2	1815	2	1852	4	1893	8	1930	11
1734	2	1816	5	1853	5	1894	14	1931	7
1739	1	1817	2	1856	2	1895	17	1932	15
1749	1	1818	2	1857	3	1896	8	1933	6
1751	1	1819	4	1858	1	1897	9	1934	11
1753	3	1820	6	1860	2	1898	8	1935	16
1754	1	1821	12	1861	1	1899	12	1936	10
1758	1	1822	9	1862	4			1937	7
1763	1	1823	13	1863	5	1900	7	1938	5
1767	1	1824	11	1864	6	1901	15	1939	9
1768	1	1825	6	1865	6	1902	6	1940	5
1772	2	1826	6	1867	5	1903	13	1941	5
1774	1	1827	12	1868	13	1904	20	1943	4
1776	1	1828	16	1869	7	1905	11	1944	2
1784	1	1829	13	1870	6	1906	20	1945	7
1786	1	1830	10	1871	5	1907	12	1946	39
1788	1	1831	12	1872	2	1908	5	1947	30
1789	1	1832	8	1873	2	1909	5	1948	23
1790	1	1833	7	1874	10	1910	5	1949	16
1791	2	1834	5	1875	4	1911	5	1950	15
1792	2	1835	4	1876	6	1912	4	1951	5
1795	3	1836	3	1877	5	1913	15	1952	7
1796	1	1837	4	1878	5	1914	6	1953	15
		1838	7	1879	6	1915	5	1954	12
1800	2	1839	1	1880	6	1917	5	1955	12
1801	2	1840	6	1881	7	1918	1	1956	10
1803	4	1841	2	1882	5	1919	11	1957	11
1804	1	1842	5	1883	7	1920	6	1958	7
1805	5	1843	5	1884	11	1921	9	1959	10
1806	4	1844	3	1885	8	1922	13	1961	4
1807	3	1845	4	1886	7	1923	13	1962	6
1808	1	1846	5	1887	5	1924	11	1963	5
1809	1	1847	8	1888	8	1925	16	1964	2
1811	3	1848	8	1889	9	1926	4	1965	3
1812	2	1849	9	1890	8	1927	14	1966	2
1813	2	1850	7	1891	7	1928	12	1967	1
1814	3	1851	6	1892	7	1929	11		

Appendix III

General Statistics

Periodicals located at the British Museum	523
Periodicals located at the British Museum Newspaper Library at Colindale	269
Periodicals located only at the British Museum	254
Periodicals located only at the British Museum Newspaper Library at Colindale	222
Periodicals destroyed at the British Museum during the Second World War	97
Periodicals destroyed at the British Museum during the Second World War, but located elsewhere	48
Periodicals destroyed at the British Museum during the Second World War, and not located elsewhere	49
Periodicals never located at any library	30
Periodicals not located, including those destroyed at the British Museum, and not found at any other library, as well as one missing from the library shelf	80
Periodicals located at the Bodleian Library, Oxford	198
Periodicals located at The New York Public Library	158
Periodicals located at Harvard University Library	168
Periodicals on microfilm at Loyola University, Chicago	260
Periodicals published less than one year	534
Periodicals of only one issue	137
Periodicals of less than five issues	258
Annuals of only one issue	46
Number of periodicals with known editors	262
Number of periodicals reproduced from typewritten copy	29
Number of cities, excluding London, where periodicals appeared	102
Number of periodicals published in cities other than London	438
Number of periodicals published in London	795

Appendix IV

Frequency of Publication

Irregular	85	Weekly	392	3 times a year	6
Daily	29	Biweekly	34	2 times a year	8
6 days a week	13	Monthly	254	Annual	121
5 days a week	1	Every 6 weeks	1	Uncertain	310
3 days a week	5	Bimonthly	14		
2 days a week	4	Quarterly	62		

References

"Births and Deaths; a Record of New Ttitles, Changed Titles and Deaths in the Periodical World." *Bulletin of Bibliography* April 1900–   .

Briggs, Asa. *Press and Public in Early Nineteenth-century Birmingham.* Oxford: Printed for the Dugdale Society by Charles Batey, Printer to the University 1949. (Dugdale Society Occasional Papers, No. 8). [Contains a list of forty-five publications.]

British Museum Catalogue. Periodicals. 18 vols. Cols 1–1716.

British Museum General Catalogue of Printed Books. Photolithographic edition to 1955. Periodical Publications. London: Published by The Trustees of the British Museum 1936. Vols 184–186.

British Museum Newspaper Catalogue. Vols 1–21, plus volume for Irish Newspapers, and volume for Scottish Newspapers.

British Union-Catalogue of Periodicals: a record of the periodicals of the world, from the seventeenth century to the present day, in British Libraries. Edited for the council of the British-Union-Catalogue of periodicals by J. D. Stewart, with M. E. Hammond, and E. Saenger. London: Butterworths 1955–1958. 4 vols.

British Union-Catalogue of Periodicals. A record of the periodicals of the world, from the seventeenth century to the present day, in British Libraries. *Supplement to 1960.* Ed by James D. Stewart, with Muriel E. Hammond, and Erwin Saenger. London: Butterworths 1962.

British Union-Catalogue of Periodicals. Incorporating World List of Scientific Periodicals. New Periodical Titles. London: Butterworths, 1964–1967. 4 supplements.

The Cambridge Bibliography of English Literature. Edited by F. W. Bateson. New York and Cambridge, England 1941. 4 vols. Supplement 1957. 1 vol.

Cameron, James. "A Bibliography of Scottish Theatrical Literature." *Papers of the Edinburgh Bibliographical Society* I (1890–1895). Session 1891–1892, No 10. [1]–8. Session 1894–1895, No 24. 1–2.

A Catalogue of the Allen A Brown Collection of Books Relating to the Stage in the Public Library of the City of Boston. Boston: Published by the Trustees 1919.

Couper, William James. *Edinburgh Periodical Press; being a Bibliographical Account of the Newspapers, Journals, and Magazines Issued in Edinburgh from the Earliest Times to 1800.* Stirling: Mackay 1908. 2 vols. Supplements appeared in *Scottish Notes and Queries* 3rd Series VIII–XIII (1930–1935).

Crane, Ronald Salmon, and F. B. Kaye. *A Census of British Newspapers and Periodicals, 1620–1800.* Chapel Hill: University of North Carolina Press 1927.

Cranfield, G. A. *A Handlist of English Provincial Newspapers and Periodicals 1700–1760.* Cambridge: Bowes & Bowes 1952. (Cambridge Bibliographical Society Monographs No 2).

Gabler, Anthony J. "Check List of English Newspapers and Periodicals before 1801 in the Huntington Library." *Huntington Library Bulletin* No 2 (November 1931) 1–66.

Graham, Walter. *English Literary Periodicals.* New York: T. Nelson and Sons 1930.

Gray, Charles Harold. *Theatrical Criticism in London to 1795.* New York: Columbia University Press 1931.

Hoffman, Frederick J., Charles Allen, Carolyn F. Ulrich. *The Little Magazines.* A history and a bibliography. Princeton, New Jersey: Princeton University Press 1947. 2nd ed.

Hope, Frederick William. *Catalogue of a Collection of Early Newspapers and Essayists, Formed by the Late John Thomas Hope, Esq., and Presented to the Bodleian Library By the Late Rev. Frederick William Hope, M.A., D.C.L.* Oxford: At the Clarendon Press 1865. [764 numbered entries].

Keen, Owen W., and Kathleen Hancock. *The London Union List of Periodicals.* Holdings of the municipal and county libraries of Greater London. 2nd ed. London: The Library Association 1958.

Loewenberg, Alfred, comp. *The Theatre of the British Isles Excluding London. A Bibliography.* [Edited by Ifan Kyrle Fletcher.] London: Society for Theatre Research 1950.

London University. Library. *List of Periodicals.* London: The University 1956.

The London Union List of Periodicals: holdings of the municipal and county libraries of Greater London. Edited by K. A. Mallaber, and P. M. de Paris. London: Library Association, London & Home Counties Branch 1951. [Typewritten].

Lowe, Robert William. *A Bibliographical Account of English Theatrical Literature from Earliest Times to the Present Day.* London: J. C. Nimmo 1888.

Madden, Richard Robert. *The History of Irish Periodical Literature, from the End of the 17th to the Middle of the 19th Century.* London 1867. 2 vols.

Milford, R. T., and D. M. Sutherland. *A Catalogue of English Newspapers and Periodicals in the Bodleian Library, 1622–1800.* Oxford: Oxford Bibliographical Society 1936.

[Muddiman, J. G.] *Tercentenary Handlist of English and Welsh Newspapers, Magazines, and Reviews.* Section I. London & Suburban. II. Provincial. London: "The Times," 1920. [Addenda were published in *Notes and Queries* 1921–1922.]

New Serial Titles. A Union List of Serials Commencing Publication after December 31 1949. Prepared under the sponsorship of the joint committee on The Union List of Serials. Supplement to The Union List of Serials. Third Edition. 1961–1965. Cumulation. New York & London: R. R. Bowker Company; New York: Arno Publishing Inc 1966. 2 vols.

New Serial Titles 1950–1960. Supplement to the Union List of Serials. Third Edition. A Union List of Serials commencing publication after December 31, 1949. Prepared under the sponsorship of the joint committee on the Union List of Serials. Washington: The Library of Congress 1961. 2 vols.

The Newspaper Press Directory and Advertisers' Guide. London: Benn 1846–   . Annual. [Not published 1941–1944; published by Mitchell 1846–1948.]

O'Neill, James J. "A Bibliographical Account of Irish Theatrical Literature." *The Bibliographical Society of Ireland* i No 6 (1920) [57]–[87].

Parkes, Samuel. "An Account of the Periodical Literary Journals Which Were Published in Great Britain and Ireland, from the Year 1681 to the Commencement of *The Monthly*

Review, in the Year 1749." *Quarterly Journal of Science, Literature and the Arts* XIII (1822) 36–58, 289–312.

Powers, John. *List of Irish Periodical Publications (Chiefly Literary) from 1729 to the Present Time.* Reprinted from *Notes and Queries* March and April 1866, and *The Irish Literary Inquirer* No 4, with additions and corrections. London: (Printed for Private Circulation Only.) [1866].

Sell's World Press; the Handbook of the Fourth Estate. London: Sell 1884–1921. Vols 1–36. [Title varies].

Sper, Felix. *The Periodical Press of London, Theatrical and Literary, Excluding the Daily Newspaper, 1800–1830.* Boston: F. W. Faxon Co 1937.

Stewart, Powell. *British Newspapers and Periodicals, 1632–1800.* A Descriptive Catalogue of a Collection at the University of Texas. Austin 1950.

Subject Index of the Modern Works Added to the Library of the British Museum in the Years 1881–1900. Ed by G. K. Fortescue. London 1902–1903. 3 vols. [See also the volumes added for the years: 1901–1910. 2 vols; 1911–1915. 1 vol; 1916–1920. 1 vol; 1921–1925. 1 vol; 1926–1930. 1 vol; 1931–1935. 2 vols; 1936–1940. 2 vols; 1941–1945. 2 vols; 1946–1950. 4 vols; 1956–1960. 6 vols. The title varies.]

Toase, Mary. *Guide to Current British Periodicals.* London: The Library Association 1962.

Ulrich, Carolyn Farquhar. *Little Magazines, a List Compiled.* New York: New York Public Library 1947.

Ulrich's Periodicals Directory. A classified guide to a selected list of current periodicals, foreign and domestic. 5th ed. Ed by Carolyn F. Ulrich. Including a list of clandestine periodicals of World War II by Adrienne Florence Muzzy. New York: Bowker 1947. [The directory began in 1932, and is continued to the present day.]

Ulrich's International Periodicals Directory. Volume 2. Arts, Humanities, Business & Social Sciences. Eleventh Edition. Ed by Eileen C. Graves. New York and London: R. R. Bowker Company, 1966.

Union Catalogue of the Periodical Publications in the University Libraries of the British Isles, with Their Respective Holdings,

Excluding Titles in the "World List of Scientific Periodicals" 1934. London: Joint Standing Committee on Library Cooperation 1937.

Union List of Serials in Libraries of the United States and Canada. 2nd ed. Edited by W. Gregory. New York: Wilson 1943. [Supplements for 1941–1943; 1944–1949. Then, *New Serial Titles*, 1953–   .]

Ward, William Smith. *Index and Finding List of Serials Published in the British Isles, 1789–1832*. Lexington: University of Kentucky Press 1953.

Weed, Katherine Kirtley, and Richmond Pugh Bond. *Studies of British Newspapers and Periodicals, from Their Beginning to 1800: a Bibliography*. Chapel Hill: University of North Carolina Press 1947.

Willing's Press Guide. A comprehensive index and handbook of the press of the United Kingdom of Great Britain, Northern Ireland, and the Irish Republic; together with the principal British Commonwealth, Dominion, Colonial and foreign publications. London: Willing, 1871–   . Annual. [Title varies. Originally, *Frederick May's London Press Directory*, 1871.]

INDEX

"A.A." (1917) 723

A.B.C. Amusement Guide & Record (1896) 545

A.C.U. Paper (1939) 920

à Beckett, Gilbert A. See Censor (1828) 155

Abbey Theatre. See Arrow (1906), 648

Abbott, G. F. See Gallery Gazette (1920) 740

Aberdeen. See Bon Accord (1880) 419

About the House (1962) 1159

Abracadabra (1946) 950

Act (1955) 1107

Act One, Scene 2 (1967) 1177

Acting Manager (1831) 192

Acting Manager and Musical Director. See Theatrical Manager (1928) 825

Actor. See Liverpool Dramatic Censor (1806) 47; Mirror of the Stage (1822) 101; Performer (1906) 659; Performer Annual (1907) 670; "Performer" Handbook (1921) 753; Playgoer's Magazine (1888) 478; Roscius (1825) 132

Actor and Elocutionist (1881) 425

Actor for Player and Public (1919) 729

Actor Illustrated (1905) 638

Actor, Playgoer, and Dramatic Directory (1891) 496

Actors Association Yearbook (1917) 724

Actors' Association. See British Equity (1931) 848; Equity Letter (1947) 996

Actors by Daylight (1838) 235

Actors by Gaslight (1838) 236

Actor's Church Union. See Call Board (1930) 839

Actors' Equity Association. See British Actors' Equity Hotel and Apartment Guide (1961) 1155; British Equity (1931) 848; Equity Letter (1947) 996

Actors' Equity Hotel and Apartment Guide. See British Actors' Equity Hotel and Apartment Guide (1961) 1155

Actor's Note-Book (1841) 249

Actresses' Franchise League (1913) 698

Age. See Tallis's Illustrated Life (1864) 339

Age and Dramatic Journal (1883) 437

Age, Theatrical, Musical, and Sporting. See Tallis's Illustrated Life (1864) 339

Alexandra Journal (1927) 806

Allday, Joseph. See Theatrical John Bull (1824) 127

Altrincham Garrick Society. See Garrick Magazine (1936) 903

Amateur. See Amateur Actor (1886) 462; Amateur Dramatic Yearbook (1928) 816; Amateur Operatic Yearbook (1923) 766; Amateur Stage (1906) 647; Amateur Stage (1926) 802; Amateur Stage (1932) 853; Amateur Stage (1946) 951; Amateur Theatre (1925) 787; Amateur Theatre and Play-

wright's Journal (1934) 874; Amateur Theatrical Review (1933) 868; Amateur Theatrical World (1925) 788; Amateur's Guide (1867) 346; Amateur's Handbook and Entertainment Guide (1897) 553; "Broadsheet" (1948) 1018; Glasgow Amateur Public Amusement Record (1856) 317; Glasgow and District Entertainment Guide (1922) 757

Amateur Actor (1886) 462

Amateur Dramatic Year Book (1928) 816

Amateur Operatic Year Book (1923) 766

Amateur Players. See "Broadsheet" (1948) 1018

Amateur Stage (1906) 647; (1926) 802; (1932) 853; (1946) 951

Amateur Theatre (1925) 787. See also Scottish Stage (1930) 845

Amateur Theatre and Playwright's Journal (1934) 874

Amateur Theatrical Review (1933) 868

Amateur Theatrical World (1925) 788

Amateur's Guide (1867) 346

Amateur's Handbook and Entertainer's Directory (1897) 553

Amateur's Place Book. See Dramatic Correspondent (1828) 156

Amphi (1873) 382

Amusement Workers' News. See N.A.T.E. Journal (1921) 752

Amusement World (1932) 854

Andrews, John. See Dobson's Theatre Year Book (1948) 1021; Magic Magazine (1952) 1077

Androssan. See Piping and Dancing (1935) 896

Anglo-French Chronicle. See Anglo-French Stage Chronicle (1899) 569

Anglo-French Stage Chronicle (1899) 569

Anmer's Hall's Company. See Festival Theatre Programme (1929) 829

Anti-Theatre (1720) 1

Annals of the Drama. See Theatrical Review (1763) 13

Annuals. See Actors Association Yearbook (1917) 724; Amateur Dramatic Year Book (1928) 816; Amateur Operatic Year Book (1923) 766; Amateur's Handbook (1897) 553; Authors', Playwrights, & Composers' Handbook (1935) 885; Ballet Annual (1947) 990; Ballroom Dancing Annual (1947) 992; Ballroom Dancing Year Book (1958) 1138; Bill of the Play (1882) 432; Birmingham Pantomime Annual (1899) 571; Boorman's Theatrical Directory (1895) 528; British Actors' Equity Hotel and Apartment Guide (1961) 1155; British Equity (1931) 848; British Theatre (1946) 955; Cinema and Theatre Annual (1947) 995; The "Comedy"

Gazette (1899) 571a; Concert Goer's Annual (1957) 1129; Cymdeithas Ddawns Werin Cymru (1955) 1081; Dance Music Annual (1951) 1070; Dancing (1906) 653; (1923) 768; Directory of London Theatrical Agents (1956) 1120; Dobson's Theatre Year Book (1948) 1021; Dramatic and Musical Directory (1883) 439; Dramatic Annual (1831) 194; Dramatic Equestrian (1862) 327; Dramatic Notes (1879) 414; Dramatic Peerage (1892) 503; Dramatic Register for 1851 (1851) 304; Dramatic Souvenir (1833) 212; Dramatic Year Book (1892) 504; Encore Annual (1895) 531; English Folk-Dance Society's Journal (1914) 713; Entr'acte Almanack (1873) 383; Era Almanac (1868) 354; Festival News (1947) 998; Flash Backs from "London Off Duty" (1943) 937; General Dramatic, Equestrian & Musical Agency (1857) 319; Glasgow Pantomime Annual (1895) 534; Glasgow Theatrical Annual (1895) 535; Grand Guignol Annual Review (1921) 750; Green Room Book (1906) 656; Guide to Selecting Plays (1914) 714; Henry Butler's Theatrical Directory (1853) 313; Imperial Society of Teachers of Dancing (1954) 1097; International Theatre Annual (1956) 1122; John Waddington's Annual (1901) 592; Journal of the English Folk Dance and Song Society (1932) 860; Leeds Pantomime Annual (1894) 522; Leisure Year (1948) 1025; London Stage Annual (1903) 614; Londoner Annual (1947) 1001; London's Fesitval Ballet Annual (1957) 1131; Magic Wand Year Book (1947) 1002; Magician Annual (1907) 669; Malvern Festival (1929) 830; Manchester Pantomime's Annual (1882) 435; Manchester Repertory Theatre Magazine (1935) 892; Music, Music and Dancing (1954) 1101; Musical Artists', Lecturers', and Entertainers' Guide (1885) 458; National Amateur Operatic and Dramatic Association (1922) 761; National Operatic and Dramatic Association Directory (1957) 1134; New Plays Annual for Women (1956) 1123; 1955 Directory of Concert and Cabaret Artistes (1955) 1110; Official Music Hall Directory and Variety ABC (1899) 577; Old Drury-Lane Christmas Annual (1882) 436; Opera Annual (1954) 1102; Oxford Repertory Company Limited (1935) 895; Pantomime Annual (1892) 505; Performer Annual (1907) 670; Playgoers' Pocket-book (1886) 467; Plays and Players (1904) 628; Plays of the Year (1948) 1030a; Puppet Year Book (1944) 942; Puppetry Year Book (1955) 1112; R. Douglas Cox's Variety Directory (1904) 630; Roberts Pantomime Annual (1895) 539; Royal Opera House Annual Report (1958) 1141; Scottish Drama (1950) 1062; Scottish Drama Year Book (1948) 1031; Scottish Music and Drama (1946) 978; Season's Concert (1912) 695; Shakespeare Club (1929) 835; Shakespeare Survey (1948) 1032; Showmen's Year Book (1956) 1126; Society for Theatre Research (1950) 1065; Souvenirs de Ballet (1949) 1046; Spotlight (1949) 1047; "Spotlight" Yearbook (1931) 851; Stage and Variety Artistes Guide (1950) 1067; Stage Society (1900) 585; Stage Year Book (1908) 678; Sunday Chronicle (1913) 706; Thalia Diary & Directory of Concert Parties (1910) 689; Theatre (1954) 1106; Theatre Annual (1884) 448; Theatre World Annual (1949) 1049; Theatrical Apartments (1920) 745; Universal Musical and Dramatic Directory (1913) 710; Variety Theatre Annual (1906) 662; Walter's Theatrical and Sporting Directory (1884) 452; Wandering Thespian Annual (1871) 379; Weekly Sporting Review (1937) 915; Will A. Bradley's Pantomime Annual (1900) 586; Yorkshire Owl Pantomime Annual (1892) 508

Anson, J. W. See Dramatic Almanac (1868) 351; Dramatic Equestrian (1862) 327; General Dramatic, Equestrian & Musical Agency (1857) 319

Apartment Guide. See British Actors' Equity Hotel and Apartment Guide (1961) 1155

Apollo (1829) 170

Arcadia, Doncaster, Monthly Post (1930) 837

Arcadia Theatre. See Arcadia, Doncaster, Monthly Post (1930) 837

Archer, William. See Theatrical World for 1893–1897 (1893) 514

Argus (1804) 40; (1925) 789

Argus Corrected (1805) 41

Armley. See Hanson's Directory of the Musicians (1894) 520

Armstrong, George. See Wizard (1947) 1016

Arram, David D. See Musicians Directory (1932) 863

Arrow (1906) 648

Art (1911) 690

Artist (1807) 50

Artiste (1887) 468

Artistes Bulletin (1947) 989

Arts Council Bulletin. See C.E.M.A. Bulletin (1940) 928

Arts Gazette (1919) 730

Arts in the USSR. See SCR. Society for Cultural Relations with the U.S.S.R. (1953) 1088

Ash-Lyons, L. See Musicians Directory (1932) 863

Ashton-under-Lynne. See Wilford Hutchinson's Conjurers Chronicle (1919) 739

Association of Touring and Producing Managers. See *Theatrical Manager* (1928) 825

Athenaeum (1828) 154

Athletic and Dramatic News. See *Liverpool Athletic & Dramatic News* (1890) 492

Audience. See *Professional World* (1892) 506

Austrian Shakespeare Society. See *Shakespeare Quarterly* (1948) 1031a

Authentic Memoirs of the Green-Room (1801) 34; (1806) 46

Author (1890) 489

Author, Playwright and Composer. See *Author* (1890) 489

Authors', Playwrights, & Composers' Handbook (1935) 885

Avon News (1930) 838

B.D.T.G. Bulletin (1948) 1017

Bacon-Shakespeare (1914) 712

Baconiana. See *Journal of the Bacon Society* (1886) 463a

Bagshawe, Edward. See *Edward Bagshawe's Magical Journal* (1927) 809; *Magical Monthly* (1923) 769

Baldrey, Henry R. See *Folk Drama* (1954) 1096

Ball Room (1911) 691; (1926) 803

Ballet. See *About the House* (1962) 1159; *Ballet* (1939) 921; (1945) 943; *Ballet Annual* (1947) 990; *Ballet Carnaval* (1946) 952; *Ballet Review* (1947) 991; *Ballet Today* (1946) 953; *British Ballet Organisation Bulletin* (1939) 922; *Dancer* (1928) 818; *Foyer* (1951) 1071; *Harlequin* (1957) 1130; *London Musical Events* (1946) 968; *London's Festival Ballet* (1957) 1131; *Opera, Ballet, and Music-Hall* (1952) 1078; *Souvenirs de Ballet* (1949) 1046; *Young Ballet Dancer* (1952) 1080

Ballet (1939) 921; (1945) 943

Ballet and Opera. See *Ballet* (1939) 921

Ballet Annual (1947) 990

Ballet Carnaval (1946) 952

Ballet Review (1947) 991

Ballet Today (1946) 953

Ballet World. See *Ballet* (1945) 943

Ballroom Dancing Annual (1947) 992

Ballroom Dancing Times (1956) 1118

Ballroom Dancing Year Book (1958) 1138

Barry, K. V. See *Monitor* (1962) 1161

Bat (1885) 454

Bath. See *Bath Theatrical Review* (1822) 98

Bath Theatrical Review (1822) 98

Baton (1865) 340

"Bayard." See *Sunday Chronicle* (1913) 706

Baylis, Wyndham C. See *In Town* (1950) 1056; *In Town* (1952) 1075

Beaumont, Cyril. See *Dance Journal* (1950) 1055

Beauties of the Magazines and Spirit of the Times (1827) 142

Beckenham and Penge Entertainment Guide (1936) 901

Behind the Scenes (1946) 954

Belfast. See *Queue* (1946) 974; *Script* (1945) 947; *Threshold* (1957) 1137

Bell, Christopher. See *Isis Theatre Supplement* (1953) 1085a

Beltaine (1899) 570

Belvedere. See *Erith, Belvedere and District Free Press* (1930) 841

Bennett, Hannaford. See *Clean Slate* (1903) 608

Bensusam, S. L. See *Bohemian* (1893) 510

Besant, Sir Walter. See *Author* (1890) 489

Bexley and Erith Bulletin. See *Erith, Belvedere and District Free Press* (1930) 841

Bijou Journal of London. See *Compass* (1898) 561

Bill of the Play (1869) 362; (1882) 432; (1892) 502

Birmingham. See *Abracadabra* (1946) 950; *Alexandra Journal* (1927) 806; *Amateur's Guide* (1867) 346; *B.D.T.G. Bulletin* (1948) 1017; *Birmingham Amusements and Souvenir of the Stage* (1893) 509; *Birmingham and Midlands Musical Journal* (1884) 444; *Birmingham Dramatic News* (1885) 455; *Birmingham Musical Examiner* (1845) 264; *Birmingham Pantomime Annual* (1899) 571; *Birmingham Programme of Amusements* (1906) 649; *Birmingham Repertory Theatre News-Letter* (1925) 790; *Birmingham Reporter* (1823) 106; *Birmingham Spectator* (1824) 119; *Caste* (1900) 581; *Children's Theatre* (1948) 1019; *Current Events* (1929) 827; *Encore* (1966) 1176; *Gong* (1921) 749; *London Museum Music Hall* (1867) 347; *Midlander* (1925) 795a; *Municipal Player* (1924) 785; *Occasional Magazine* (1932) 864; *Pleasure and Pastime in the City* (1901) 597; *Prince of Wales Courier* (1929) 833; *Prince of Wales' Journal and Shows' Gazette* (1885) 460; *Prince of Wales Theatre* (1863) 331; *Proscenium* (1965) 1174; *Royal Tatler* (1929) 834; *Scallop-Shell* (1911) 692; *Seats* (1954) 1103; *Spotlight* (1950) 1066; *Theatrical Argus and Stage Reporter* (1830) 190; *Theatrical John Bull* (1824) 127; *Theatrical Looker-on* (1822) 105; *Theatrical Note-Book* (1824) 128; *Theatrical Observer* (1830) 190a; *Theatrical Tatler* (1830) 191; *What's On in Birmingham* (1922) 765; (1943) 940

Birmingham Amusements and Souvenir of the Stage (1893) 509

Birmingham and Midlands Musical Journal (1844) 444

Birmingham Dramatic News (1885) 455
Birmingham Hospitality Committee. See *What's On in Birmingham* (1943) 940
Birmingham Musical Examiner (1845) 264
Birmingham Pantomime Annual (1899) 571
Birmingham Programme of Amusements (1906) 649
Birmingham Repertory Theatre. See *Gong* (1921) 749; *Occasional Magazine* (1932) 864; *Proscenium* (1965) 1174
Birmingham Repertory Theatre News-letter (1925) 790
Birmingham Reporter, and Theatrical Review (1823) 106
Birmingham Spectator (1824) 119
Bishop, G. W. See *Amateur Dramatic Year Book* (1928) 816
Blackadder, Rosemary. See *Parade* (1925) 797
Blackpool. See *Blackpool Amusements* (1894) 515a; *Blackpool Carnival Pictorial & Programme* (1924) 777a; *Blackpool Programme* (1893) 509a; *Blackpool Visitor* (1868) 350a; *Blackpool Visitor and Programme* (1884) 444a; *Sights and Shows* (1899) 579
Blackpool Amusements (1894) 515a
Blackpool Carnival Pictorial & Programme (1924) 777a
Blackpool Programme (1893) 509a
Blackpool Programme and Visitor. See *Blackpool Programme* (1893) 509a
Blackpool Visitor (1868) 350a
Blackpool Visitor and Advertiser (1868) 350b
Blackpool Visitor and Programme (1884) 444a
Blackpool Visitor and Programme. See *Blackpool Programme* (1893) 509a
Bland, Alan. See *Birmingham Repertory Theatre News-letter* (1925) 790; *Gong* (1921) 749
Blue Review (1913) 699
Bohemian (1893) 510
Bon Accord (1880) 419
Book of the Play (1906) 650
Book World (1890) 490
Books and Art, Films, Theatre (1957) 1128
Books of the Month. See *Books and Art* (1957) 1128
Boorman, J. H. See *Boorman's Theatrical Directory* (1895) 528
Boorman's Theatrical Directory (1895) 528
Boosey's Musical and Dramatic Review. See *Musical and Dramatic Review* (1864) 337
Booth, John. See *London Shakespeare League Journal* (1914) 715
Boscombe. See *Bournemouth and Boscombe Amusements* (1894) 515b
Bourn, Tom. See *Amateur Operatic Year Book* (1923) 766
Bourne, John. See *Amateur Theatre and Playwright's Journal* (1934) 874; *John Bourne's*

Newsletter (1959) 1148; *New Plays Annual for Women* (1956) 1123; *New Plays Quarterly* (1947) 1004; *Theatrecraft* (1938) 919; *Theatrecraft News-Letter* (1941) 936
Bournemouth. See *Bournemouth and Boscombe Amusements* (1894) 515b; *Bournemouth Visitors' Programme* (1907) 665a; *Mercury* (1948) 1028
Bournemouth and Boscombe Amusements (1894) 515b
Bournemouth & District Visitors' & Residents' Weekly Guide. See *Bournemouth Visitors' Programme* (1907) 665a
Bournemouth Visitors' Daily Events. See *Bournemouth Visitors' Programme* (1907) 665a
Bowen, G. M. See *Shakespeare Fellowship News-Letter* (1947) 1007a
Box Office Entertainment Guide (1884) 445
Bradford. See *Leeds Playgoer* (1924) 779; *Magical Record* (1915) 720; *Theatre* (1945) 948
Bradley, Will A. See *Will A. Bradley's Pantomime Annual* (1900) 586
Bramall, Eric. See *Puppetry Year Book* (1955) 1112
Bramcote. See *Peter Warlock's Pentagram* (1946) 971
Brereton, Austin. See *Dramatic Notes* (1879) 414
Brewer, Geo. See *Man in the Moon* (1803) 38
Brighton. See *Brighton Amusements* (1903) 607a; *Brighton and Hove Entertainment Chronicle* (1891) 496a; *Brighton Dramatic Miscellany* (1838) 237; *Brighton Echo and Daily Bill of the Play* (1874) 383a; *Brighton Entertainments* (1906) 651; *Brighton Record* (1850) 297; *Brighton Theatrical Observer* (1836) 228; *Now-a-days* (1947) 1005; *Potpourri* (1946) 972; *Stage Door* (1947) 1011; *Theatre Royal* (1935) 898
Brighton Amusements (1903) 607a
Brighton and Hove Entertainment Chronicle (1891) 496a
Brighton Dramatic Miscellany (1838) 237
Brighton Echo and Daily Bill of the Play (1874) 383a
Brighton Entertainments (1906) 651
Brighton Illustrated Sporting Mail. See *Brighton Entertainments* (1906) 651
Brighton Programme. See *Brighton Entertainments* (1906) 651; *Now-a-days* (1947) 1005
Brighton Record (1850) 297
Brighton Repertory Theatre Magazine. See *Theatre Royal* (1935) 898
Brighton Theatrical Observer (1836) 228
Brighton Weekly Programme. See *Brighton Entertainments* (1906) 651

Bristol. See *Bristol & Clifton Amusements* (1900) 580; *Bristol Diary of Events* (1947) 993; *Bristol Playgoer* (1915) 718; *Call Boy* (1946) 956; *Call-boy* (1949) 1039; *New Theatre Magazine* (1959) 1150; *Thespian* (1823) 116; *What's On?* (1901) 601

Bristol & Clifton Amusements (1900) 580

Bristol Development Department. See *Bristol Diary of Events* (1947) 993

Bristol Diary of Events (1947) 993

Bristol Guild of Players. See *Call Boy* (1946) 956

Bristol Playgoer (1915) 718

Bristol Playgoer's Club. See *Bristol Playgoer* (1915) 718

British Actor's Equity Association. See *British Actors' Equity Hotel and Apartment Guide* (1961) 1155; *British Equity* (1931) 848; *Equity Letter* (1947) 996

British Actors' Equity Hotel and Apartment Guide (1961) 1155

British Ballet Organisation. See *Dancer* (1928) 818

British Ballet Organisation Bulletin (1939) 922

British Drama and Literary Humorist (1832) 204

British Drama League. See *Amateur Dramatic Year Book* (1928) 816; *B.D.T.G. Bulletin* (1948) 1017; *Drama* (1919) 731; *War-time Drama* (1939) 927; *Working Light* (1948) 1036

British Empire Shakespeare Society. (1915) 719

British Equity (1931) 848

British Puppet and Model Theatre Guild. See *Puppetry Year Book* (1955) 1112

British Puppet and Model Theatre Guild Junior News (1941) 933

British Puppet and Model Theatre Guild Newsletter (1951) 1069

British Puppet and Model Theatre Guild. *War-time Bulletin* (1939) 923

British Puppet Theatre (1949) 1038

British Stage (1823) 107; (1831) 193

British Stage and Literary Cabinet (1817) 72

British Theatre (1800) 32; (1946) 955

"Broadsheet" (1948) 1018

Broadstairs. See *Broadstairs Day by Day* (1925) 791

Broadstairs Day By Day (1925) 791

Brother, Barnaby. See *Theatrical Tickler* (1828) 168

Broughton, J. See *British Stage and Literary Cabinet* (1817) 72

Brown, Ivor. See *Theatre* (1954) 1106

Browning, Fred. See *Dancing* (1903) 609

Brynildsen, E. N. See *Dancing Annual* (1923) 768

Buckle, Richard. See *Ballet* (1939) 921

Butler, Henry. See *Manager's Circular* (1851) 306

C.E.M.A. Bulletin (1940) 928

Call Board (1930) 839

Call-boy (1838) 238; (1949) 1039

Call Boy (1906) 652

Call Boy (1946) 956

Call Sheet (1937) 910

Cambridge. See *Cambridge Guide to "What's On?"* (1922) 754a; *Shakespeare Survey* (1948) 1032; *What's On* (1955) 1116; *What's On in Cambridge* (1953) 1094

Cambridge Guide to "What's On?" (1922) 754a

Cameron, Donald. See *Scots Theatre* (1946) 976

Canterbury Hall. See *South London Palace and Canterbury Hall Journal* (1871) 376

Capper, Alfred. See *Professional World* (1892) 506

Cardiff. See *What's On* (1904) 637a; *What's On in the West Country* (1949) 1053

Carlile, R. See *Prompter* (1830) 188

Carnival Parade (1956) 1119

Carson, Lionel. See *"Stage" Guide* (1912) 696; *Stage Year Book* (1908) 678

Carter, Lionel. See *Masque* (1946) 969

Cast (1947) 994

Caste (1900) 581

Cecchetti Society. See *Dance Journal* (1950) 1055

Censor (1807) 51; (1821) 86; (1828) 155

Censor. See *Covent-Garden Journal* (1752) 8

Chapbook. See *Poetry and Drama* (1913) 705

Chat of the Week (1830) 183

Chatham. See *What's On* (1927) 813a

Cheltenham. See *Hardey's Universal Theatrical Directory* (1928) 819; *National Amateur Operatic and Dramatic Association* (1922) 761

Cheltnam, Charles S. See *Dramatic Year Book* (1892) 504

Cheron, Alfred. See *Moliere and Shakespeare* (1858) 322

Chesterfield. See *In Town* (1950) 1056

Chesterton, A. K. See *Shakespeare Review* (1928) 821

Children's Theatre (1948) 1019

Chislehurst. See *Marlovian Chronicle* (1957) 1133

Choir, and Musical Record. See *Saturday Musical Review* (1879) 417

Christian Drama (1946) 957

Cicerone (1843) 256

Cinema and Theatre Annual Review (1947) 995

Circle (1905) 639

Circular. See *Dramatic Reform Association* (1878) 410

Circulating Library (1886) 463

Citizens' Theatre Society. See *Prompter* (1943) 938

City of Nottingham Civic News. See *Diary of Entertainment and Events* (1958) 1139

Civic Entertainment (1948) 1020

Clacton. See *Clacton Programme of Entertainment* (1901) 587; *Clacton Visitors' Guide* (1923) 766a

Clacton Programme of Entertainment (1901) 587

Clacton Visitors' Guide (1923) 766a

Clarion (1882) 433; (1930) 840

Clarke, Charles M. See *Dramatic Opinion* (1889) 481

Clarke, Charles. See *Show* (1925) 798

Clarke, Mary. See *Ballet Annual* (1947) 990

Clean Slate (1903) 608

Clifton. See *Bristol & Clifton Amusements* (1900) 580; *What's On* (1901) 601

Clown of London (1845) 265

Codlin, Ellen M. See *Puppet Year Book* (1944) 942

Colchester. See *What's On* (1955) 1116

Collier, Jun., Jeremy. See *Prompter Prompted* (1816) 70

Collis, J. B. See *Inspector* (1819) 77

Columbine and Weekly Review of Literature (1829) 171

Combes, W. H. See *Entr' acte Almanack* (1873) 383

Comedy (1889) 480a

"Comedy" Gazette (1899) 571a

Commentary (1941) 933a

Companion to the Theatre. See *Dramatic Tatler* (1829) 175

Companion to the Theatres (1852) 310

Compass (1898) 561

Compton, Herbert. See *Dramatic Peerage* (1892) 503

Con Brio (1946) 958

Concert. See *Amateur's Guide* (1867) 346; *Drama* (1846) 268; *Folkestone Amusement Guide* (1901) 590; *Garraway's Directory of Concert* (1934) 876; *London Amusements* (1925) 793; *London Entertainer and Concert Artiste* (1953) 1086; *London Guide and Photographic Album* (1876) 400; *London Musical Events* (1946) 968; *London Singer's Magazine* (1838) 240; *London Theatre Entertainment* (1900) 582; *Lytton's Theatre Seating Plans and Concert Halls* (1957) 1132; *Musician, and Music-Hall Times* (1862) 329; *1955 Directory of Concert* (1955) 1110; *Pullman Casting Directory* (1956) 1125; *Season's Concert* (1912) 695; *Seats* (1954) 1103; *Thalia Diary & Directory of Concert Parties* (1910) 689; *Theatrical and Concert Companion* (1840) 247

Concert Goer's Annual (1957) 1129

Concert, Lecture, Dramatic Guide. See *Season's Concert* (1912) 695

Conjuror's Magazine (1791) 25

Connoisseur (1845) 266

Conway, F. W. See *Stage* (1821) 92

Cooke, James. See *Actor's Note-Book* (1841) 249

Copper, Alfred. See *Professional World* (1892) 506

Corder, Robert. See *Masque* (1954) 1099

Cornish Pixie (1944) 941

Cornucopia (1820) 80

Corrector (1816) 67

Cote's Weekly Journal (1734) 3

Coulter, W. M. See *Scots Theatre* (1946) 976

Country Correspondent (1739) 5

Courier (1932) 855; (1932) 856

Court Journal (1829) 172

Courtney, Gordon. See *Courier* (1932) 856

Coveney, Ralph. See *Showgirl Glamour Review* (1955) 1114

Covent Garden Chronicle (1768) 14a

Covent-Garden Journal (1752) 8

Covent Garden Journal (1810). See year 1810

Covent-Garden Theatrical Gazette (1816) 68

Coventry. See *Footlights* (1945) 944; *Hippodrome Tatler* (1935) 888; *Theatre Guild News* (1958) 1143; *What's On in Coventry and District* (1921) 754

Craig-Raymond, Peter. See *Ballet Today* (1946) 953

Creative Drama (1949) 1040; See also *Children's Theatre* (1948) 1019

Cribbes, G. O. See *Scottish Drama Year Book* (1948) 1031

Critic (1820) 81; (1843) 257; (1874) 384; (1880) 420; (1928) 817

Critic. See *Critic of Literature, Art, Science and Drama* (1843) 258

Critic of Literature, Art, Science and the Drama (1843) 258

Critical and Biographical Illustrations. See *Dramatic Censor* (1811) 55

Critical Companion. See *Dramatic Censor* (1770) 15

Critical Remarks on the Amusements. See *Vauxhall Observer* (1823) 117

Critical Remarks on the Daily Performances. See *Theatrical Examiner* (1823) 114

Critics' Circle. See *Critics' Circular* (1923) 767

Critics' Circular (1923) 767

Critique (1898) 562

Croker, Thomas F. See *Dramatic Register for 1851* (1851) 304

Croydon. See, *Purley and Couldson Entertainment Guide* (1936) 906; *Rep* (1934) 881

Cruikshank, G., and I. R. See *Monthly Theatrical Reporter* (1814) 63; *Scourge* (1811) 57

Crystal Palace Herald (1853) 312a

Crystal Palace Herald and London Amusement Guide. See *Crystal Palace Herald* (1853) 312a

Crystal Palace Herald and Shareholders' Monthly Circular. See *Crystal Palace Herald* (1853) 312a

Crystal Palace Herald and Visitors' Guide. See *Crystal Palace Herald* (1853) 312a

Cue (1949) 1041

Current Events (1929) 827

Curtain (1847) 273; (1862) 326; (1878) 408; (1922) 755

Curtain Call (1949) 1042

Cylchgrawn Undeb y Ddrama Gymreig (1927) 807

Cymdeithas Ddawns Werin Cymru (1953) 1081; (1955) 1108

Daily Bills of the Performances. See *Theatrical Mirror* (1827) 153

Daily Chronicle of Public Amusements. See *Theatrical Guide* (1822) 104

Daily Programme and Playbill (1899) 572

Daily Theatrical Mirror. See *Looking Glass* (1832) 208

Dance. See *Ball Room* (1911) 691; *Ball Room* (1926) 803; *Ballet* (1939) 921; (1945) 943; *Ballet Annual* (1947) 990; *Ballet Carnaval* (1946) 952; *Ballet Review* (1947) 991; *Ballet Today* (1946) 953; *Ballroom Dancing Annual* (1947) 992; *Ballroom Dancing Times* (1956) 1118; *Ballroom Dancing Year Book* (1958) 1138; *Dance and Dancers* (1950) 1054; *Dance Journal* (1950) 1055; *Dance Music Annual* (1951) 1070; *Dance News Weekly* (1946) 959; *Dance Notes* (1953) 1082; *Dance Review* (1939) 924; *Dance Tone* (1935) 886; *Danceland* (1922) 756; *Danceland* (1937) 911; *Dancer* (1928) 818; *Dancer and Cabaret* (1932) 857; *Dancing* (1891) 497; (1903) 609; (1906) 653; *Dancing Annual* (1923) 768; *Dancing Life* (1921) 746; *Dancing Record* (1924) 778; *Dancing Times* (1894) 516; *English Dance and Song* (1936) 902; *English Folk Dance and Song Society* (1948) 1022; *English Folk Dance Society News* (1921) 748; *English Folk-Dance Society's Journal* (1914) 713; *Ethnic* (1959) 1146; *Folk Dancer* (1954) 1096; *Gazette* (1941) 934; *Imperial Society of Teachers of Dancing* (1954) 1097; *Journal of the English Folk Dance* (1932) 860; *Lancashire Dance News* (1946) 963; *Link* (1924) 780; *London Amusements* (1925) 793; *London Dance News* (1946) 966; *London Weekly Programme* (1935) 891; *London's Festival Ballet Annual* (1957) 1131; *Music, Music and Dancing* (1954) 1101; *Musicians Directory* (1932) 863; *Operatic*

Association Gazette (1930) 843; *Palais Dancing News* (1920) 742; *Parados* (1940) 931; *Piping and Dancing* (1935) 896; *Piping, Drumming and Highland Dancing* (1948) 1030; *Quarterly News Sheet* (1950) 1060; *Scottish Dance News* (1946) 977; *Top-Spin* (1940) 932; *Who's Who in Dancing* (1932) 867

Dance and Dancers (1950) 1054

Dance Journal (1950) 1055

Dance Music Annual (1951) 1070

Dance News. See *Dance News Weekly* (1946) 959; *Danceland* (1937) 911; *Ethnic* (1959) 1146

Dance News Weekly (1946) 959

Dance News Weekly. See *Scottish Dance News* (1946) 977

Dance Notes (1953) 1082

Dance Review (1939) 924

Dance Teachers Association. See *Ballroom Dancing Year Book* (1958) 1138

Dance Tone (1935) 886

Danceland (1922) 756; (1937) 911

Dancer (1928) 818

Dancer and Cabaret (1932) 857

Dancing (1891) 497; (1903) 609; (1906) 653

Dancing and Film News. See *Dancer and Cabaret* (1932) 857

Dancing Annual (1923) 768

Dancing Life (1921) 746

Dancing Record and London Amusements (1924) 778

Dancing Times (1894) 516

Dancing Times, Ltd. See *Ballroom Dancing Annual* (1947) 992; *Ballroom Dancing Times* (1956) 1118

Dancing World. See *Dancing Life* (1921) 746; *Palais Dancing News* (1920) 742

Dangerfield, Fred. See *Playgoer* (1901) 595; *Stage Souvenir* (1903) 619

Dangerfield Entertainment Guide (1895) 529

Dark, Sidney. See *London Stage Annual* (1904) 614

Darlington. See *Living Theatre* (1948) 1027

Darlington Repertory Theatre. See *Living Theatre* (1948) 1027

Darnley, Herbert. See *Wanted* (1904) 637

Davenport, L. See *Davenport's The Demon Telegraph* (1933) 869

Davenport's The Demon Telegraph (1933) 869

Davies, Byron. See *Danceland* (1937) 911

Davis, James. See *Bat* (1885) 454

Davis, Rowland T. See *Dance News Weekly* (1946) 959; *Lancashire Dance News* (1946) 963; *London Dance News* (1946) 966; *Scottish Dance News* (1946) 977

Dawe, R. See *Highlights from the Folkestone-Hythe Operatic and Dramatic Society* (1953) 1084

Day's Doings (1870) 369

De Pinna, I. Wm. See *Green Register* (1947) 1000

Deacon, James. See *Artiste* (1887) 468

Debrett's Coming Events (1901) 588

Deckmann, George. See *Movement* (1948) 1029

'Demon' Telegraph. See *Davenport's The Demon Telegraph* (1933) 869

Denbigh. See *Drama* (1959) 1145; *Welsh Folk Drama Society News-Letter* (1953) 1092

Denbury, Garry. See *Magazine 4* (1952) 1076

Derby. See *In Town* (1952) 1075

Diary of Entertainment and Events (1958) 1139

Digbeth, Humphrey. See *Birmingham Reporter* (1823) 106

Directory. See *Actor, Player, and Dramatic Directory* (1891) 496; *Amateur's Handbook* (1897) 553; *Call Sheet* (1938) 910; *Cinema and Theatre Annual Review* (1947) 995; *Directory of London Theatrical Agents* (1956) 1120; *Dramatic and Musical Directory* (1883) 439; *Garraway's Directory* (1934) 876; *Green Register* (1947) 1000; *Hanson's Directory of the Musicians* (1894) 520; *Hardey's Universal Theatrical Directory* (1928) 819; *Henry Butler's Theatrical Directory* (1853) 313; *Kirkley's Theatrical Apartments Directory* (1901) 594; *Manager's Circular* (1851) 306; *Musical Artists', Lecturers', and Entertainers' Guide* (1885) 458; *1955 Directory of Concert and Cabaret Artistes* (1955) 1110; *Official Music Hall Directory* (1899) 577; *Photo-Cast* (1957) 1136; *Pullman Casting Directory* (1956) 1125; *R. Douglas Cox's . . . Variety Directory* (1904) 630; *Spotlight* (1949) 1047; *"Spotlight" Casting Directory* (1927) 813; *Spotlight Gazette of Artists* (1934) 884; *"Spotlight" Pocket Telephone Directory* (1935) 897; *Stage Directory* (1880) 424; *Stagecast Directory* (1963) 1167; *Theatrical Apartments* (1920) 745; *Universal Musical and Dramatic Directory* (1913) 710; *Walter's Theatrical and Sporting Directory* (1884) 452; *Wm. Haslam's Apartment Directory* (1906) 665

Directory of London Theatrical Agents (1956) 1120

District Club News and Local Entertainment (1952) 1074

Dobbs, Dr. See *My Journal* (1907) 669a

Dobson's Theatre Year Book (1948) 1021

Doncaster. See *Arcadia, Doncaster, Monthly Post* (1930) 837

Dorman, Sean. See *Commentary* (1941) 933a

Douglas, Albert. See *Amateurs' Handbook* (1897) 553

Douglass' Directory. See *Amateurs' Handbook and Entertainers' Directory* (1897) 553

Dragoman (1927) 808

Drama (1821) 88; (1846) 268; (1847) 274; (1883) 438; (1919) 731; (1959) 1145

Drama, a Daily Register of Histrionic Performances on the Dublin Stage (1821) 87

Drama, Music, Art, Literature. See *Arts Gazette* (1919) 730

Dramatic Almanac (1868) 351

Dramatic Almanack for 1867. See *Dramatic Equestrian* (1862) 327

Dramatic & Musical Almanack. See *Dramatic Equestrian* (1862) 327

Dramatic and Musical Circular (1879) 413

Dramatic and Musical Directory of the United Kingdom (1883) 439

Dramatic and Musical Mirror. See *Dramatic and Musical Circular* (1879) 413

Dramatic and Musical Review (1842) 251

Dramatic Annual (1831) 194

Dramatic Argus (1824) 120

Dramatic Art Circular (1875) 393

Dramatic Authors' Society (1878) 409

Dramatic Authors' Society Tariff. See *Dramatic Authors' Society* (1878) 409

Dramatic Censor (1752) 9; (1770) 15; (1800) 33; (1811) 55; (1829) 173

Dramatic Chronicle and Observer (1870) 370

Dramatic Correspondent and Amateur's Place Book (1828) 156

Dramatic Criticism (1899) 573

Dramatic Debates. See *First-Nighter* (1904) 620

Dramatic Diary (1906) 654

Dramatic, Equestrian, and Musical Sick Fund Almanack. See *General Dramatic, Equestrian & Musical Agency* (1857) 319

Dramatic Equestrian and Musical Sick Fund Almanack (1862) 327

Dramatic Gazette (1830) 184

Dramatic Indicator. See *Scene Shifter* (1848) 285

Dramatic Inspector (1819) 76

Dramatic Intelligence. See *Corrector* (1816) 67

Dramatic Magazine (1786) 21; (1829) 174

Dramatic Mirror. See *Thespian Telegraph* (1796) 31

Dramatic Mirror and Review of Music (1847) 275

Dramatic Miscellany (1820) 82

Dramatic News (1847) 276; (1868) 352

Dramatic Notes (1879) 414

Dramatic Observer (1877) 403

Dramatic Observer and Musical Review (1823) 108

Dramatic Omnibus (1849) 288

Dramatic Opinion (1889) 481; (1891) 498

Dramatic Peerage (1892) 503

Dramatic Record and Theatrical Advertiser (1874) 385
Dramatic Reform Association (1878) 410
Dramatic Register (1828) 157
Dramatic Register for 1851 (1851) 304
Dramatic Review (1795) 28; (1821) 89; (1847) 277; (1848) 281; (1851) 305; (1868) 353; (1885) 456; (1906) 655
Dramatic Review, and Register of the Fine Arts (1814) 62
Dramatic Review and Weekly Miscellany (1837) 231
Dramatic Souvenir (1833) 212
Dramatic Spectator (1837) 232
Dramatic Speculum (1826) 136
Dramatic Tatler (1829) 175
Dramatic Telegram (1865) 341
Dramatic Times (1895) 530
Dramatic World (1894) 517
Dramatic Year Book (1892) 504
Dramatical and Musical Magazine (1823) 109
Drape, A. C. See *Dramatic Diary* (1906) 654
Drinkwater, John. See *Scallop-Shell* (1911) 692
"Dromio." See *Will A. Bradley's Pantomime Annual* (1900) 586
Drury Lane Gazette (1907) 666
Drury-Lane Journal. See *Have At You All* (1752) 10
Drury-lane Theatrical Gazette (1816) 69
Du Maurier, G. See *Stage Props* (1923) 776
Dublin. See *Arrow* (1906) 648; *Cinema and Theatre Annual* (1947) 995; *Commentary* (1941) 933a; *Covent-Garden Journal* (1752) 8; *Drama* (1821) 88; *Dramatic Argus* (1824) 120; *Dramatic Inspector* (1819) 76; *Dramatic Review* (1821) 89; *Genuine Theatrical Observer* (1823) 111; *Independent Theatrical Observer* (1822) 100; *Irish Dramatic Censor* (1811) 56; *Irish Limelight* (1917) 725; *Irish Playgoer and Amusement Record* (1899) 575; *Irish Turf Telegraph and Dramatic Gazette* (1875) 394; *Motley* (1932) 862; *Nettle* (1751) 7; *New Theatrical Observer* (1833) 216; *Original Theatrical Observer* (1821) 91; *Play-house Journal* (1749) 6; *Public Advertiser* (1774) 18; *Samhain* (1901) 598; *Stage* (1821) 92; *Stagecast Directory* (1963) 1167; *Tatler and Theatrical Mirror* (1834) 222; *Theatre* (1822) 103; *Theatric Magazine* (1805) 44; *Weekly Theatrical Reporter* (1829) 182
Dublin Gate Theatre Magazine. See *Motley* (1932) 862
Dudley. See *Dance Notes* (1953) 1082
Dudley, John. See *British Puppet and Model Theatre* (1951) 1069
Duffy, Henry A. See *Hague's Minstrel and Dramatic Journal* (1882) 434; *Manchester*

Pantomime's Annual (1882) 435; *Pantomime Annual* (1892) 505
Dundee. See *What's On and Where* (1949) 1051
Dundee Theatrical Review (1826) 137
Dunstable. See *What's On* (1955) 1116
Durham. See *Exits and Entrances* (1947) 997
Durham County Drama Association. See *Exits and Entrances* (1947) 997
Dutton, Thomas. See *Dramatic Censor* (1800) 33; *Monthly Theatrical Reporter* (1814) 63

E.F.D.S. News (1921) 747
EPA Spotlight (1966) 1175
EPA Year Book. See *Puppet Year Book* (1944) 942
Ealing. See *Fore-Stage* (1956) 1121; *What's On in Ealing* (1949) 1052
Earl, Thomas. See *Country Correspondent* (1739) 5
East Barnet. See *Gen* (1946) 961
East London Sports and Entertainment Mirror (1934) 875
East Surrey and District Entertainment Guide (1935) 887
East Yorkshire Comet. See *Hull, Grimsby & East Yorkshire Programme* (1894) 521
Eastbourne Amusements (1901) 589
Eastbourne Courier. See *Eastbourne Programme* (1908) 676
Eastbourne Mirror. See *Eastbourne Programme* (1908) 676
Eastbourne Programme of Entertainments (1908) 676
Eclipse and Theatrical Programme (1876) 397
Edgar, Sir John. See *Theatre* (1720) 2
Edile (1784) 20
Edinburgh. See *Ballet Review* (1947) 991; *Companion to the Theatres* (1852) 310; *Courier* (1932) 855; *Dramatic Censor* (1829) 173; *Dramatic Review* (1851) 305; *Dramatic Review and Weekly Miscellany* (1837) 231; *Dramatic Spectator* (1837) 232; *Dramatic Tatler* (1829) 175; *Edinburgh Dramatic Censor* (1842) 252; *Edinburgh Dramatic and Musical Magazine* (1827) 143; *Edinburgh Dramatic Journal* (1828) 158; *Edinburgh Dramatic Recorder* (1825) 130; *Edinburgh Dramatic Review* (1822) 99; *Edinburgh Dramatic Review, and Thespian Inquisitor* (1827) 144; *Edinburgh Dramatic Tête-à-tête* (1828) 159; *Edinburgh Programme* (1879) 415; *Edinburgh Theatrical and Musical Review* (1835) 224; *Edinburgh Theatrical Casket* (1832) 205; *Edinburgh Theatrical Censor* (1803) 36; *Edinburgh Theatrical Observer and Musical Review* (1823) 110; *Festival News* (1947) 998; *Literary Cynosure* (1824) 122; *New Edinburgh Dramatic Re-*

view (1832) 209; *Opera* (1832) 210; *Opera Glass* (1840) 244; *Piping, Drumming and Highland Dancing Journal* (1948) 1030; *Printers Devil* (1850) 300; *Prompter and Scottish Dramatic Review* (1842) 255; *S.C.D.A. Advisory Service* (1947) 1007a; *Scottish Community Drama* (1964) 1170; *Scottish Drama* (1950) 1062; *Scottish Drama Year Book* (1948) 1031; *Scottish Dramatic Mirror* (1844) 262; *Scottish Music and Drama* (1946) 978; *Scottish Musical Magazine* (1919) 736; *Stage and Scottish Musical and Theatrical Omnibus* (1849) 291; *Theatre* (1813) 60; (1831) 201; (1851) 309; *Theatrical Record* (1823) 115; *Theatrical Speculum* (1831) 203; *Thespian Censor* (1818) 75; *Thespian Critique* (1816) 71; *Weekly Dramatic Review* (1828) 169; *Weekly Review and Dramatic Critic* (1852) 312; *What's On* (1925) 800

Edinburgh Dramatic and Musical Magazine (1827) 143

Edinburgh Dramatic Censor (1842) 252

Edinburgh Dramatic Journal (1828) 158

Edinburgh Dramatic Recorder (1825) 130

Edinburgh Dramatic Review (1822) 99

Edinburgh Dramatic Review, and Thespian Inquisitor (1827) 144

Edinburgh Dramatic Tête-à-tète (1828) 159

Edinburgh General Review. See *Printers Devil* (1850) 300

Edinburgh Programme (1879) 415

Edinburgh Theatrical and Musical Review (1835) 224

Edinburgh Theatrical Casket (1832) 205

Edinburgh Theatrical Censor (1803) 36

Edinburgh Theatrical Observer and Musical Review (1823) 110

Educational Drama Association. See *Creative Drama* (1949) 1040

Educational Puppetry Association. See *EPA Spotlight* (1966) 1175; *Puppet Post* (1947) 1007; *Puppet Year Book* (1944) 942

Edward Bagshawe's Magical Journal (1927) 809

Edwards, Kathleen. See *Unemployed Drama News* (1936) 908

El-BA Direction. See *Artistes Bulletin* (1947) 989

Ellis, Benedict. See *Laban Art of Movement Guide* (1948) 1024

Ellison, Cary. See *Artistes Bulletin* (1947) 989

Ellison, Christopher. See *New Theatre Magazine* (1959) 1150

Ellison-Barlow Productions. See *Cast* (1947) 994

Elmer, G. See *Swan* (1958) 1142

Elocution. See *Hanson's Directory of the Musicians* (1894) 520

Encore (1954) 1095; (1966) 1176

Encore Annual (1895) 531

Encore Annual (1905) 639a

Enfield. See *Peter Warlock's Pentagram* (1946) 971

English Dance and Song (1936) 902

English Entr'acte. See *Curtain* (1847) 273

English Folk Dance. See *E.F.D.S. News* (1921) 747; *English Dance and Song* (1936) 902; *English Folk Dance & Song Society Bulletin* (1948) 1022; *English Folk Dance Society News* (1921) 748; *English Folk-Dance Society's Journal* (1914) 713; *Ethnic* (1959) 1146; *Journal of the English Folk Dance and Song Society* (1932) 860

English Folk Dance & Song Society Bulletin (1948) 1022

English Folk Dance Society News (1921) 748

English Folk-Dance Society's Journal (1914) 713

English Folk Music. See *Ethnic* (1959) 1146

English Review. See *Theatre-Craft* (1919) 738

English Society in Town and Country (1870) 371

English Stage-Player. See *Cote's Weekly Journal* (1734) 3

Entertainer (1913) 700

Entertainment Gazette and Echoes of the Week. See *Entertainment Gazette and Guide to London* (1887) 469

Entertainment Gazette and Guide to London (1887) 469

Entertainment Gazette Illustrated. See *Entertainment Gazette and Guide to London* (1887) 469

Entertainment World. See *Music Box* (1927) 811

Entr' Acte. See *London Entr' Acte* (1869) 366

Entr'acte Almanack (1873) 383

Equity. See *British Actors' Equity Hotel and Apartment Guide* (1961) 1155; *British Equity* (1931) 848; *Equity Letter* (1947) 996

Equity Letter (1947) 996

Era (1838) 239

Era Almanac (1868) 354

Era Almanac and Annual. See *Era Almanac* (1868) 354

Era Screen and Stage Pictorial (1931) 849

Erith, Belvedere and District Free Press (1930) 841

Erith Theatre Guild. See *Proscenium* (1946) 973

Erskine, Mrs. Steuart. See *Kensington* (1901) 593

Espinosa, Louisa Kay. See *Dancer* (1928) 818

Ethnic (1959) 1146

Eureka (1897) 554

Evans, Jon. See *Mercury* (1948) 1028

Eve, Edward. See *Music Box and British Entertainer* (1927) 811

Events in Bristol. See *What's On in the West Country* (1949) 1053
Everyman (1929) 828
Examiner (1808) 53
Exeter. See *Exeter Day by Day* (1911) 691a
Exeter Day by Day (1911) 691a
Exits and Entrances (1947) 997
Eyre, Samuel. See *Samuel Eyre's Theatrical Programme* (1872) 381

Falstaffe, Sir John. See *Anti-Theatre* (1720) 1
Favourite (1907) 667
Favourite Magazine. See *Eureka* (1897) 554
Fayerman, A. T. See *Norwich Theatrical Observer* (1827) 148
Felixstowe. See *What's On* (1955) 1117
Fennell, James. See *Prompter* (1789) 23; *Theatrical Guardian* (1791) 26
Fennell's Shakespeare Repository. See *Shakespeare Repository* (1853) 315
Ferret (1870) 372
Festival Gate Review. See *Festival Theatre Review* (1926) 804
Festival News (1947) 998
Festival Review. See *Festival Theatre Review* (1926) 804
Festival Theatre. See *Festival Theatre Review* (1926) 804
Festival Theatre Programme (1929) 829. See also *Festival Theatre Review* (1926) 804
Festival Theatre Review (1926) 804
Festival Theatre Review'd. See *Festival Theatre Review* (1926) 804
Figaro in Liverpool (1833) 213
Figaro in London (1831) 195
Figaro Programme (1874) 386
Film and Stage Digest (1946) 960
Film and Theatre Today. See *Theatre Today* (1946) 984
Findlay, J. See *Cornucopia* (1820) 80
Fire Fly (1876) 398
First-Nighter (1904) 620
Fitzgerald, S. J. Adair. See *Playgoer* (1901) 595
Flash Backs from "London off Duty" (1943) 937
Fly Leaves of the Ladies Guild of Francis St. Alban. See *Ladies Guild of Francis St. Alban* (1905) 640a
Fly Paper (1884) 446
Folk Dance. See *English Dance and Song* (1936) 902; *English Folk Dance & Song Society* (1948) 1022; *English Folk Dance Society News* (1921) 748; *English Folk-Dance Society's Journal* (1914) 713; *Folk Dancer* (1954) 1096; *Journal of the English Folk Dance and Song Society* (1932) 860
Folk Dancer (1954) 1096
Folk Musician and Singer. See *Folk Dancer* (1954) 1096

Folkestone. See *Folkestone Amusement Guide* (1901) 590; *Folkestone Amusements* (1894) 518; *Folkestone-Hythe Operatic and Dramatic Society* (1959) 1147; *Folkestone Programme* (1895) 532; *Highlights from the Folkestone-Hythe Operatic and Dramatic Society* (1953) 1084
Folkestone Amusement Guide (1901) 590
Folkestone Amusements (1894) 518
Folkestone-Hythe Operatic and Dramatic Society (1959) 1147
Folkestone Programme (1895) 532
Folklorist. See *Folk Dancer* (1954) 1096
Footlights (1864) 334; (1869) 363; (1884) 447; (1890) 491; (1897) 555; (1899) 574; (1945) 944; (1948) 1023
Forest, W. See *Managers' Guide and Artistes' Advertiser* (1878) 411
Fore-Stage (1956) 1121
Fowler, C. T. See *Theatrical Chronicle and Dramatic Review* (1840) 248
Foyer (1951) 1071
France. See *Anglo-French Stage Chronicle* (1899) 569; *Gaulois and the Universal Caricature* (1861) 325
Franchise League. See *Actresses' Franchise League* (1913) 698
Francis & Day's Book of Dialogues. See *Mohawk Minstrels' "Nigger" Dramas* (1878) 412
Fraser, A. See *This Week in London* (1946) 985
French, Samuel. See *Guide to Selecting Plays* (1914) 714
French's Play Parade (1953) 1083
Friendship (1937) 911a
Frinton-On-Sea. See *Clacton Programme of Entertainment* (1901) 587
Friswell, James H. See *Play-goer* (1851) 307

Gaiety (1869) 364; (1869) 365
Gale, B. T. See *Licensed Victuallers' Mirror* (1883) 473
Gallery Gazette (1903) 610; (1909) 681; (1920) 740
Gambit (1963) 1165
Gardner, Douglas. See *Lytton's Theatre Seating Plans and Concert Halls* (1957) 1132
Garraway's Directory of Concert and Variety Artistes (1934) 876
Garrick Magazine (1936) 903
Garrick Spectator (1932) 858
Gaulois and the Universal Caricature (1861) 325
Gazette (1941) 934
Gen (1946) 961
General Dramatic, Equestrian & Musical Agency (1857) 319
General Repository. See *Theatric Magazine* (1805) 44

General Theatrical Directory. See *Manager's Circular* (1851) 306

General Theatrical Programme (1883) 440

Gent, W. G. H. See *Journal of the Institute of Magicians* (1934) 878

Gentleman, Francis. See *Dramatic Censor* (1770) 15

Genuine Theatrical Observer (1823) 111

Giddins, W. J. See *Journal of the Institute of Magicians* (1934) 878

Gilbert and Sullivan Journal (1925) 792

Gilbert and Sullivan Society. See *Gilbert and Sullivan Journal* (1925) 792

Giles, Rae. See *Highlights from the Folkestone-Hythe Operatic and Dramatic Society* (1953) 1084

Gillingham. See *What's On* (1927) 813a

Ginner-Mawer School. See *Link* (1924) 780; *Quarterly News Sheet* (1950) 1060

Glasgow. See *Age and Dramatic Journal* (1883) 437; *Con Brio* (1946) 958; *Drama* (1847) 274; *Dramatic Omnibus* (1849) 288; *Dramatic Review* (1847) 277; *Dramatic Review* (1868) 353; *Entertainer* (1913) 700; *Film and Stage Digest* (1946) 960; *Glasgow Amateur Public Amusement Record* (1856) 317; *Glasgow and District Entertainment Guide* (1922) 757; *Glasgow Dramatic Review* (1826) 138; (1844) 261; *Glasgow Entertainment Guide* (1927) 810; *Glasgow Harlequin* (1895) 533; *Glasgow Pantomime Annual* (1895) 534; *Glasgow Programme* (1897) 556; *Glasgow Programme and List of Entertainments* (1905) 640; *Glasgow Satirist and Dramatic Critic* (1848) 282; *Glasgow Theatrical Annual* (1895) 535; *Glasgow Theatrical Observer* (1824) 121; *Glasgow Theatrical Register* (1803) 37; (1805) 42; *Glasgow Theatrical Review* (1827) 145; (1846) 269; *Glasgow Weekly Programme* (1896) 546; *New Opera Glass* (1830) 186; *Opera Glass* (1829) 178; (1848) 283; *Pepper Box* (1840) 245; *Play-Goer* (1831) 200; *Playgoer and Public Amusement Guide* (1850) 299; *Prompter* (1893) 513; (1943) 938; *Scots Theatre* (1946) 976; *Scottish Opera News* (1964) 1171; *Scottish Player* (1923) 775; *Scottish Stage* (1930) 845; *Stage and Literary and Musical Review* (1848) 286; *Stage News* (1897) 559; *Theatre de Luxe Gazette* (1914) 717; *Theatrical Critic* (1845) 223; *Theatrical Examiner* (1833) 152; *Theatrical Observer* (1820) 85; *Theatrical Visitor* (1835) 227; *Thistle* (1829) 181; *Weekly Spectator* (1857) 321

Glasgow Amateur Public Amusement Record (1856) 317

Glasgow and District Entertainment Guide (1922) 757; See also *Glasgow Programme and List of Entertainments* (1905) 640

Glasgow Dramatic Review (1826) 138; (1844) 261

Glasgow Entertainment Guide (1927) 810; See also *Glasgow Programme and List of Entertainments* (1905) 640

Glasgow Harlequin (1895) 533

Glasgow Pantomime Annual (1895) 534

Glasgow Programme (1897) 556; See also *Glasgow Programme and List of Entertainments* (1905) 640; *Glasgow Weekly Programme* (1896) 546

Glasgow Programme and List of Entertainments (1905) 640

Glasgow Punch. See *Glasgow Satirist and Dramatic Critic* (1848) 282

Glasgow Satirist and Dramatic Critic (1848) 282

Glasgow Theatrical Annual (1895) 535

Glasgow Theatrical Observer (1824) 121

Glasgow Theatrical Register (1803) 37; (1805) 42

Glasgow Theatrical Review (1827) 145; (1846) 269

Glasgow Unity Theatre. See *Scots Theatre* (1946) 976

Glasgow Weekly Programme (1896) 546

Glastonbury. See *Magazine 4* (1952) 1076; *What's On in the West Country* (1949) 1053

Gloucester. See *Footlights* (1948) 1023

Gloucester Theatre Guild. See *Footlights* (1948) 1023

Glover, James M. See *Theatre Manager's Handbook* (1928) 824

Gold's London Magazine. See *The London Magazine* (1820) 84

Goldston, Will. See *Goldston's Magical Quarterly* (1934) 877; *Magician Annual* (1907) 669; *Pantomime and Vaudeville Favourites* (1913) 703

Goldston's Magical Quarterly (1934) 877

Gong (1921) 749

Goodliffe. See *Abracadabra* (1946) 950; *Goodliffe's Magic Monthly* (1947) 999

Goodliffe's Magic Monthly (1947) 999

Graham, W. J. See *Museum* (1822) 102

Grand Guignol Annual Review (1921) 750

Grand Theatre Magazine Programme. See *Magazine Programme* (1906) 657a

Graphic Guide to the London Theatres (1894) 519

Grays. See *District Club News* (1952) 1074

Great Yarmouth. See *What's On* (1953) 1093

Greater London Players' Magazine (1932) 859

Greek Dance Association. See *Quarterly News-Sheet* (1950) 1060

Greek Drama. See *Broadsheet* (1948) 1018; *Link* (1924) 780

Green, Isidore. See *Show Pictorial* (1961) 1156

Green, L. Dunton. See *Arts Gazette* (1919) 730

Green Register (1947) 1000

Green Room. See *Authentic Memoirs of the Green-Room* (1801) 34; (1806) 46; *Monitor* (1767) 14

Green Room (1880) 421

Green Room Book (1906) 656

Green-Room Laid Open. See *Monitor* (1767) 14

Green Room Mirror (1946) 962

Gregory, John. See *Harlequin* (1957) 1130

Grein, J. T. See *Arts Gazette* (1919) 730; *Comedy* (1889) 480a; *Independent Theatre Goer* (1912) 694; *Playgoer's Review* (1891) 500; *To-Morrow* (1896) 573

Grein, Thomas. See *Dramatic Criticism* (1899) 573

Guide to Selecting Plays (1914) 714

Hadley, Michael. See *London Musical Events* (1946) 968; *Pot-pourri* (1946) 972

Hague's Minstrel and Dramatic Journal (1882) 434

Hall, A. George. See *London's Festival Ballet Annual* (1957) 1131

Hall Green Little Theatre. See *Spotlight* (1950) 1066

Hallucinate, Hanibal. See *Edinburgh Dramatic Review* (1827) 144

Hammerton, J. A. See *Prompter* (1893) 513

Hampstead. See *Harmonic Olio* (1812) 58

Hanson's Directory of the Musicians (1894) 520

Hardacre, J. Pitt. See *"Comedy" Gazette* (1899) 571a

Hardey's Universal Theatrical Directory (1928) 819

Harland-Edgcumbe. See *Leeds Playgoer* (1924) 779

Harlequin. See *Glasgow Harlequin* (1895) 533; *Yorkshire Harlequin* (1896) 552

Harlequin (1829) 176; (1957) 1130

Harmonic Olio (1812) 58

Harpenden. See *Offstage* (1956) 1124; *What's On* (1955) 1116

Haskell, Arnold. See *Ballet Annual* (1947) 990; *Who's Who in Dancing* (1932) 867

Haslam, William. See *Wm. Haslam's Apartment Directory* (1906) 665

Hastings. See *Hastings Day by Day* (1928) 819a; *Hastings, St. Leonards & Bexhill Amusements* (1896) 547

Hastings, St. Leonards & Bexhill Amusements (1896) 547

Have At You All (1752) 10

Hawkes, D. See *Puppet Post* (1947) 1007

Haydn, J. T. See *Stage* (1821) 92

Healy, Michael. See *Act One, Scene 2* (1967) 1177

Helmann, C. L. See *Danceland* (1937) 911

Henderson, William. See *Prompter* (1899) 578

Henry Butler's Theatrical Directory (1853) 313

Heraud, John A. See *Henry Butler's Theatrical Directory* (1853) 313

Herf, Estelle. See *Ballet Today* (1946) 953

Hickman, Charles D. See *P.A.D.* (1902) 604; *Playlet and Monologue Magazine* (1901) 596

Hiffernan, Paul. See *Tuner* (1754) 11

Highbury Bulletin. See *Highbury Players' Bulletin* (1936) 904

Highbury Players' Bulletin (1936) 904

Highbury Theatre Centre. See *Intimate Theatre Group Newsletter* (1950) 1057

Highlights from the Folkestone-Hythe Operatic and Dramatic Society (1953) 1084

Hill, Aaron. See *Prompter* (1734) 4

Hippodrome (1901) 591

Hippodrome Tatler (1935) 888

Hitchin. See *What's On* (1955) 1116

Hitching, Francis. See *Scene* (1962) 1163

Hoare, Prince. See *Artist* (1807) 50

Hobson, Harold. See *International Theatre Annual* (1956) 1122

Hogg, J. See *English Society in Town and Country* (1870) 371

Holcroft, Thomas. See *Theatrical Recorder* (1805) 45; *Theatrical Review* (1807) 52

Holland, G. F. See *Curtain* (1922) 755

Holme, Stamford. See *Repertory* (1931) 850a

Holme, Thea. See *Repertory* (1931) 850a

Honey Pot (1919) 732

Honorary Secretary. See *Readable Recitations* (1888) 479

Hood, Tom. See, *Our Plays and Players* (1925), 796

Hook, F. See *Puppet Post* (1947) 1007

Hope, Charles. See *Curtain* (1922) 755

Hopkins, J. B. See *Players* (1860) 323

Hotel Guide. See *British Actors' Equity Hotel and Apartment Guide* (1961) 1155

House, Jack. See *Scottish Drama Year Book* (1948) 1031

Hove. See *Stage Door* (1947) 1011

Howard, Cecil. See *Dramatic Notes* (1879) 414

Howes, Frank. See *Journal of the English Folk Dance and Song Society* (1932) 860

Huddersfield. See *Spear* (1922) 763

Hudson, J. W. See *Lyre* (1841) 250

Hughes, John. See *Hughes News* (1953) 1085

Hughes News (1953) 1085

Hull. See *Hull Dramatic Censor* (1826) 139; *Hull, Grimsby & East Yorkshire Programme* (1894) 521

Hull, Basil. See *Fore-Stage* (1956) 1121
Hull and East Yorkshire Illustrated. See *Hull, Grimsby & East Yorkshire Programme* (1894) 521
Hull Dramatic Censor (1826) 139
Hull Entr' Acte. See *Hull, Grimsby & East Yorkshire Programme* (1894) 521
Hull, Grimsby & East Yorkshire Programme (1894) 521
Hunt, Leigh. See *Chat of the Week* (1830) 183; *Examiner* (1808) 53
Hutchinson, Wilford. See *Wilford Hutchinson's Conjurers Chronicle* (1919) 739
Hythe. See *Folkestone-Hythe Operatic and Dramatic Society* (1959) 1147

Idler, and Breakfast-Table Companion (1837) 233
Ilford. See *Ilford and District Shoppers' Guide* (1927) 810a; *Ilford What's On* (1922) 758; *What's On in Ilford* (1948) 1035
Ilford and District Shoppers' Guide & Amusement Programme (1927) 810a
Ilford What's On (1922) 758
Illustrated Life in London (1881) 426
Illustrated Review (1870) 373
Illustrated Sporting and Dramatic News (1874) 387
Illustrated Sporting and Theatrical News. See *Illustrated Sporting News* (1862) 328
Illustrated Sporting Mail and Brighton Weekly. See *Brighton Entertainments* (1906) 651
Illustrated Sporting News (1862) 328
Imperial Society of Teachers of Dancing. See *Dance Journal* (1950) 1055
Imperial Society of Teachers of Dancing (1954) 1097
In London Now (1954) 1098
In Town (1950) 1056; (1952) 1075
Independent Theatre Goer (1912) 694
Independent Theatrical Observer (1822) 100
Inspector (1819) 77
Institute of Magicians. See *Journal of the Institute of Magicians* (1934) 878
Interlude (1885) 457
International Entertainer (1902) 602
International Festival of Music and Drama. See *Festival News* (1947) 998
International Stage & Film Review (1962) 1160
International Theatre (1903) 611
International Theatre Annual (1956) 1122
Intimate Theatre Group News-letter (1950) 1057
Ipswich. See *Proscenium* (1950) 1059; *What's On* (1955) 1116
"Iris" Guide to London Amusements (1913) 701
Irish Cinema. See *Commentary* (1941) 933a

Irish Commentary. See *Commentary* (1941) 933a
Irish Dramatic Censor (1811) 56
Irish Limelight (1917) 725
Irish Literary Theatre. See *Beltaine* (1899) 570; *Samhain* (1901) 598
Irish Playgoer and Amusement Record (1899) 575
Irish Turf Telegraph (1875) 394
Isis Theatre Supplement (1953) 1085a

Jackson, P. L. See *Gallery Gazette* (1909) 681
Jeannette, G. K. See *Theatre Digest* (1948) 1034
John Bourne's Newsletter (1959) 1148
John Waddington's Annual (1901) 592
Jones, Henry A. See *Dramatic Opinion* (1889) 481
Jonson, Wilfrid G. See *Magical News* (1924) 784
Journal of the Bacon Society (1886) 463a
Journal of Dramatic Reform. See *Dramatic Reform Association* (1878) 410
Journal of Manners and Society. See *News of Literature and Fashion* (1824) 124
Journal of Music and Drama (1823) 112
Journal of the English Folk Dance. See *English Folk-Dance Society's Journal* (1914) 713
Journal of the English Folk Dance and Song Society (1932) 860
Journal of the Institute of Magicians (1934) 878
Journal of the Leeds College of Music, Drama and Art (1897) 557
Jury (1965) 1172

Keene, W. See *Keene's Theatrical Evening Mirror* (1820) 83
Keene's Theatrical Evening Mirror (1820) 83
Kempton, E. W. See *Optic* (1885) 459; *Walter's Theatrical and Sporting Directory* (1884) 452
Kenrick, Thomas. See *British Stage and Literary Cabinet* (1817) 72
Kensington (1901) 593
Kettering. See *Friendship* (1937) 911a
Kirkley, F. Russell. See *Kirkley's Theatrical Apartments Directory* (1901) 594
Kirkley's Theatrical Apartments Directory (1901) 594
Klein, Herman. See *Independent Theatre Goer* (1912) 694
Knight Errant (1817) 73

L.A.G. (1919) 733
Laban Art of Movement Guild. See *Movement* (1948) 1029
Laban Art of Movement Guild News Sheet (1948) 1024
Ladies Guild of Francis St. Alban (1905) 640a

Lamonte, Jack. See *Wizard* (1947) 1016

Lancashire Dance News (1946) 963

Lancashire Stage-land (1908) 677

Landa, M. J. See *First-Nighter* (1904) 620

Lantern (1946) 964

Lavigerie, M. de. See *Gaulois and the Universal Caricature* (1861) 325

Lawrence, Edward. See *Encore Annual* (1895) 531

Le Roy, George. See *London Entertainer and Concert Artiste* (1953) 1086

Leading Stars of the London Stage (1864) 335

Ledger, Edward. See *Era Almanac* (1868) 354

Leeds. See *Amateur Actor* (1886) 462; *John Waddington's Annual* (1901) 592; *Journal of the Leeds College of Music* (1897) 557; *Leeds Pantomime Annual* (1894) 522; *Leeds Playgoer* (1924) 779; *Leeds Programme of Amusements* (1894) 523; *Roberts Pantomime Annual* (1895) 539; *Season's Concert* (1912) 695; *Student Theatre* (1963) 1168; *Yorkshire Harlequin* (1896) 552; *Yorkshire Owl Pantomime Annual* (1892) 508

Leeds Pantomime Annual (1894) 522

Leeds Playgoer (1924) 779

Leeds Programme of Amusements (1894) 523

Leeds Triad. See *Journal of the Leeds College of Music* (1897) 557

Leeds University Union. See *Student Theatre* (1963) 1168

Legat, N. See Nicolaeva-Legat, Mme.

Leggett, W. See *Covent-Garden Theatrical Gazette* (1816) 68

Leicester. See *Showgirl* (1954) 1105

Leisure Topix (1946) 965

Leisure Year (1948) 1025

Leith, Alicia A. See *Ladies Guild of Francis St. Alban* (1905) 640a

Leporello in Liverpool (1835) 225

Letchworth. See *N.A.T.E. Journal* (1921) 752

Let's Go (1933) 870

Levey, Sivori. See *Maskerpiece* (1922) 760

Lewis, Leopold. See *Mask* (1868) 356

Licensed Victuallers' Mirror (1888) 473

Licensed Victuallers' Mirror. See *Sporting and Dramatic Mirror* (1892) 507

Licensed Victuallers' Sportsman (1888) 474

Lincoln. See *Lincoln Dramatic Censor* (1809) 54; *What's On* (1951) 1073

Lincoln Dramatic Censor (1809) 54

Link (1904) 621; (1924) 780

Literary and Dramatic Mirror. See *Cornucopia* (1820) 80

Literary Beacon (1831) 196

Literary Cabinet and Journal of Belles Lettres (1827) 146

Literary Cynosure (1824) 122

Literary Guardian and Spectator of Books (1831) 197

Literary Mirror. See *Monthly Theatrical Reporter* (1814) 63

Literary Museum. See *Museum* (1822) 102

Literary Observer. See *Weekly Magazine* (1823) 118

Literary Review and Stage Manager. See *Stage-Manager* (1849) 292

Literary Test (1832) 206

Literary, Theatrical and Miscellaneous Magazine. See *Scourge* (1811) 57

Literary, Theatrical, and Police Reporter. See *Thistle* (1829) 181

"Little" Magazine (1937) 912

Little Showman (1864) 336

Little Theatre. See *Grand Guignol Annual Review* (1921) 750; *"Little" Magazine* (1937) 912; *Little Theatre News* (1948) 1026; *Spotlight* (1950) 1066

Little Theatre News (1948) 1026

Liverpool. See *Amphi* (1873) 382; *Censor* (1821) 86; *Clarion* (1882) 433; *Corrector* (1816) 67; *Curtain* (1862) 326; *Dramatic Speculum* (1826) 136; *Figaro in Liverpool* (1833) 213; *Footlights* (1864) 334; (1897) 555; *Hague's Minstrel and Dramatic Journal* (1882) 434; *Leporello in Liverpool* (1835) 225; *Liverpool and District Programme* (1903) 612; *Liverpool Athletic & Dramatic News* (1890) 492; *Liverpool Busy Bee* (1886) 464; *Liverpool Dramatic Argus* (1846) 270; *Liverpool Dramatic Censor* (1806) 47; (1834) 219; *Liverpool Dramatic Journal* (1832) 207; *Liverpool Entertainment and Pleasure Programme* (1903) 613; *Liverpool Entr' Acte* (1881) 427; *Liverpool Programme of Amusements* (1875) 395; *Liverpool Programme of Entertainments* (1920) 741; *Liverpool Theatrical Investigator* (1821) 90; *Liverpool Theatrical News* (1907) 668; *Liverpool Thespian Register* (1836) 229; *Liverpool "Week-by-Week"* (1924) 781; *Lloyds Programme* (1883) 441; *Looking Glass* (1832) 208; *Magician* (1904) 623; *Merseyside Unity Theatre* (1940) 930; *Musical and Dramatic World* (1881) 428; *Paul Pry in Liverpool* (1834) 220; *Play* (1867) 348; *Playgoer* (1924) 786; *Plays and Players* (1904) 628; *Prompt Box* (1907) 672; *Prompter* (1899) 578; *Rotunda Prompter* (1876) 402; *Star* (1865) 344; *Theatrical Apartments* (1920) 745; *Theatrical News* (1926) 805; *Thespian* (1821) 97; *Will A. Bradley's Pantomime Annual* (1900) 586

Liverpool and District Programme (1903) 612

Liverpool and Merseyside Programme of Entertainments. See *Liverpool Programme of Entertainments* (1920) 741

Liverpool Athletic & Dramatic News (1890) 492

Liverpool Busy Bee (1886) 464

Liverpool Dramatic Argus (1846) 270

Liverpool Dramatic Censor (1806) 47; (1834) 219

Liverpool Dramatic Journal (1832) 207

Liverpool Entertainment and Pleasure Programme (1903) 613

Liverpool Entr' Acte (1881) 427

Liverpool Programme (1888) 475

Liverpool Programme of Amusements (1875) 395

Liverpool Programme of Entertainments (1920) 741

Liverpool Stage Club. See *Prompt Box* (1907) 672

Liverpool Theatrical Investigator (1821) 90

Liverpool Theatrical News (1907) 668

Liverpool Thespian Register and Mirror (1836) 229

Liverpool "Week-by-Week" (1924) 781

Lives and Traits of the Bon Ton Theatricals (1790) 24

Living Theatre (1948) 1027

Lloyd, F. See *Amateur Stage* (1926) 802; *Amateur Theatre* (1925) 787; *Amateur Theatrical World* (1925) 788

Lloyd, Francis. See *Theatrical Looker-on at the Birmingham Theatre* (1822) 105

Lloyds Programme (1883) 441

Lockwood, E. See *Dangerfield Entertainment Guide* (1895) 529

Locum, Septem. See *Drury Lane Gazette* (1907) 666

London (1853) 314; (1936) 905

London Album (1876) 399

London Amusement Guide (1836) 230; See also *L.A.G.* (1919) 733

London Amusement Guide and Theatrical Reporter (1835) 226

London Amusements (1925) 793

London and Edinburgh General Review. See *Printers Devil* (1850) 300

London and New York Dramatic Exchange. See *Footlights* (1899) 574

London and Provincial Entr' Acte. See *London Entr' Acte* (1869) 366

London and Suburban Programme and Amusement Guide (1932) 861

London Artiste (1945) 945

London Attractions (1919) 734

London Bridge Theatre Diary (1895) 536

London by Night (1965) 1173

London Dance News (1946) 966

London Dance News Weekly. See *Dance News Weekly* (1946) 959

London Entertainer and Concert Artiste (1953) 1086

London Entertainment. See *Murray's London Entertainment Guide* (1888) 476

London Entr'acte (1869) 366

London Guide and Photographic Album (1876) 400

London Illustrated Standard (1895) 537

London Leisure. See *London Off Duty* (1940) 929

London Magazine (1820) 84

London Mercury (1868) 355

London Mirror. See *Dramatic and Musical Circular* (1879) 413

London Museum Music Hall, Bull Ring (1867) 347

London Music Diary (1946) 967

London Musical Events (1946) 968

London Off Duty (1940) 929

London Playgoer and Comedy (1890) 493

London Program (1913) 702

London Programme (1924) 782

London Programme and Sketch-Book. See *Figaro Programme* (1874) 386

London Programme of Amusements (1906) 657

London Record (1904) 622

London Review. See *London Programme* (1924) 782

London School of Dramatic Art Magazine (1934) 879

London Shakespeare League Journal (1914) 715

London Singer's Magazine (1838) 240

London Society of Magicians. See *Magical Gazette* (1941) 935

London Sports and Entertainments (1935) 889

London Stage Annual (1903) 614

London Theatre Entertainment (1900) 582

London Theatrical Observer (1823) 113

London Week (1935) 890

London Weekly Diary of Social Events (1921) 751

London Weekly Programme and Guide to Theatres (1935) 891

Londoner. See *In London Now* (1954) 1098

Londoner Annual (1947) 1001

London's Daily Guide (1902) 603

London's Entertainments (1922) 759

London's Festival Ballet Annual (1957) 1131

Looking Glass (1832) 208; (1877) 404

Lorgnette (1883) 442

Lorgnette Programme (1874) 388

Lotinga's Weekly (1910) 685

Love, M. See *London School of Dramatic Art Magazine* (1934) 879

Lowestoft. See *Theatre Royal* (1961) 1157; *What's On* (1953) 1093

Lucas, Perceval. See *English Folk-Dance Society's Journal* (1914) 713

Luton. See *What's On* (1955) 1116

Lyre (1841) 250

Lyric Players. See *Threshold* (1957) 1137

Lyster, A. C. See *International Entertainer* (1902) 602

Lytton's Theatre Seating Plans (1957) 1132

M.H.A.A. Gazette (1886) 465

Mac Innes, Angus. See *Repertory* (1950) 1061

Macaroni, Scavoir Vivre, and Theatrical Magazine (1772) 16

Mace, E. J. P. See *S.C.D.A. Advisory Service* (1947) 1007a

Macfarren, Sir George Alexander. See *Musical Artistes', Lecturers', and Entertainers' Guide* (1885) 458

Macready, T. See *Compass* (1898) 561

Magazine 4 (1952) 1076

Magazine Programme (1906) 657a

Magazine Programme (1924) 783

Magic (1900) 583

Magic. See *Abracadabra* (1946) 950; *Edward Bagshawe's Magical Journal* (1927) 809; *Goldston's Magical Quarterly* (1934) 877; *Goodliffe's Magic Monthly* (1947) 999; *Journal of the Institute of Magicians* (1934) 878; *Magic* (1900) 583; *Magic and Conjuring Magazine* (1795) 29; *Magic Circular* (1906) 658; *Magic Magazine* (1952) 1077; *Magic Wand* (1910) 686; *Magic Wand Year Book* (1947) 1002; *Magical Digest* (1949) 1043; *Magical Gazette* (1941) 935; *Magical Monthly* (1923) 769; *Magical News* (1924) 784; *Magical Record* (1915) 720; *Magical World* (1910) 687; *Magician* (1904) 623; *Magician Annual* (1907) 669; *P.A.D.* (1902) 604; *Wizard* (1947) 1016; *World of Magic* (1865) 345

Magic and Conjuring Magazine (1795) 29

Magic Circular (1906) 658

Magic Magazine (1952) 1077

Magic Wand (1910) 686

Magic Wand Year Book (1947) 1002

"*Magical Digest*" (1949) 1043

Magical Gazette (1941) 935

Magical Monthly (1923) 769

Magical News (1924) 784

Magical Record (1915) 720

Magical World (1910) 687

Magician (1904) 623

Magician. See *Journal of the Institute of Magicians* (1934) 878; *Magic* (1900) 583

Magician Annual (1907) 669

Magician's Club. See *Goldston's Magical Quarterly* (1934) 877

Maidstone. See *What's On in Maidstone* (1927) 814a

Maidstone and District What's On. See *What's On in Maidstone* (1927) 814a

Malvern Festival (1929) 830

Malvern Theatres Monthly Post (1930) 842

Man of Today (1913) 702a

Man in the Moon (1803) 38

Manager and Stage Business Gazette (1925) 794

Manager's Circular (1851) 306

Manager's Guide and Artistes' Advertiser (1878) 411

Manchester, P. W. See *Ballet Today* (1946) 953

Manchester. See *Argus* (1804) 40; *Argus Corrected* (1805) 41; *Censor* (1807) 51; *Courier* (1932) 855; *Dramatic Reform Association* (1878) 410; *Footlights* (1884) 447; *Lancashire Stage-land* (1908) 677; *Looking Glass* (1877) 404; *Magical World* (1910) 687; *Managers' Guide and Artistes' Advertiser* (1878) 411; *Manchester Amusements* (1893) 511; *Manchester Dramatic and Musical Review* (1846) 271; *Manchester Observer* (1865) 342; *Manchester Pantomime's Annual* (1882) 435; *Manchester Playgoer* (1910) 688; (1925) 795; *Manchester Repertory Theatre* (1935) 892; *Manchester Theatrical Censor* (1828) 160; *Millgate Monthly* (1905) 641; *Playgoers' Club Journal* (1915) 722; *Programme of Manchester Amusements* (1891) 501; *Prompter* (1815) 65; *Prompter Prompted* (1816) 70; *Proscenium* (1898) 565; *Sphinx* (1868) 359; *Stage and Field* (1904) 631; *Sunday Chronicle* (1913) 706; *Theatrical Censor* (1828) 167; *Theatrical Programme and General Amusements Advertiser* (1890) 495a; *Thespian Review* (1806) 49; *Townsman* (1803) 39; *What's On?* (1896) 551; (1946) 988; (1947) 1015; *What's On in the City* (1936) 909; *Wm. Haslam's Apartment Directory* (1906) 665

Manchester Amusements (1893) 511

Manchester Dramatic and Musical Review (1846) 271

Manchester Observer (1865) 342

Manchester Pantomime's Annual (1882) 435

Manchester Playgoer (1910) 688; (1925) 795

Manchester Repertory Theatre (1935) 892

Manchester Theatrical Censor (1828) 160

Mann, E. M. See *Spotlight* (1949) 1047

Manning, Mary. See *Motley* (1932) 862

Margate. See *Hastings Day by Day* (1928) 819a; *What's On in Margate* (1923) 777

Marks, Ellen M. See *Puppet Year Book* (1944) 942

Marlovia (1957) 1132a

Marlovian Chronicle (1957) 1133

Marlowe, Christopher. See *Marlovia* (1957) 1132a; *Marlovian Chronicle* (1957) 1133

Martin, G. See *Music and Theatre Digest* (1951) 1072

Mascot (1894) 524

Mask (1868) 356; (1879) 416

Maskerpiece (1922) 760

Masque (1946) 969; (1954) 1099; (1954) 1100

Mayall's Celebrities of the London Stage (1863) 329a

McFadden, Roy. See *Threshold* (1957) 1137

Melpomene's Memorandum Book. See *Thalia's Tablet* (1821) 93

Melvin, Duncan. See *Souvenirs de Ballet* (1949) 1046

Mercury (1948) 1028

Mermaid Theatre Review (1959) 1149

Merryn, Anthony. See *Theatre Digest* (1948) 1034

Merseyside Unity Theatre (1940) 930

Meteor (1949) 1044

Metropolitan Times (1947) 1003

Midland Amusements. See *Birmingham Programme of Amusements* (1906) 649

Midlander (1925) 795a

Midlands. See *Birmingham and Midlands Musical Journal* (1884) 444; *Birmingham Dramatic News* (1885) 455; *Birmingham Programme of Amusements* (1906) 649; *Dance Notes* (1953) 1082

Miles, Kenneth. See *Highlights from the Folkestone-Hythe Operatic and Dramatic Society* (1953) 1084

Millgate and Playgoer. See *Millgate Monthly* (1905) 641

Millgate Monthly (1905) 641

Mills, H. P. See *Theatrical Journal* (1839) 242

Mime. See *Parados* (1940) 931

Mime Review (1935) 893

Minim (1893) 512

Minstrel (1876) 401

Minstrel. See *Hague's Minstrel and Dramatic Journal* (1882) 434; *Mohawk Minstrels' "Nigger" Dramas* (1878) 412; *P.A.D.* (1902) 604

Mirror (1872) 380

Mirror of the Stage (1822) 101

Mirror of the Stage. See *Dramatic Review* (1795) 28

Model Stage (1946) 970

Model Theatre. See *British Puppet and Model Theatre Guild Junior News* (1941) 933; *British Puppet and Model Theatre Guild Newsletter* (1951) 1069; *British Puppet and Model Theatre Guild Wartime Bulletin* (1939) 923

Modern Dance (1934) 880

Modern Dance and Dancer. See *Modern Dance* (1934) 880

Mohawk Minstrels' "Nigger" Dramas (1878) 412

Moliere. See *Moliere and Shakespeare* (1858) 322

Moliere and Shakespeare (1858) 322

Monitor (1767) 14; (1962) 1161

Monmouthshire Drama League. See *Monitor* (1962) 1161

Monthly Expositor of Imposture. See *Scourge* (1811) 57

Monthly Mirror (1795) 30; See also *Theatrical Inquisitor* (1812) 59

Monthly Mirror of the Drama. See *Oxberry's Theatrical Inquisitor* (1828) 162

Monthly Museum (1776) 19

Monthly Register of Events. See *Public Reporter* (1806) 48

Monthly Register of Taste. See *Macaroni, Scavoir Vivre* (1772) 16

Monthly Theatrical Reporter (1814) 63

Monthly Theatrical Review (1829) 177

Moss, W. Keith. See *"Spotlight" Yearbook* (1931) 851

Motley (1932) 862

Movement (1948) 1029

Mummer. See *Municipal Player* (1924) 785

Municipal Player (1924) 785

Munro, Harold. See *Poetry and Drama* (1913) 705

Murray, John M. See *Blue Review* (1913) 699

Murray, William. See *Thespian Critique* (1816) 71

Murray's London Entertainment Guide (1888) 476

Murray's London Recreation Guide (1896) 548

Museum (1822) 102

Music. See *Actor and Elocutionist* (1881) 425; *Amateur's Guide* (1867) 346; *Apollo* (1829) 170; *Arts Gazette* (1919) 730; *Athenaeum* (1828) 154; *Baton* (1865) 340; *Birmingham and Midlands Musical Journal* (1884) 444; *Birmingham Musical Examiner* (1845) 264; *Blue Review* (1913) 699; *Bon Accord* (1880) 419; *Books and Art* (1957) 1128; *Brighton Record* (1850) 297; *Circulating Library* (1886) 463; *Civic Entertainment* (1948) 1020; *Concert Goer's Annual* (1957) 1129; *Connoisseur* (1845) 266; *Critic* (1843) 257; (1874) 384; *Critic, Literature, Art, Music, Drama* (1928) 817; *Critique* (1898) 562; *Dance Music Annual* (1951) 1070; *Dancing Times* (1894) 516; *Dramatic Equestrian* (1862) 327; *Dramatic Gazette* (1830) 184; *Dramatic Mirror and Review of Music* (1847) 275; *Dramatic News* (1868) 352; *Dramatic Observer* (1877) 403; *Dramatic Observer and Musical Review* (1823) 108; *Dramatic Review* (1885) 456; *Entr'acte Almanack* (1873) 383; *Ethnic* (1959) 1146; *Everyman* (1929) 828; *Festival News* (1947) 998; *Fly Paper* (1884) 446; *Footlights* (1869) 363; *Foyer* (1951) 1071; *Gaiety* (1869) 364; *General Dramatic, Equestrian & Musical Agency* (1857) 319; *Green Register* (1947) 1000; *Green Room* (1880) 421; *Hanson's Directory of the Musicians* (1894) 520; *Harmonic Olio* (1812) 58; *Journal of Music and the Drama* (1823) 112; *Journal of the English Folk Dance and Song Society* (1932) 860; *Journal of the Leeds College of Music* (1897) 557; *Literary Beacon* (1831)

196; *Liverpool and District Programme* (1903) 612; *Liverpool Busy Bee* (1886) 464; *Lloyds Programme* (1883) 441; *London* (1853) 314; *London Museum Music Hall* (1867) 347; *London Music Diary* (1946) 967; *London Musical Events* (1946) 968; *London Singer's Magazine* (1838) 240; *Looking Glass* (1877) 404; *Lyre* (1841) 250; *M.H.A.A. Gazette* (1886) 465; *Magazine 4* (1952) 1076; *Managers' Guide and Artistes' Advertiser* (1878) 411; *Manchester Dramatic and Musical Review* (1846) 271; *Minim* (1893) 512; *Music Box and British Entertainer* (1927) 811; *Music Hall* (1889) 482; *Music Hall Critic* (1870) 374; *Music Hall Pictorial* (1904) 624; *Music Halls' Gazette* (1868) 357; *Music, Music and Dancing* (1954) 1101; *Musical and Dramatic Review* (1864) 337; *Musical and Dramatic World* (1881) 428; *Musical Artists', Lecturers', and Entertainers' Guide* (1885) 458; *Musical Exchange Journal* (1894) 525; *Musical Journal* (1840) 243; *Musical Monthly* (1864) 338; *Musical World and Dramatic Observer* (1895) 538; *Musician, and Music-Hall Times* (1862) 329; *Musicians Directory* (1932) 863; *National Omnibus* (1831) 198; *National Standard of Literature* (1833) 214; *New Anti-Jacobin* (1833) 215; *1955 Directory of Concert and Cabaret Artistes* (1955) 1110; *Now-a-days* (1947) 1005; *Official Music Hall Directory and Variety ABC* (1899) 577; *Olio of Literature, Music, the Drama* (1871) 375; *Opera* (1832) 210; *Opera, Ballet, and Music-Hall* (1952) 1078; *Orchestra* (1863) 330; *Panton Magazine* (1927) 812; *Pictorial Sporting and Theatrical Guide* (1868) 358; *Play* (1869) 367; *Playgoer's Magazine* (1898) 563; *Proscenium* (1898) 565; *Psyche* (1840) 246; *Salon* (1888) 480; *Saturday Musical Review* (1879) 417; *Sketch* (1879) 418; *Sock and Buskin* (1867) 349; *Soho Courier* (1856) 318; *Sphinx* (1868) 359; *Sporting Telegraph* (1860) 324; *Stage and Literary and Musical Review* (1848) 286; *Stage and Scottish Musical and Theatrical Omnibus* (1849) 291; *Stage-Manager* (1849) 292; *Stroller* (1905) 643; *Tallis's Dramatic Magazine* (1850) 302; *Tallis's Illustrated Life in London* (1864) 339; *Theatrical and Musical Guide* (1884) 449; *Theatrical and Musical Review* (1868) 361; *Theatrical Speculum* (1831) 203; *Universal Musical and Dramatic Directory* (1913) 710; *Week-End Review of Politics* (1930) 846; *Weekly Comedy* (1889) 488; *Weekly Musical Transcript* (1853) 316. See also Ballet, Concert, Dance, Folk Dance, Music Hall, Opera

Music and Theatre Digest (1951) 1072
Music Box and British Entertainer (1927) 811
Music Hall. See *A.B.C. Amusement Guide* (1896) 545; *Artiste* (1887) 468; *Compass* (1898) 561; *Entr' Acte Almanack and Theatrical and Music Hall Annual* (1873) 383; *M.H.A.A. Gazette* (1886) 465; *Managers' Guide and Artistes Advertiser* (1878) 411; *Music Hall* (1889) 482; *Music Hall Critic* (1870) 374; *Music Hall Pictorial* (1904) 624; *Music Halls' Gazette* (1868) 357; *Musician, and Music-Hall Times* (1862) 329; *Official Music Hall Directory and Variety ABC* (1899) 577; *Opera, Ballet, and Music Hall* (1952) 1078; *Playgoer's Magazine* (1898) 563; *Prompter and the Footlights* (1889) 483; *Sporting Globe* (1905) 642; *Stage* (1868) 360; *Sunday Mirror* (1897) 560; *Thalia Diary & Directory* (1914) 716; *Theatre, Music Hall & Cinema Blue Book* (1917) 727; *Theatrical and Music Hall Life* (1898) 566; *Variety Stage and Music Hall Pictorial* (1905) 644; *Weekly Theatrical Reporter* (1867) 350
Music Hall (1889) 482
Music Hall and Theatre. See *Music Hall* (1889) 482
Music Hall and Theatre Review. See *Music Hall* (1889) 482
Music Hall Critic (1870) 374
Music Hall Pictorial (1904) 624
Music Halls' Gazette (1868) 357
Music, Music and Dancing (1954) 1101
Musical and Dramatic Review (1864) 337
Musical and Dramatic World (1881) 428
Musical Artists', Lecturers', and Entertainers' Guide (1885) 458
Musical Exchange Journal (1894) 525
Musical Journal (1840) 243
Musical Monthly (1864) 338
Musical Transcript. See *Weekly Musical Transcript* (1853) 316
Musical World and Dramatic Observer (1895) 538
Musician, and Music-Hall Times (1862) 329
Musicians Directory (1932) 863
My Journal (1907) 669a
My Programme (1904) 625

N.A.T.E. Journal (1921) 752
N.O.D.A. Bulletin (1935) 894
Nash, A. L. See *Ballet Carnaval* (1946) 952
National Amateur and Operatic and Dramatic Association. See *Amateur Stage* (1926) 802; *Amateur Theatre* (1925) 787; *Amateur Theatrical World* (1925) 788
National Amateur Operatic and Dramatic Association (1922) 761
National Association of Theatrical Employees. See *N.A.T.E. Journal* (1921) 752

National Omnibus (1831) 198

National Operatic and Dramatic Association. See *N.O.D.A. Bulletin* (1935) 894

National Operatic and Dramatic Association Directory (1957) 1134

National Operatic and Dramatic Association. Member's Handbook (1957) 1135

National Standard of Literature (1833) 214

National Union of Townswomen's Guilds. See *Play Reviews* (1955) 1111

Negro. See *Mohawk Minstrels' "Nigger" Dramas* (1878) 412

Nettle (1751) 7

New Anti-Jacobin (1833) 215

New Companion to the Playhouse. See *Theatrical Review* (1772) 17

New Edinburgh Dramatic Review (1832) 209

New Elizabethan (1955) 1109

New Era. See *Touchstone* (1877) 407

New Evening Theatrical Observer (1830) 185

New Opera Glass (1830) 186

New Plays Annual for Women (1956) 1123

New Plays from Old Stories (1924) 785a

New Plays Quarterly (1947) 1004

New Puppet Show. See *Puppet Show* (1848) 284

New Shakespeare Society's Transactions (1874) 389

New Theatre (1939) 925

New Theatre Magazine (1959) 1150

New Theatrical Observer (1833) 216

New York. See *Footlights* (1899) 574

New York Shakespeare Society in Europe. See *Shakespearean* (1895) 541

Newcastle. See *Newcastle Theatrical Observer* (1824) 123; *Theatrical Critique* (1829) 180; *Working Light* (1948) 1036

Newcastle Theatrical Observer (1824) 123

Newcastle Upon Tyne. See *Dramatic Register* (1828) 157; *Phoenix* (1947) 1006; *Rep* (1930) 844; *Theatrical Examiner* (1827) 152; *Tyneside Phoenix* (1947) 1014

Newport. See *Monitor* (1962) 1161; *Shakespeare Fellowship News-Letter* (1947) 1007a

News of Literature and Fashion (1824) 124

News-Sheet. See *Quarterly News-Sheet* (1950) 1060

Newton, Wilson. See *Professional World* (1892) 506

Nicolaeva-Legat. Mme. See *Ballet* (1945) 943; *Young Ballet Dancer* (1952) 1080

Nicholson's Noctes; or, Nights and Sights in London (1842) 253

Nicoll, Allardyce. See *Shakespeare Survey* (1948) 1032

Night Life. See *Variety Fare* (1946) 986

Nightly Reflector of the Theatres Royal. See *Theatrical Gazette* (1818) 74

Nights and Sights in London. See *Nicholson's Noctes* (1842) 253

1955 Directory of Concert and Cabaret Artistes (1955) 1110

Noble, Peter. See *Stage and Screen Miscellany* (1947) 1010

Nolan's Theatrical Observer. See *Theatrical Observer* (1821) 94

North London Dancers. See *Top-Spin* (1940) 932

North London Programme (1877) 405

North Shields. See *North Shields Dramatic Censor* (1827) 147; *Paul Pry* (1827) 149

North Shields Dramatic Censor (1827) 147

Northern Dance News. See *Dance News Weekly* (1946) 959

Northgate. See *Repertory* (1950) 1061

Norwich. See *Lorgnette* (1883) 442; *Norwich Theatrical Observer and Dramatic Review* (1827) 148; *Theatrical Tickler* (1828) 168

Norwich Theatrical Observer and Dramatic Review (1827) 148

Notcutt, Percy. See *Musical Exchange Journal* (1894) 525

Nottingham. See *Diary of Entertainment and Events* (1958) 1139; *Nottingham Amusements* (1899) 576

Nottingham Amusements (1899) 576

Nottingham Diary of Entertainments & Events. See *Diary of Entertainment and Events* (1958) 1139

Now-a-days (1947) 1005

Oates, John A. See *Highlights from the Folkestone-Hythe Operatic and Dramatic Society* (1953) 1084

Occasional Magazine (1932) 864

Official Music Hall Directory (1899) 577

Offstage (1956) 1124

Old Drury-Lane Christmas Annual (1882) 436

Old Oak Chest. See *Cicerone* (1843) 256

Old Vic. See *Shakespeare at the Old Vic* (1954) 1104

Old Vic. and Sadler's Wells Magazine. See *"Old Vic." Magazine* (1919) 735

"Old Vic." Magazine (1919) 735

Oldham. See *Oldham Amusements and Shopping Programme* (1923) 770; *Oldham Repertory Club* (1938) 916

Oldham Amusements and Shopping Programme (1923) 770

Oldham Repertory Club (1938) 916

Olio of Literature, Music, the Drama (1871) 375

O'Malley, Mary. See *Threshold* (1957) 1137

On Stage (1959) 1151

Opera. See *About the House* (1962) 1159; *Amateur Operatic Year Book* (1923) 766; *Bill of the Play* (1882) 432; *Courier* (1932) 855; *Curtain* (1847) 273; *Dramatic Maga-*

zine (1786) 21; *Folkestone-Hythe Operatic and Dramatic Society* (1959) 1147; *Foyer* (1951) 1071; *Highlights from the Folkestone-Hythe Operatic and Dramatic Society* (1953) 1084; *London Musical Events* (1946) 968; *Minstrel* (1876) 401; *N.O.D.A. Bulletin* (1935) 894; *National Amateur Operatic and Dramatic Association* (1922) 761; *National Operatic and Dramatic Association Directory* (1957) 1134; *National Operatic and Dramatic Association. Member's Handbook* (1957) 1135; *Opera* (1832) 210; (1923) 771; (1950) 1058; *Opera Annual* (1954) 1102; *Opera, Ballet and Music-Hall* (1952) 1078; *Opera Box* (1849) 289; *Opera Glass* (1829) 178; (1840) 244; (1848) 283; *Opera Glass, for Peeping into the Microcosm* (1826) 140; *Operatic Association Gazette* (1930) 843; *Royal Opera House Annual Report* (1958) 1141; *Scottish Opera News* (1964) 1171; *Stage Door* (1947) 1011; *Stage Mirror* (1850) 301

Opera (1832) 210; (1923) 771; (1950) 1058
Opera and Ballet. See *Opera* (1923) 771
Opera Annual (1954) 1102
Opera, Ballet and Music-Hall (1952) 1078
Opera Box (1849) 289
Opera Glass (1829) 178; (1840) 244; (1848) 283
Opera Glass, for Peeping into the Microcosm of the Fine Arts (1826) 140
Operatic Association Gazette (1930) 843
Optic (1885) 459
Orchestra (1863) 330
Original Theatrical Observer (1821) 91
Oswald, Oscar. See *Magical Digest* (1949) 1043
Ould, H. L. See *New Plays from Old Stories* (1924) 785a
Our Plays and Players (1925) 796
Ourselves (1886) 466
Owl (1831) 199
Oxberry, Catherine E. See *Oxberry's Theatrical Inquisitor* (1828) 162
Oxberry's Dramatic Biography (1825) 131
Oxberry's Dramatic Mirror (1828) 161
Oxberry's Theatrical Inquisitor (1828) 162
Oxberry's Weekly Budget of Plays (1843) 259
Oxford. See *Act One, Scene 2* (1967) 1177; *Isis Theatre Supplement* (1953) 1085a; *Oxford and District and Oxfordshire Amusement Guide* (1903) 615; *Oxford Repertory Company* (1935) 895; *Repertory* (1931) 850a; *Theatre Forum* (1938) 919a
Oxford and District and Oxfordshire Amusement Guide (1903) 615
Oxford Playhouse Company. See *Act One, Scene 2* (1967) 1177
Oxford Repertory Company. See *Repertory* (1931) 850a

Oxford Repertory Company Limited (1935) 895

P.A.D. (1902) 604
Paignton. See *Paignton's Amusements* (1903) 616
Paignton's Amusements (1903) 616
Paisley. See *Paisley Society and Dramatic Mirror* (1894) 526
Paisley Mirror. See *Paisley Society and Dramatic Mirror* (1894) 526
Paisley Society and Dramatic Mirror (1894) 526
Palais Dancing News (1920) 742
Pandora (1842) 254
Pantomime. *Birmingham Pantomime Annual* (1899) 571; *Glasgow Harlequin* (1895) 533; *Glasgow Pantomime Annual* (1895) 534; *Leeds Pantomime Annual* (1894) 522; *Manchester Pantomime Annual* (1882) 435; *Pantomime and Vaudeville Favourites* (1913) 703; *Pantomime Annual* (1892) 505; *Roberts Pantomime Annual* (1895) 539; *Will A. Bradley's Pantomime Annual* (1900) 586; *Yorkshire Owl Pantomime Annual* (1892) 508
Pantomime and Vaudeville Favourites (1913) 703
Pantomime Annual (1892) 505
Panton Magazine (1927) 812
Parade (1925) 797
Parados (1940) 931
Paris. See *International Theatre* (1903) 611
Parker, John. See *Green Room Book* (1906) 656
Pascoe, Charles E. See *Dramatic Notes* (1879) 414
Pasquin (1847) 278
Pastime (1937) 913
Paterson, Alfred. See *Professional World* (1892) 506
Paul Pry (1827) 149
Paul Pry in Liverpool (1834) 220
Peacock, William. See *Our Plays and Players* (1925) 796
Peddie, James. See *Sporting Summary and Theatrical Tatler* (1890) 494
Pedlars Pack. See *People's National Theatre Magazine* (1933) 871
Penge Entertainment Guide. See *Beckenham and Penge* (1936) 901
Penny Pictorial Play (1850) 298
People's National Theatre Magazine (1933) 871
People's Theatre Arts Group. See *Phoenix* (1947) 1006; *Tyneside Phoenix* (1947) 1014
Pepper Box (1840) 245
Percy, R. See *Circle* (1905) 639
Performer (1906) 659

Performer Annual (1907) 670
"*Performer*" *Handbook* (1921) 753
Performing Right Bulletin. See *Performing Right Gazette* (1922) 762
Performing Right Gazette (1922) 762
Performing Right Society Ltd. See *Performing Right Gazette* (1922) 762
Perforwritings (1938) 917
Peter Warlock's Pentagram (1946) 971
Peterson, Arthur E. See *British Puppet and Model Theatre Guild* (1939) 923
Pettett, Victor L. See *Leisure Topix* (1946) 965
Philo-Danmonion (1830) 187
Philpott, A. R. See *Puppet Post* (1947) 1007
Phoenix (1947) 1006
Photo-Cast (1957) 1136
Pictorial Sporting and Theatrical Guide (1868) 358
Pictorial Times (1843) 260
Picture Hire Club. See *Commentary* (1941) 933a
Pictures, Pleasures, Pastimes (1929) 831
Picus. See *Woodpecker* (1887) 472
Pierce Egan's Weekly Courier (1829) 179
Pilgrim Players. See *Scallop-Shell* (1911) 692
Pilgrim Review. See *Scallop-Shell* (1911) 692
Piping and Dancing (1935) 896
Piping, Drumming and Highland Dancing (1948) 1030
Pit, Patrick. See *Thespian Critique* (1816) 71
Planet (1907) 671
Play (1867) 348; (1869) 367; (1881) 429; (1904) 626
Play Pictorial (1902) 605; See also *Play* (1904) 626
Play Reviews (1955) 1111
Plays of the Year (1948) 1030a
Playbill (1913) 704
Playbill. See *Daily Programme and Playbill* (1899) 572
Players (1860) 323; (1891) 499
Play-Goer (1831) 200; (1851) 307; (1888) 477; (1897) 558; (1901) 595; (1924) 786
Playgoer and Literary Tatler. See *Play-goer* (1851) 307
Playgoer and Millgate. See *Millgate Monthly* (1905) 641
Playgoer, and Public Amusement Guide (1850) 299
Playgoer and Society. See *Theatre* (1909) 684
Playgoer's Calendar for 1915 (1915) 721
Playgoer's Club. See *Playgoer's Review* (1891) 500
Playgoers' Club Journal (1915) 722
Playgoers' Guide and Theatrical Notes (1896) 549
Playgoers' Magazine (1888) 478; (1898) 563
Playgoers' Pocket-book (1886) 467
Playgoer's Review (1891) 500

Playhouse (1904) 627
Play-house Journal (1749) 6
Playhouse News. See *Sheffield Repertory Company* (1934) 883
Playlet and Monologue Magazine (1901) 596
Plays and Players (1904) 628; (1929) 832; (1953) 1087. See also *Encore* (1954) 1095
Playwright. See *Amateur Theatre and Playwright's Journal* (1934) 874
Pleasure and Pastime in the City (1901) 597
Plumptre, Charles J. See *Musical Artists', Lecturers', and Entertainers' Guide* (1885) 458
Plymouth. See *Philo-Danmonion* (1830) 187; *Plymouth Theatrical Spy* (1828) 163
Plymouth Theatrical Spy (1828) 163
Poetry (1918) 728
Poetry and Drama (1913) 705
Poetry and the Play. See *Poetry* (1918) 728
Poetry Quarterly and Dramatic Review (1933) 872
Pollock, Benjamin. See *Model Stage* (1946) 970
Pollock's Toy Theatre Club. See *Model Stage* (1946) 970
Pool, D. L. See *Drury Lane Gazette* (1907) 666
Popple, William. See *Prompter* (1734) 4
Porcupine, Proteus. See *Dramatic Censor* (1829) 173
Portsmouth. See *Green Room Mirror* (1946) 962; *Little Theatre News* (1948) 1026; *Portsmouth and Southsea Amusements* (1894) 527; *What's On in Portsmouth and Southsea* (1913) 711
Portsmouth and Southsea Amusements (1894) 527
Pot-pourri (1946) 972
Potter, J. See *Theatrical Review* (1772) 17
Poulter, M. R. See *Puppet Post* (1947) 1007
Poz, Quiz and Company. See *Dramatic Spectator* (1837) 232
Prest, T. See *London Singer's Magazine* (1838) 240
Preston. See *Manager and Stage Business* (1925) 794
Price, Nancy. See *People's National Theatre Magazine* (1933) 871
Priestly-Greenwood, H. P. See *Graphic Guide to the London Theatres* (1894) 519
Prince of Wales Courier (1929) 833
Prince of Wales' Journal (1885) 460
Prince of Wales Theatre (1863) 331
Printers Devil (1850) 300
Probe, Pertinax. See *Stage* (1805) 43
Proceedings of the Sheffield Shakespeare Club (1819) 78
Professional World (1892) 506
Programme (1903) 617; (1923) 772
Programme and Dramatic Review (1875) 396
Programme and Playbill (1898) 564

Programme of Manchester Amusements (1891) 501. See also *Theatrical Programme and General Amusements Advertiser* (1890) 495a

Prompt (1962) 1162

Prompt Box (1907) 672

Prompter (1734) 4; (1789) 23; (1815) 65; (1824) 125; (1830) 188; (1834) 221; (1880) 422; (1893) 513; (1899) 578; (1907) 673; (1909) 682; (1943) 938; (1945) 946

Prompter and Scottish Dramatic Review (1842) 255

Prompter and the Footlights (1889) 483

Prompter Prompted (1816) 70

Proprietors and Managers Reference Book (1904) 628a

Proscenium (1898) 565; (1920) 743; (1946) 973; (1950) 1059; (1965) 1174

Psyche (1840) 246

Public Advertiser (1774) 18

Public Ledger. See *Theatrical Review* (1772) 17

Public Life. See *Theatrical and Public Life* (1898) 567

Public Reporter (1806) 48

Pulham, J. See *British Stage and Literary Cabinet* (1817) 72

Pullman Casting Directory (1956) 1125

Puppetry. See *British Puppet and Model Theatre Guild Junior News* (1941) 933; *British Puppet and Model Theatre Guild Newsletter* (1951) 1069; *British Puppet and Model Theatre Guild Wartime Bulletin* (1939) 923; *British Puppet Theatre* (1949) 1038; *Puppet Post* (1947) 1007; *Puppet Show* (1848) 284; *Puppet Year Book* (1944) 942; *Puppetry Year Book* (1955) 1112

Puppet Master. See *British Puppet and Model Theatre Guild Wartime Bulletin* (1939) 923

Puppet Post (1947) 1007

Puppet Show (1848) 284

Puppet Year Book (1944) 942

Puppetry Year Book (1955) 1112

Purdom, C. B. See *Shakespeare Stage* (1953) 1089

Purley and Couldson Entertainment (1936) 906

Quaestors. See *Fore-Stage* (1956) 1121

Quarterly News-Sheet (1950) 1060

Queen. See *Pictorial Times* (1843) 260

Querry, Edmund. See *Ball Room* (1926) 803

Questors Theatre (1958) 1140

Queue (1946) 974

Quixote, Sir Hercules. See *Knight Errant* (1817) 73

RADA Magazine. See *Royal Academy of Dramatic Art Magazine* (1946) 975

R. Douglas Cox's Theatrical and C. Douglas Stuart's Variety Directory (1904) 630

R. P. Watson's Weekly (1904) 629

Rada News (1923) 773

Range, Edward. See *Theatre* (1813) 60

Readable Recitations (1888) 479

Reanden News-Sheet (1923) 774

Recitations. See *Apollo* (1829) 170; *Readable Recitations* (1888) 479

Red Stage (1931) 850

Reed, Erskine. See *Dramatic Peerage* (1892) 503

Reid's London Entertainment Guide. See *Murray's London Entertainment Guide* (1888) 476

Religious Drama Society of Great Britain. See *Christian Drama* (1946) 957

Rep (1930) 844; (1934) 881

Repertoire (1959) 1152

Repertory (1931) 850a

Repertory (1950) 1061

Repertory Theatre. See *Birmingham Repertory Theatre News-letter* (1925) 790; *Living Theatre* (1948) 1027; *Manchester Repertory Theatre Magazine* (1935) 892; *Occasional Magazine* (1932) 864; *Oldham Repertory Club* (1938) 916; *Proscenium* (1965) 1174; *Rep* (1930) 844; *Repertory* (1950) 1061; *Repertory World* (1939) 925a; *Sheffield Repertory Company* (1934) 883; *Southampton Repertory Magazine* (1936) 907; *Southport Playbill* (1949) 1045

Repertory Theatre Co., Ltd. See *Rep* (1930) 844

Repertory World (1939) 925a

Review of World Theatre. See *Encore* (1954) 1095

Reynolds, F. See *Dramatic Annual* (1831) 194

Rialto (1889) 484

Richardson, P. J. S. See *Who's Who in Dancing* (1932) 867

Richardson, R. J. See *Kensington* (1901) 593

Rideing, William H. *Dramatic Notes* (1879) 414

Rietty, Robert. See *Gambit* (1963) 1165

Robbins, Glynn. See *Act One, Scene 2* (1967) 1177

Robert Arthur Theatres Illustrated (1907) 674

Roberts, D. Kilham. See *Authors', Playwrights, & Composers* (1935) 885

Roberts Pantomime Annual (1895) 539

Rochester. See *What's On* (1927) 813a

Romford. See *On Stage* (1959) 1151

Roope, F. C. See *Showmen's Year Book* (1956) 1126

Roscius (1825) 132

Rosenberg, Adolphus. See *Umpire* (1881) 431

Rosenthal, Harold. See *Opera Annual* (1954) 1102

Rotherham. See *Meteor* (1949) 1044

Rotunda Prompter (1876) 402

Round Table (1895) 540

Round the Town. See *London's Entertainments* (1922) 759

Round the Town Illustrated. See *London's Entertainments* (1922) 759

Roxana Tergamant. See *Have At You All* (1752) 10

Royal Academy of Dancing. See *Gazette* (1941) 934

Royal Academy of Dramatic Art. See *Masque* (1954) 1100; *Parade* (1925) 797; *Rada News* (1923) 773

Royal Academy of Dramatic Art Magazine (1946) 975

Royal Dramatic College News (1863) 332

Royal Opera House Annual Report (1958) 1141

Royal Opera House, Covent Garden. See *Royal Opera House Annual Report* (1958) 1141

Royal Shakespeare Company. See *Shakespeare Memorial Theatre* (1955) 1112a

Royal Shakespeare Theatre. See *Shakespeare Memorial Theatre* (1955) 1112a

Royal Tatler (1929) 834

Russell, Clifford W. See *Marlovia* (1957) 1132a; *Marlovian Chronicle* (1957) 1133

Russian Ballet. See *Ballet* (1945) 943; *Harlequin* (1957) 1130

Russian Ballet League. See *Ballet* (1945) 943

S.C.D.A. Advisory Service (1947) 1007a

SCR. Society for Cultural Relations with the U.S.S.R. (1953) 1088

Sadler's Wells. See *"Old Vic." Magazine* (1919) 735; *Repertoire* (1959) 1152

St. Pancras People's Theatre Magazine (1928) 822

Sala, George A. See *London* (1853) 314

Salisbury. See *Salisbury Observer* and *What's On* (1929) 834a

Salisbury Observer and *What's On* (1929) 834a

Salon (1888) 480

Samhain (1901) 598

Samuel Eyre's Theatrical Programme (1872) 381

Saturday Musical Review (1879) 417

Saturday Programme and Great City. See *Figaro Programme* (1874) 386

Saturday Programme and Sketch-Book. See *Figaro Programme* (1874) 386

Scallop-Shell (1911) 692

Scene (1962) 1163

Scene Shifter (1848) 285

School Drama (1938) 918

Scots Theatre (1946) 976

Scott, Clement. See *Theatre Annual* (1884) 448

Scottish Amateur Theatre (1934) 882

Scottish Community Drama Association. See *S.C.D.A. Advisory Service* (1947) 1007a; *Scottish Stage* (1930) 845

Scottish Community Drama Association Bulletin (1964) 1170

Scottish Dance News. See *Dance News Weekly* (1946) 959; *Scottish Dance News* (1946) 977

Scottish Dance News (1946) 977

Scottish Drama (1950) 1062

Scottish Drama Year Book (1948) 1031

Scottish Dramatic Mirror (1844) 262

Scottish Music and Drama (1946) 978

Scottish Music and Drama. See *Con Brio* (1946) 958

Scottish Musical Magazine (1919) 736

Scottish National Theatre Society. See *Scottish Player* (1923) 775

Scottish Opera News (1964) 1171

Scottish Player (1923) 775

Scottish Stage (1930) 845. See also *Amateur Theatre and Playwright's Journal* (1934) 874

Scourge (1811) 57

Screen and Stage (1920) 744

Script (1945) 947

Season's Concert and Entertainment Calendar (1912) 695

Seats (1954) 1103

Senior, Evan. See *Concert Goer's Annual* (1957) 1129

Seton, R. See *Tatler* (1830) 189

Seven Arts (1962) 1164

Seven Arts Digest (1959) 1153

Shakespeare. See *Bacon-Shakespeare* (1914) 712; *Baconiana* (1886) 463a; *British Empire Shakespeare Society* (1915) 719; *Dramatic Souvenir* (1833) 212; *Ladies Guild of Francis St. Alban* (1905) 640a; *London Shakespeare League Journal* (1914) 715; *New Elizabethan* (1955) 1109; *New Shakespeare Society's Transactions* (1874) 389; *Proceedings of the Sheffield Shakespeare Club* (1819) 78; *Shakespeare Almanack for 1869* (1869) 368; *Shakespeare Association Papers* (1917) 726; *Shakespeare at the Old Vic* (1954) 1104; *Shakespeare Club* (1929) 835; *Shakespeare Fellowship News-Letter* (1947) 1007a; *Shakespeare Gazette* (1863) 333; *Shakespeare Memorial Theatre* (1950) 1063; *Shakespeare Memorial Theatre* (1955) 1112a; *Shakespeare Newspaper* (1847) 279; *Shakespeare Pictorial* (1928) 820; *Shakespeare Quarterly* (1947) 1008; *Shakespeare Quarterly* (1948) 1031a; *Shakespeare Repository* (1853) 315; *Shakespeare Review* (1928) 821; *Shakespeare Stage* (1953) 1089; *Shakespeare Survey* (1948) 1032; *Shakespearean* (1895) 541; *Shakespearean Authorship Review* (1959) 1154; *Spear*

(1922) 763; *Tallis's Shakespeare Gallery* (1852) 311; *University Shakespeare Journal* (1887) 471

Shakespeare Almanack for 1869 (1869) 368

Shakespeare Association Papers (1917) 726

Shakespeare at the Old Vic (1954) 1104

Shakespeare Club (1929) 835

Shakespeare Fellowship News-Letter (1947) 1007a

Shakespeare Gazette (1863) 333

Shakespeare Journal. See *London Shakespeare League Journal* (1914) 715

Shakespeare League Journal. See *London Shakespeare League Journal* (1914) 715

Shakespeare Memorial Theatre (1950) 1063

Shakespeare Memorial Theatre (1955) 1112a

Shakespeare Newspaper (1847) 279

Shakespeare Pictorial. See *Shakespeare Pictorial and Visitor's Weekly Guide* (1928) 820. See also *Avon News* (1930) 838

Shakespeare Pictorial and Visitor's Weekly Guide (1928) 820

Shakespeare Quarterly (1947) 1008

Shakespeare Quarterly (1948) 1031a

Shakespeare Repository (1853) 315

Shakespeare Review (1928) 821

Shakespeare Stage (1953) 1089

Shakespeare Stage Society. See *Shakespeare Stage* (1953) 1089

Shakespeare Survey (1948) 1032

Shakespearean (1895) 541

Shakespeare Authorship Review (1959) 1154

Shavian Tract (1950) 1064

Shaw-Mackenzie, G. See *London School of Dramatic Art Magazine* (1934) 879

Shaw-Script (1963) 1166

Shaw Society. See *Shavian Tract* (1950) 1064

Shaw Society Bulletin (1946) 979

Sheffield. See *Laban Art of Movement Guide* (1948) 1024; *Proceedings of the Sheffield Shakespeare Club* (1819) 78; *Sheffield Guide* (1909) 683; *Sheffield Repertory Company* (1934) 883; *Stage* (1880) 423; *Theatrical Examiner for Sheffield* (1824) 126; *What's On in Sheffield and District* (1931) 852a

Sheffield Guide and Advertiser (1909) 683

Sheffield Repertory Company (1934) 883

Sheridan-Bickers. See *Theatre World and Illustrated Stage Review* (1925) 799

Show (1925) 798; (1955) 1113

Show Business and Weekly Sporting Review. See *Weekly Sporting Review* (1937) 915

Show Pictorial (1961) 1156

Show World (1946) 980

Showgirl (1954) 1105

Showgirl Glamour Review (1955) 1114

Showman (1900) 584

Showman. See *Music Hall* (1889) 482

Showmen's Year Book (1956) 1126

Sights and Shows (1899) 579

"Sir Oracle." See *Glasgow Pantomime Annual* (1895) 534

Sketch (1879) 418

Sketchy Bits (1895) 542

Skinsley, A. C. See *Vaudeville Magazine* (1871) 378

Slater, M. See *Theatre Today* (1946) 984

Sleigh, Charles. See *Dramatic Circular* (1875) 393; *Wings* (1884) 453

Smallwood, Edward. See *Psyche* (1840) 246

Smith, W. Hawkes. See *Birmingham Spectator* (1824) 119

Smith's Liverpool Weekly. See *Liverpool Entertainment and Pleasure Programme* (1903) 613; *Plays and Players* (1904) 628

Smithson, David J. See *Speech* (1889) 485

Society and Dramatic World. See *Dramatic World* (1894) 517

Society for Theatre Research (1950) 1065

Society Herald (1887) 470

Society of Authors. See *Author* (1890) 489

Society of Teachers of Speech and Drama. See *Speech and Drama* (1952) 1079

Sock and Buskin (1867) 349; (1885) 461

Soho Courier (1856) 318

South London Palace and Canterbury Hall Journal (1871) 376

South Wales. See *Curtain Call* (1949) 1042

Southall. See *West Middlesex Entertainment Review* (1949) 1050

Southampton. See *Prompter* (1945) 946; *Southampton Repertory Magazine* (1936) 907; *What's On in Southampton* (1908) 680; *What's On in Southampton* (1909) 684a

Southampton Repertory Magazine (1936) 907

Southend. See *New Elizabethan* (1955) 1109; *Southend Guide to What's On* (1927) 812a

Southend Shakespeare Society. See *New Elizabethan* (1955) 1109

Southport. See *Amateur Theatrical Review* (1933) 868; *Garrick Spectator* (1932) 858; *"Little" Magazine* (1937) 912; *Southport Dramatic Club Magazine* (1932) 865; *Southport Playbill* (1949) 1045

Southport Dramatic Club Magazine (1932) 865; See also *Amateur Theatrical Review* (1933) 868

Southport Playbill (1949) 1045

Southsea. See *Portsmouth and Southsea Amusements* (1894) 527; *Show* (1925) 798; *Stage, Screen and Variety News* (1947) 1012; *What's On in Portsmouth and Southsea* (1913) 711; *What's On in Southsea & Portsmouth* (1925) 801

Souvenirs de Ballet (1949) 1046

Soviet Theatre Bulletin. See *SCR. Society for Cultural Relations with the U.S.S.R.* (1953) 1088

Spear (1922) 763
Speech (1889) 485
Speech and Drama (1952) 1079
Spectator (1828) 164
Speed, F. Maurice. See *Londoner Annual* (1947) 1001
Sphinx (1868) 359
Sport and Country. See *Illustrated Sporting and Dramatic News* (1874) 387
Sport & Show News (1953) 1090
Sporting and Dramatic Mirror (1892) 507
Sporting and Dramatic Standard. See *London Illustrated Standard* (1895) 537
Sporting and Theatrical Review. See *Sporting Review* (1889) 486
Sporting Globe (1905) 642
Sporting Herald (1895) 543
Sporting Mirror. See *Sporting and Dramatic Mirror* (1892) 507
Sporting Pilot and the Age. See *Tallis's Illustrated Life* (1864) 339
Sporting Review (1889) 486
Sporting Summary and Theatrical Tatler (1890) 494
Sporting Telegraph (1860) 324
Sporting Times (1865) 343
Sporting Truth & Dramatic Record (1889) 487
Sportive Snatches (1890) 495
Spotlight (1947) 1009; (1949) 1047; (1950) 1066
"Spotlight" Casting Directory (1927) 813
Spotlight-Contacts (1949) 1048
Spotlight Gazette of Artists (1934) 884
"Spotlight" Pocket Telephone Directory of Subscribers (1935) 897
"Spotlight" Yearbook (1931) 851
St. J. Murphy, C. See *Danceland* (1937) 911
St. John, Vivian. See *Cornish Pixie* (1944) 941
Stage (1805) 43; (1814) 64; (1821) 92; (1822) 102a; (1828) 165; (1844) 263; (1848) 290; (1868) 360; (1871) 377; (1874) 391; (1874) 390; (1880) 423. See also *Stage Directory* (1880) 424
Stage and Field (1904) 631
Stage and Literary and Musical Review (1848) 286
Stage and Scottish Musical and Theatrical Omnibus (1849) 291
Stage and Screen Miscellany (1947) 1010
Stage and Sport (1906) 660
Stage and Television Today. See *Stage Directory* (1880) 424
Stage and Variety Artistes Guide (1950) 1067
Stage Directory (1880) 424
Stage Door (1906) 661; (1947) 1011
"Stage" Guide (1912) 696
Stage Land. See *Stage Door* (1906) 661
Stage Management and Green-Room. See *Monitor* (1767) 14

Stage-Manager (1849) 292
Stage Mirror (1850) 301; (1919) 737
Stage Monitor. See *Country Correspondent* (1739) 5
Stage News (1897) 559
Stage Pictorial (1904) 632
Stage Props (1923) 776
Stage, Screen and Variety News (1947) 1012
Stage Society (1900) 585
Stage Society News (1903) 618
Stage Souvenir (1903) 619
Stage Staff Journal (1901) 599
Stage Stars of To-day (1932) 866
Stage Year Book (1908) 678
Stagecast Directory (1963) 1167
Stageland. See *Lancashire Stageland* (1908) 677; *Stage Door* (1906) 661
Stanley, Harry. See *Gen* (1946) 961
Stanyon, Ellis. See *Magic* (1900) 583
Star (1865) 344
Steele, Sir Richard. See *Anti-Theatre* (1720) 1; *Theatre* (1720) 2
Stephans, Walter. See *Wandering Thespian* (1871) 379
Sterling, Max. See *Magical World* (1910) 687
Stinson, E. J. See *Vaudeville Magazine* (1871) 378
Stockport. See *What's On* (1947) 1015
Stockqueler, J. H. See *Cicerone* (1843) 256
Stoneley, Herbert. See *Carnival Parade* (1956) 1119
Strand Electric and Engineering Co. See *Tabs* (1943) 939
Stratford-upon-Avon. See *Avon News* (1930) 838; *Shakespeare Club* (1929) 835; *Shakespeare Memorial Theatre* (1955) 1112a; *Shakespeare Pictorial* (1928) 820; *Shakespeare Review* (1928) 821; *Shakespearean* (1895) 541; *Stratford Theatrical Review* (1827) 150; *Theatrecraft* (1938) 919; *Theatrecraft News-Letter* (1941) 936
Stratford Theatrical Review and Stage Reporter (1827) 150
Stratford-upon-Avon Scene (1946) 981
Stroller (1905) 643
Strood. See *What's On* (1927) 813a
Stuart, Charles D. See *Encore Annual* (1895) 531
Student Theatre (1963) 1168
Sunday Chronicle (1913) 706
Sunday Mirror and Dramatic and Music Hall Record (1897) 560
Supplement to New Plays Quarterly (1948) 1033
Supplement to "The Opera Box" (1849) 293
Surrey Dramatic Spectator (1827) 151
Sutton Coldfield. See *Highbury Players' Bulletin* (1936) 904; *Intimate Theatre Group News-Letter* (1950) 1057
Swan (1958) 1142

Swan Players. See *Swan* (1958) 1142
Swansea. See *Curtain Call* (1949) 1042;
    Cylchgrawn Undeb y Ddrama Gymreig
    (1927) 807; *Magazine Programme* (1906)
    657a
Swindon. See *Spotlight* (1947) 1009
Swindon and District Theatre Guild. See
    Spotlight (1947) 1009
Sydenham. See *Crystal Palace Herald* (1853)
    312a

T.M.A. Monthly Report (1922) 764
Tabs (1943) 939
Tales of the Drama (1848) 287
Tallis's Dramatic Magazine (1850) 302
*Tallis's Drawing Room Table Book of Theatri-
    cal Portraits* (1851) 308
Tallis's Illustrated Life in London (1864) 339
Tallis's Shakespeare Gallery (1852) 311
Tatler (1830) 189; (1901) 600
Tatler and Bystander. See *Tatler* (1901) 600
Tatler and Theatrical Mirror (1834) 222
Taunton. See *What's On in the West Country*
    (1949) 1053
Taylor, George. See *Amateur Stage* (1946) 951
Taylor, Lester. See *Stratford-upon-Avon Scene*
    (1946) 981
Termagant, Roxana. See *Have At You All*
    (1752) 10
Thalia Diary & Directory for Music Halls
    (1914) 716
Thalia Diary & Directory of Concert Parties
    (1910) 689
*Thalia's Tablet and Melpomene's Memoran-
    dum Book* (1821) 93
Theatre (1720) 2; (1813) 60; (1819) 79;
    (1822) 103; (1828) 166; (1831) 201;
    (1851) 309; (1877) 406; (1904) 633;
    (1908) 679; (1909) 684; (1913) 707;
    (1937) 914; (1939) 926; (1945) 948;
    (1954) 1106
Theatre and Film Illustrated (1928) 823
Theatre Annual (1884) 448
Theatre-Craft (1919) 738
Theatre de Luxe Gazette (1914) 717
Theatre Digest (1948) 1034
Theatre Forum (1938) 919a
Theatre Guide. See *Graphic Guide to the
    London Theatres* (1894) 519
Theatre Guild News (1958) 1143
Theatre Guild Review. See *B.D.T.G.
    Bulletin* (1948) 1017
Theatre Holiday Bulletin (1950) 1068
Theatre Illustrated Quarterly (1933) 873
Theatre in Education (1947) 1013
Theatre Industry. See *T.M.A. Monthly Report*
    (1922) 764
Theatre Industry Journal. See *T.M.A. Monthly
    Report* (1922) 764
Theatre Journal-Programme (1902) 606

Theatre Magazine. See *Book of the Play*
    (1906) 650
Theatre Manager's Handbook (1928) 824
Theatre Managers Journal. See *T.M.A.
    Monthly Report* (1922) 764
Theatre Mirror (1946) 982
Theatre, Music Hall & Cinema Blue Book
    (1917) 727
Theatre News. See *Hippodrome Tatler* (1935)
    888
Theatre Newsletter (1946) 983
Theatre Notebook (1945) 949
Theatre Organ Club. See *Theatre Organ
    Review* (1955) 1115
Theatre Organ Review (1955) 1115
Theatre Programme-Journal. See *Theatre Jour-
    nal-Programme* (1902) 606
Theatre Royal (1961) 1157
*Theatre Royal: Brighton Repertory Theatre
    Magazine* (1935) 898
Theatre Today (1946) 984
Theatre World (1925) 799. See also *Amateur
    Stage* (1932) 853
Theatre World Annual (1949) 1049
Theatre World Monographs (1953) 1091
Theatrecraft (1938) 919
Theatrecraft News-Letter (1941) 936
Theatreland (1912) 697
Theatric Magazine (1805) 44
Theatrical Agents. See *Directory of London
    Theatrical Agents* (1956) 1120
Theatrical and Concert Companion (1840) 247
Theatrical and Concert Guide. See *Prompter*
    (1834) 221
Theatrical and Music Hall Life (1898) 566
Theatrical and Musical Guide (1884) 449
Theatrical and Musical Review (1868) 361
Theatrical and Public Life (1898) 567
Theatrical and Variety Apartments. See *Kirk-
    ley's Theatrical Apartments Directory*
    (1901) 594
Theatrical Apartments and Business Directory
    (1920) 745
Theatrical Argus, and Stage Reporter (1830)
    190
Theatrical Artistes Road Book (1929) 836
Theatrical Athenaeum (1833) 217
Theatrical Beauties and Reigning Stars (1847)
    280
Theatrical Censor (1828) 167
Theatrical Chronicle. See *Public Advertiser*
    (1774) 18
Theatrical Chronicle and Dramatic Review
    (1840) 248
Theatrical Critic (1834) 223; (1845) 267
Theatrical Critique (1829) 180
Theatrical Employees Journal (1904) 634
Theatrical Examiner (1823) 114; (1827) 152;
    (1833) 218
Theatrical Examiner for Sheffield (1824) 126

Theatrical Gazette (1813) 61; (1815) 66; (1818) 74

Theatrical Guardian (1791) 26

Theatrical Guide (1822) 104

Theatrical Inquisitor (1812) 59. See also *Stage* (1828) 165

Theatrical Investigator. See *Prompter* (1815) 65

Theatrical Investigator Dissected. See *Prompter Prompted* (1816) 70

Theatrical John Bull (1824) 127

Theatrical Journal, and Stranger's Guide (1839) 242

Theatrical Looker-on (1822) 105

Theatrical Manager (1928) 825

Theatrical Manager's Association. See *T.M.A. Monthly Report* (1922) 764

Theatrical Manager's Register (1884) 450

Theatrical Mince Pie (1825) 133

Theatrical Mirror (1827) 153

Theatrical Mirror and Playgoer's Companion (1849) 294. See also *Theatrical Programme and Entr' Acte* (1849) 295

Theatrical Monitor. See *Monitor* (1767) 14

Theatrical News (1926) 805

Theatrical Note-Book (1824) 128

Theatrical Observer (1820) 85; (1821) 94; (1821) 95. See also *Argus* (1804) 40; *Original Theatrical Observer* (1821) 91; *Theatrical News* (1926) 805

Theatrical Paul Pry (1848) 287a

Theatrical Pocket Magazine. See *Drama* (1821) 88

Theatrical Programme. See *General Theatrical Programme* (1883) 440; *Samuel Eyre's Theatrical Programme* (1872) 381

Theatrical Programme, and Entr' Acte (1849) 295

Theatrical Programme and General Amusements Advertiser (1890) 495a

Theatrical Public Guide (1898) 568

Theatrical Record (1823) 115

Theatrical Recorder (1805) 45. See also *Liverpool Dramatic Censor* (1806) 47

Theatrical Register (1788) 22

Theatrical Register and General Amusement (1838) 241

Theatrical Repertory (1801) 35

Theatrical Review (1763) 13; (1772) 17; (1807) 52. See also *Prompter* (1824) 125

Theatrical Review and Author's Miscellany (1849) 296

Theatrical Review: for the Year 1757 (1758) 12

Theatrical Rod (1831) 202

Theatrical Spectator (1821) 96

Theatrical Speculum and Musical Review (1831) 203

Theatrical Tattler (1830) 191

Theatrical Tickler (1828) 168

Theatrical Times (1846) 272; (1883) 443

Theatrical Touchstone. See *Stage* (1805) 43

Theatrical Tribunal. See *New Opera Glass* (1830) 186

Theatrical Vademecum. See *Thespian Sentinel* (1825) 134

Theatrical Visitor (1835) 227

Theatrical World (1881) 430

Theatrical World for 1893–1897 (1893) 514

Theatricals (1893) 515

Thespian (1821) 97; (1823) 116; (1913) 708

Thespian and Dramatic Record (1857) 320

Thespian Censor (1818) 75

Thespian Critique (1816) 71. See also *Theatrical Observer* (1820) 85

Thespian Magazine (1792) 27

Thespian Review (1806) 49

Thespian Sentinel (1825) 134

Thespian Telegraph (1796) 31

This Is London (1956) 1127

This Week in London (1946) 985

Thistle (1829) 181

Thomas, A. E. See *Children's Theatre* (1948) 1019

Thompson, Alfred. See *Mask* (1868) 356; *Mask* (1879) 416

Thompson, H. W. See *West Middlesex Entertainment Review* (1949) 1050

Thompson, Harry. See *New Theatre Magazine* (1959) 1150

Thornell, J. Higden. See *Bill of the Play* (1882) 432

Thornton, Bonnel. See *Have At You All* (1752) 10

Three Arts Club Journal (1913) 709

Threshold (1957) 1137

Thurston, Hugh A. See *Folk Dancer* (1954) 1096

Tickler, and Dramatic Intelligencer (1837) 234

Timbs, John. See *Harlequin* (1829) 176

To-day in Eastbourne. See *Eastbourne Programme* (1908) 676

To-Day's London Guide (1904) 635

To-Morrow (1896) 550

Top-Spin (1940) 932

Torquay. See *Torquay Amusements* (1904) 636

Torquay Amusements (1904) 636

Tottenham. See *Top-Spin* (1940) 932; *What's On in Tottenham* (1928) 826

Touchstone (1877) 407

Townsman (1803) 39

Toy Theatre Club. See *Model Stage* (1946) 970

Tragic, Comic and Operatic Library. See *Dramatic Magazine* (1786) 21

Trewin, J. C. *Plays of the Year* (1948) 1030a; *Year's Work in the Theatre* (1948) 1037

Trilling, Ossia. See *Dobson's Theatre Year Book* (1948) 1021; *Theatre Newsletter* (1946) 983
Tunbridge Wells. See *Ballet* (1945) 943
Tuner (1754) 11
Tyneside Phoenix (1947) 1014

Ulster Dramatic Societies. See *Script* (1945) 947
Umpire (1881) 431
Under the Clock (1884) 451
Unemployed Drama News (1936) 908
Universal Guide to the Amusements & Fashions (1852) 311a
Universal Musical and Dramatic Directory (1913) 710
University Shakespeare Journal (1887) 471

Variety. See *Garraway's Directory of Concert and Variety Artistes* (1934) 876; *Interlude* (1885) 457; *London Amusements* (1925) 793; *Official Music Hall Directory and Variety ABC* (1899) 577; *Performer* (1906) 659; *Photo-Cast* (1957) 1136; *Pullman Casting Directory* (1956) 1125; *R. Douglas Cox's . . . Variety Directory* (1904) 630; *Stage and Variety Artistes Guide* (1950) 1067; *Stage, Screen and Variety News* (1947) 1012; *Variety Fare* (1946) 986; *Variety, Music, Stage and Film News* (1931) 852; *Variety Stage* (1895) 544; *Variety Stage and Music Hall Pictorial* (1905) 644; *Variety Stage Illustrated* (1905) 645; *Variety Theatre* (1905) 646; *Variety Theatre Annual* (1906) 662; *Variety Time Table and Programme* (1906) 663
Variety Cabaret Film News. See *Variety, Music, Stage and Film News* (1931) 852
Variety Fare (1946) 986
Variety, Music, Stage and Film News (1931) 852
Variety Stage (1895) 544
Variety Stage and Music Hall Pictorial (1905) 644
Variety Stage Illustrated (1905) 645
Variety Theatre (1905) 646
Variety Theatre Annual (1906) 662
Variety Time Table and Programme (1906) 663
Vaudeville. See *Entertainer* (1913) 700; *Hippodrome* (1901) 591; *Pantomime and Vaudeville Favourites* (1913) 703; *Vaudeville Magazine* (1871) 378
Vaudeville Magazine (1871) 378
Vauxhall Observer (1823) 117
Vedder, Paul. See *Playgoer's Magazine* (1888) 478; *Playgoer's Pocket-book* (1886) 467; *Printer's Devil* (1850) 300
Vic-Wells Association (1946) 987
Victualler. See *Licensed Victuallers' Mirror* (1888) 473; *Licensed Victuallers' Sportsman* (1888) 474

Villiers-Chapman, Charles. See *Favourite* (1907) 667
Visitor's Guide and Journal of Amusements (1874) 392
Voici Londres (1935) 899
Voyce, Albert. See *Official Music Hall Directory and Variety ABC* (1899) 577
Vues from Revues (1958) 1144

Waddington, John. See *Birmingham Pantomime Annual* (1899) 571; *John Waddington's Annual* (1901) 592; *Roberts Pantomime Annual* (1895) 539
Waivewright, R. M. D. See *Shakespeare Fellowship News-Letter* (1947) 1007a
Wales. See *Curtain Call* (1949) 1042; *Cylchgrawn Undeb y Ddrama Gymreig* (1927) 807; *Cymdeithas Ddawns Werin Cymru* (1953) 1081; *Cymdeithas Ddawns Werin Cymru* (1955) 1108
Walker, Ray. See *Theatre Newsletter* (1946) 983
Wall, Alfred H. See *Shakespearean* (1895) 541
Wallington. See *Puppetry Year Book* (1955) 1112; *Wallington Entertainment Guide* (1936) 908a
Walter's Theatrical and Sporting Directory (1884) 452
Walton-On-Naze. See *Clacton Programme of Entertainment* (1901) 587
Wanderer (1832) 211
Wandering Thespian Annual (1871) 379
Wanted (1904) 637
Warr, John. See *"Performer" Handbook* (1921) 753
War-time Drama (1939) 927
Warwickshire. See *Stratford-upon-Avon Scene* (1946) 981
Wasp (1826) 141
Watson, James. See *Townsman* (1803) 39
Watson, R. P. See *R. P. Watson's Weekly* (1904) 629
Waugh, A. See *Playgoers' Guide and Theatrical Notes* (1896) 549
Wednesday Programme and Sketch Book. See *Figaro Programme* (1874) 386
Week-End Review of Politics (1930) 846
Weekly Comedy (1889) 488
Weekly Dramatic Chronicle (1824) 129
Weekly Dramatic Journal. See *Thespian Censor* (1818) 75
Weekly Dramatic Register (1825) 135
Weekly Dramatic Review (1828) 169
Weekly Entertainment Guide (1902) 607
Weekly Magazine (1823) 118
Weekly Musical Transcript (1853) 316
Weekly Playgoer (1911) 693
Weekly Record of the Stage. See *Dramatic Gazette* (1830) 184

Weekly Review and Dramatic Critic (1852) 312

Weekly Spectator (1857) 321

Weekly Sporting Review (1937) 915

Weekly Theatrical Report. See *Dramatic Censor* (1800) 33

Weekly Theatrical Reporter (1829) 182. See also *Critic* (1820) 81

Weekly Theatrical Reporter and Music Hall Review (1867) 350

Wells. See *What's On in the West Country* (1949) 1053

Welsh Drama League. See *Cylchgrawn Undeb y Ddrama Gymreig* (1927) 807; *Y Llwyfan* (1927) 815

Welsh Folk Dance Society. See *Cymdeithas Ddawns Werin Cymru* (1955) 1108; *Welsh Folk Dance Society News-letter* (1953) 1092

Welsh Folk Dance Society News-letter (1953) 1092

West Dulwich. See *Mime Review* (1935) 893

West End (1897) 560a

West End Review. See *West End* (1897) 560a

West Middlesex Entertainment Review (1949) 1050

Weston-super-Mare. See *What's On in the West Country* (1949) 1053

Wharton, J. C. See *University Shakespeare Journal* (1887) 471

What's Doing. See *Birmingham Programme of Amusements* (1906) 649

What's On (1896) 551; (1901) 601; (1904) 637a; (1907) 675; (1925) 800; (1927) 813a; (1927) 814; (1946) 988; (1947) 1015; (1951) 1073; (1953) 1093; (1955) 1116; (1955) 1117. See also *London Week* (1935) 890; *Sheffield Guide* (1909) 683

What's On and Where (1930) 847

What's On and Where (1949) 1051

What's On at the Theatres This Week? (1906) 664

What's On in Birmingham (1922) 765; (1943) 940

What's On in Cambridge (1953) 1094

What's On in Coventry and District (1921) 754

What's On in Ealing (1949) 1052

What's On in Ilford (1948) 1035

What's On in London (1935) 900. See also *London Week* (1935) 890

What's On in Maidstone (1927) 814a

What's On in Margate (1923) 777

What's On in Portsmouth and Southsea (1913) 711

What's On in Sheffield and District (1931) 852a

What's On in Southampton (1908) 680; (1909) 684a

What's On in Southsea and Portsmouth (1925) 801

What's On in the City (1936) 909

What's On in the West Country (1949) 1053

What's On in Tottenham (1928) 826

Whitley Bay. See *Amateur Operatic Year Book* (1923) 766

Who's Who in Dancing (1932) 867

Who's Who in Show Biz (1963) 1169

Who's Who in Show Business (1961) 1158

Who's Who in the Theatre. See *Green Room Book* (1906) 656

Who's Who on the Stage. See *Green Room Book* (1906) 656

Wilford Hutchinson's Conjurers Chronicle (1919) 739

Wilkes, Ian. See *On Stage* (1959) 1151

Will A. Bradley's Pantomime Annual (1900) 586

Williams, J. M. See *Dramatic Censor* (1811) 55

Williams, Peter. See *Dance and Dancers* (1950) 1054

Wilson, Walter. See *Dramatic Notes* (1879) 414

Wings (1884) 453

Wisgast, W. See *Players* (1860) 323

Wizard (1947) 1016

Wm. Haslam's Apartment Directory and Theatrical Guide (1906) 665

Wolverhampton. See *Cornish Pixie* (1944) 941

Wood, Frederick. See *Prompter* (1909) 682

Woodpecker (1887) 472

Worcester. See *British Puppet and Model Theatre Guild Junior News* (1941) 933; *Shaw-Script* (1963) 1166

Workers' Theatre Movement. See *Red Stage* (1931) 850

Working Light (1948) 1036

World (1850) 303

World of Magic (1865) 345

Wrexam. See *Cymdeithas Ddawns Werin Cymru* (1953) 1081

Y Llwyfan (1927) 815

Year's Work in the Theatre (1948) 1037

Yeats, W. B. See *Beltaine* (1899) 570; *Samhain* (1901) 598

Yiddish Theatre. See *Theatre Mirror* (1946) 982

"Yorick." See *Theatre World and Illustrated Stage Review* (1925) 799

York. See *Repertory World* (1939) 925a; *Theatrical Register* (1788) 22

Yorkshire Harlequin (1896) 552

Yorkshire Owl Pantomime Annual (1892) 508

Young, Clifford. See *Theatre* (1909) 684

Young, Derek. See *Stagecast Directory* (1963) 1167

Young Ballet Dancer (1952) 1080